Crime and Criminality

SECOND EDITION

Crime and

Criminality

Causes and Consequences

Ronald D. Hunter
Mark L. Dantzker

LYNNE
RIENNER
PUBLISHERS

BOULDER
LONDON

Published in the United States of America in 2012 by
Lynne Rienner Publishers, Inc.
1800 30th Street, Boulder, Colorado 80301
www.rienner.com

and in the United Kingdom by
Lynne Rienner Publishers, Inc.
3 Henrietta Street, Covent Garden, London WC2E 8LU

Library of Congress Cataloging-in-Publication Data
Hunter, Ronald D.
    Crime and criminality : causes and consequences / Ronald D. Hunter and
Mark L. Dantzker. — 2nd ed.
        p. cm.
    Includes bibliographical references and index.
    ISBN 978-1-58826-773-3 (alk. paper)
    1. Criminal psychology. 2. Criminal behavior. 3. Criminology.
I. Dantzker, Mark L., 1958– II. Title.
    HV6080.H85 2011
    364—dc24
                                                            2011025194

British Cataloguing in Publication Data
A Cataloguing in Publication record for this book
is available from the British Library.

Printed and bound in the United States of America

    The paper used in this publication meets the requirements
        of the American National Standard for Permanence of
        Paper for Printed Library Materials Z39.48-1992.

    5 4 3 2 1

To our families

From Ron to
Vi, Kelly, Jason, Butch, Sarah, Anthony,
Caroline, and Kate

From Mark to
Gail, Lance, Sherri, Lenn, Jeanette, Lauren,
Brandon, Victoria, and Sebastian

Contents

Tables and Figures

Tables

Figures

Preface

In writing the first edition of *Crime and Criminality,* our desire was to produce a brief yet thorough primer on crime and criminality for undergraduates. We developed a text that covered all significant issues and concepts to which undergraduate students taking introductory courses in criminology, criminal behavior, juvenile delinquency, deviance, or theories of crime causation should be exposed. With this second edition, consistent with our original aim, we have updated our materials, revised all chapters, and added important new chapters.

In Chapter 1, "The Nature of Crime and Justice," we define crime and criminal behavior. We acquaint the student with the various perspectives on crime and criminality and how different perspectives on human behavior influence definitions of crime, as well as responses to criminal behavior.

In Chapter 2, "The Problem of Crime," we explore the extent and costs of crime, contrast the various strategies for predicting and measuring crime, and present typologies of crime and criminals. Included within this discussion are overviews of the various types of violent crimes, property crimes, occupational crimes, organized crime, public order crimes, and political crimes.

In Chapter 3, "The Study of Crime," we define criminology, describe the five models of criminology, and discuss the classical and positive schools of criminology and their impacts on both the study of crime and the administration of criminal justice. In addition, several current influences on the study of crime are presented and discussed.

In Chapter 4, "Deterrence and Opportunity Theories," we present the tenets of classical criminology as the basis of the legal model upon which justice administration is founded. We examine deterrence theory and its applications within the components of policing, adjudication, and corrections. Modern theories that focus on the reduction of opportunity are included within this presentation.

In Chapter 5, "Biological and Biosocial Theories," we begin the review of positivist theories with a historical assessment of the major biological explanations for human and criminal behavior (for example, genetics, physical abnormalities, neurological disorders, and environmental pollution) and their incorporation into modern biosocial explanations that provide for both nature and nurture.

In Chapter 6, "Psychological and Psychosocial Theories," we review the major psychological explanations for human and criminal behavior (such as Freudian psychoanalysis, behavioral theory, and cognitive theory) and the development of social psychological and psychosocial explanations of crime and criminality.

In Chapter 7, "Social Structure Theories," we introduce the major class-based sociological theories that emphasize the effects of poverty and the individual's location within the lower class as explanations for crime and criminality.

In Chapter 8, "Social Interaction Theories," we investigate the major social psychological and sociological theories for crime and criminal behavior. These theories focus on the social interactions through which criminal and deviant behaviors are learned and reinforced. Social reaction theories are included as the bridge between functionalist and conflict theories.

In Chapter 9, "Social Conflict Theories," we present those theories that explain crime as the product of political and economic struggles among those in power and those who are without power or are seeking power. This chapter includes non-Marxist explanations as well as the Marxist perspectives of critical theory and radical theory. Of particular interest is the inclusion of elitist theory.

In Chapter 10, "Integrated and Holistic Theories," we contrast the leading efforts to combine different perspectives regarding crime and criminality into more comprehensive explanations that draw from two or more previous theories. Included is our own identity theory.

In Chapter 11, "Victimization Theories," we describe the development of victimology as an area of study and explore the various theoretical explanations of victimization.

In Chapter 12, "Dealing with Lawbreakers," we contrast the various perspectives on how to deal appropriately with those who are found to have committed crimes (including the rationales for retribution, deterrence, incapacitation, reintegration, and rehabilitation). The merits of corporal punishment and capital punishment are also examined.

In Chapter 13, "Dealing with Victims," we examine the treatment of victims by society and explain how "victim justice" differs from criminal justice.

In Chapter 14, "Dealing with the Law Abiding," we critique various views on how the criminal justice system both affects and is affected by the law-abiding public. The influence of politics on the administration of justice is discussed, and the different justice perspectives (social responsibility, social problems, and social engineering) are reviewed. In addition, we introduce the use of law and punishment as "symbolic reassurance."

In Chapter 15, "Theory in Practice," we conclude our primer by reviewing the previous chapters and discussing contemporary efforts at crime prevention and control. Here we also call for a holistic model of crime prevention to deal with future crime and criminality.

The text includes real world examples relative to each chapter's subject matter, a summary and discussion questions at the end of every chapter, a glossary that provides short definitions for key concepts, and complete references.

We hope that you find this book to be a useful guide in exploring the complexities of crime and criminality.

* * *

We thank the Lynne Rienner production team for their efforts. We also are grateful to the students of CJCR 3200 Criminology at Georgia Gwinnett College, who served as guinea pigs, contributed their insights, and participated in the development of the glossary for this edition.

—*Ronald D. Hunter*
Mark L. Dantzker

1

The Nature of
Crime and Justice

Despite our being frequently told not to discuss them, the most interesting topics in the world are **sex**,* **religion**, **politics**, and crime. The most interesting stories often include all four. The purpose of this text is to explore crime and criminality. However, before we narrow our emphasis, we need to discuss how crime and criminality relate to the myriad other important issues within our lives (of which sex, religion, and politics happen to belong). In other words, to study crime and its derivatives (criminality, **criminology**, criminal justice, crime science) we must first study **human nature**.

On Being Human

Being human is complicated; that is why we have so many disciplines that try to explain human behavior. We will examine many of those explanations in subsequent chapters. Regardless of the approach that one takes to the study of human behavior, there are commonalities found within all. Humans have a need for acceptance. By this we mean that we need to feel that other people like us and welcome our association. Even diehard loners often need a "people fix" in which they feel a connection with others. We also need to feel that there is hope for the future. Even those who are fatalistic want to believe that at some point life will become easier for them and/or their loved ones. We have a need for peace. Even though many of us seem to create, if not even welcome, turmoil, we frequently need for things to calm down. While most would probably deny it, we also have a need for understanding. In fact, in this effort,

---

* Key terms that are defined in the Glossary appear in **boldface** the first time they are used in the book.

1

we often tend to reveal too much about ourselves to those who are not interested. More frequently, we feel the need to share our views with those who would prefer not to know what we think.

Our needs are often focused in two central wants that we as humans have. The first is self-worth. *No matter how vile or contemptible individuals may be in the eyes of others or how charismatic and successful they may be, it is a person's image of him- or herself that matters the most.* Whether it is conscious or subconscious, most of our activities are geared to promoting our own self-image. This need can lead people to be obsessed with work, wealth, possessions, piety, enhanced social status, or other means of impressing others along with ourselves.

The second vital need is that of **justice**. At the time that this edition was being finalized, a charismatic pastor was ruffling feathers within traditional Christianity with his controversial views on heaven and hell. In an interview on *Good Morning America,* the Reverend Rob Bell stated that a crucial element within his "love wins" philosophy was that "the core of human existence is a longing for justice" (Bell, 2011). While most of us don't agree on what justice is, we believe that it is vital to us, our loved ones, and our society. That is why we wrote this primer. We hope that is why you are reading it.

Catalysts and Impediments to Justice

As we mentioned above, how people see the world is shaped by how they view themselves. *These two perspectives, **worldview** and self-image, provide the means by which we evaluate all other aspects of life, particularly crime and justice.* The following are what we consider to be the primary influences upon our self-image (or to use a term from a later chapter, our **identity**).

The impact of family. An old adage is that you can choose your friends, but you can't choose your family. The love and nurture provided within most families are the foundation most of us rely on during difficult times. They are the ones upon whom we may depend even though we may not at times deserve their support. Unfortunately, as many of you who are reading this are well aware, family can also be the bane of our existence. Neglect and abuse of children, battering of spouses, and mistreatment of elders occur too frequently within our communities.

The impacts of family, both in influencing criminal behaviors and in thwarting them, will be discussed within a number of the theories presented in the following chapters.

The impact of religion. We all believe in something; it may be in a supreme being, it may be in a system of living, it may be in our own perceived majesty, but we all practice some form of religion. Havilland (2002, p. 364) defines religion as "organized beliefs in the supernatural that rationalize rituals aimed at interpreting and controlling aspects of the universe otherwise beyond human control." For our purposes, we will adopt a definition consistent with that of the US Supreme Court in *Torcaso v. Watkins* (1961). In that decision, Justice Hugo Black commented in a footnote, "Among religions in this country which do not teach what would generally be considered a belief in the existence of God are Buddhism, Taoism, Ethical Culture, **Secular Humanism**, and others." The term *secular humanism* became prominent soon afterward.

Our definition is as follows: "Religion is a system of beliefs that we hold sacred and that form the basis of rituals and expectations that we live by and that we encourage others to live by." Using this perspective, we are able to classify secular humanism as third among the largest religions of the world (see Table 1.1). We do this not as a criticism of its philosophies—most of my secular humanist friends do not like it being called a religion—but in recognition of its influence in all aspects of American life we are doing so.

Table 1.1 Major Religions of the World (ranked by number of adherents)

Christianity	2.1 billion
Islam	1.5 billion
Secular/nonreligious/agnostic/atheist	1.1 billion
Hinduism	900 million
Chinese traditional religion	394 million
Buddhism	376 million
Primal-indigenous	300 million
African traditional and diasporic	100 million
Sikhism	23 million
Juche	19 million
Spiritism	15 million
Judaism	14 million
Baha'i	7 million
Jainism	4.2 million
Shinto	4 million
Cao Dai	4 million
Zoroastrianism	2.6 million
Tenrikyo	2 million
Neopaganism	1 million
Unitarian-Universalism	.8 million
Rastafarianism	.6 million
Scientology	.5 million

Source: http://www.adherents.com/Religions_By_Adherents.html (retrieved March 15, 2011).

No matter your personal religious (or nonreligious) views, the impact of religion is essential for the student of criminal justice and criminology to understand because of its importance within the lives of so many people and its influence on the making and enforcement of laws around the world. This is particularly relevant due to the ongoing aftermath of the 9/11 attacks on the Twin Towers and the Pentagon and the unrest within the Muslim world due to **Radical Islam** (see the Reality Check at the end of the chapter).

One of the interesting aspects of reviewing religions is that the ethical and moral frameworks are so similar. **Caring** for others, working for common good, sharing, and promoting justice are common tenets. Unfortunately, all religions (including **atheism**) also suffer from the adverse effects of hypocrisy and intolerance on the part of some devotees.

The greatest impacts of religion within contemporary US society have been the support of mainstream Protestants, Catholics, and Jews for civil and **human rights**; the opposition of Christian Fundamentalists to abortion, as well as their support for harsher penalties (including the death penalty) for criminal offenders; and the threat of terrorism from radical Islam both here and abroad.

The impact of gender. Does crime discriminate? According to **crime statistics**, males are the dominant criminal perpetrators. For example, in 2009, 74.7 percent of all the persons arrested, 81.2 percent arrested for violent crimes, and 62.6 percent arrested for property crimes were male (Federal Bureau of Investigation [FBI], 2010a, Table 42). Males were arrested most often for drug abuse violations and driving under the influence, while females were most often arrested for larceny-theft.

Despite the fact that males dominate criminal behavior, statistics indicate that the percentage of female arrests continues to increase. Females now account for 25.3 percent of all arrests. They have increased to 18.8 percent of arrests for violent crimes and 37.4 percent of arrests for property crimes (Federal Bureau of Investigation, 2010a). Based on these statistics, it can be said that crime does not discriminate but instead has welcomed females with open arms. Of course, the concern is why female crime rates have increased. While no one definitive answer has yet been identified, one could argue that the increase in female involvement in occupations historically dominated by males, in combination with the population numbers (women comprise 51–53 percent of the overall population in the United States), would influence the growing number of females arrested. Furthermore, equal rights and equal application of the law may have some influence. Regardless of the reason, the reality is that females are becoming more criminal.

The impact of race and ethnicity. One of the greatest misnomers in criminal justice is that minorities are arrested more than whites. In 2009, 69.1 percent of all individuals arrested were white and 28.3 percent were African American (Federal Bureau of Investigation, 2010a, Table 43). This statistic alone would indicate that minorities are not arrested more than whites. However, this statistic is misleading in that minority group members tend to be arrested disproportionately to their population base. That is, African Americans make up less than 20 percent of the population, yet nearly 30 percent of those arrested are African Americans. This disproportion has created a great debate in criminal justice over racial equality. The question of whether race influences the commission of crime or merely the prosecution of it has yet to be properly addressed.

We wish to note that the above paragraph is a bit misleading because the **Uniform Crime Reports** cite White, Black, American Indian or Alaskan Native, and Asian or Pacific Islander. Hispanics and members of other ethnic groups (including Arab Americans) are classified within White or Black. Since Hispanics/Latinos are now the largest ethnic minority in the United States, this is an oversight that needs correcting.

The impact of age. With respect to age, according to 2009 data, 43.5 percent of all those arrested in the United States were under the age of twenty-five. Of those arrested for violent crimes, 44.7 percent were under the age of twenty-five. Because 3.8 percent of those arrested were under fifteen, one could suggest that criminality is greatest among individuals ages fifteen to twenty-four (Federal Bureau of Investigation, 2010a, Table 38). Perhaps immaturity prevents this group from accepting the responsibility of being in a society that requires certain rules to be followed regardless of how doing so might hamper reaching one's goals. More likely it is being young, vigorous, and wishing to assert independence. In addition, responsibility is easily connected with the idea of free will, which one might argue younger people have more opportunity to exercise. However, it should be noted that misbehavior is not limited to the young. Our group of "Baby Boomers," aka the "Me Generation," has a well-deserved reputation for being self-centered that is irksome to both prior and later generations (Jayson, 2011).

Another issue in considering age and criminality is the increasing number of elderly offenders who are being tried and sentenced within the criminal justice system. The problems of dealing with elderly offenders in both community and institutional corrections will be of increasing concern within the coming years.

The impact of education. While higher education does not stop people from committing crimes (as demonstrated by the numbers of doctors, lawyers, judges, politicians, and professors who have been arrested), it does correspond with lesser involvement in street crimes. It also matches up with increased involvement in corporate and political crimes. The key factor in the relationship between education and crime is opportunity. Those with higher education have better opportunities for social and economic advancement, thus not having to engage in street-level crimes. However, their loftier positions create more opportunities for crimes such as embezzlement, fraud, and other types of white-collar crime. These opportunities (or the lack thereof) will be discussed within several theories in the following chapters.

The impact of social class. Among all the variables one could claim have an influence on criminality, one of the more difficult to quantify is social class. Most commonly, society has been viewed as three-tiered in terms of class: upper, middle, and lower. Each tier can then itself be divided into an upper, middle, and lower. These tiers have long been determined by economic status, which in the United States is usually defined by yearly income. Pundits, politicians, and political activists often claim that crime results from poverty, which is associated with the lower class. However, depending upon one's political ideology, class interpretations can be used to blame the poor and label them as inherently criminal or to excuse their behaviors as the result of social injustice. We investigate these views in detail within later chapters. Suffice it to say at this point that there are more than enough examples of crime among the upper and middle classes to counter this claim. In truth, criminality is found among all levels of society; it is just that many refuse to acknowledge that factors other than poverty and class conflict can contribute to crime.

The impact of ecological/geographical differences. Examining national crime data reveals that crime rates in rural and suburban areas tend to be lower than crime in large urban areas. This difference might suggest that crime is influenced by those factors found more often in urban areas, such as overcrowding, poverty, social inequality, drug use, racial conflict, and economic instability. Crime rates are also often higher in the western and southern parts of the country and during the summer, suggesting that warmer climates have some influence on criminal behavior (Doerner and Lab, 2012).

Regional differences may also be reflected in cultural issues. Massive immigration from Europe, the westward migration of white settlers, the taking of lands occupied by Native Americans and Mexicans, slavery, and the other conflicts between the industrial North and the agrarian South that led to civil war all had lasting impacts on the **culture** and traditions within the different regions of the country. As seen in Figure 1.1, these differences are seen in the nature and extent of crimes within separate regions as well as in their dissimilar responses to crime. They may also be seen in incarceration rates. For example, the national average is one out of thirty-one adults under some type of correctional supervision, while in the state of Georgia, the rate for those under correctional supervision is one out of thirteen adults (Melton, 2011).

Figure 1.1 Regional Crime Rates, 2009

	Violent and Property Crime per 1,000,000 Inhabitants
Northeast	
Property crime	2,123.2
Violent crime	358.3
Midwest	
Property crime	2,901.4
Violent crime	385.8
South	
Property crime	3,607.4
Violent crime	494.3
West	
Property crime	2,962.5
Violent crime	422.4

Source: Federal Bureau of Investigation, 2010a, table 3.

The impact of culture. In the previous sections, we have discussed geography, religion, ethnicity, family, gender, education, and social class as factors that influence criminality. All of these factors may be seen at play within the category of culture. They may support one another or they may counteract one another in regard to criminality. For example, a person may live in abject poverty with little chance of obtaining the educational or vocational skills necessary to obtain a decent job. But if that individual has strong family support and deep religious beliefs, she/he may not be susceptible to criminal behavior. Conversely, as seen by the antics of many of today's celebrities, people with money, status, and acclaim may engage in criminal activity because they have come to believe that they are entitled to do so.

Cultural aspects may be seen in the lifestyles of diverse groups: religious austerity of the Amish, tribal societies of Native Americans, patriotism of military personnel, self-reliance of rural dwellers, street lives of the homeless, and opulence among the affluent. Interestingly, cultural factors may result in diametric opposites within various groups. **Xenophobes** tend to fear and/or oppose people and cultures that are foreign to them. This can result in bias and discrimination against anyone whom they consider to be different and/or inferior. To the contrary, **xenophiles** tend to favor things that are foreign or different, often to the point of being antagonistic toward others within their own cultural group. This view can lead to bias and discrimination against their own kind in order to demonstrate their "tolerance and superiority" (Hunter and Barker, 2012).

The impact of science. In Chapter 3 we will discuss the scientific method and how important it is to the study of criminology. However, the context of this discussion is the impact science has had on the everyday lives of citizens as well as the conflicts that it has created. The advancements that have been made in the physical sciences (astronomy, chemistry, physics, earth science, and environmental science), the life sciences (biology and medicine), the formal sciences (computer science, mathematics, statistics, systems science), the social sciences (anthropology, economics, linguistics, psychology, geography, philosophy, political science, and sociology), as well as the applied sciences (agronomy, architecture, education, health sciences, management, military science, and spatial science) have dramatically influenced humans and the world we live in.

The impacts of science have not been pain-free. Many advances, such as the development of nuclear energy and the use of fossil fuels, pose serious risks to our physical environment. Likewise, the challenges created by the sciences, particularly **Darwin's theory of evolution**, continue to cause turmoil within our social environment. Debates about science versus religion (particularly evolution versus creationism) can be especially nasty. Historically, scientific explanations of human evolution have been shunned by many religions. Currently, physical scientists who express faith in a supreme being are frequently ostracized and denigrated by their peers (Lovan, 2011; Merali, 2011).

The impact of technology. The advances in science have led to the development of many marvelous inventions that have made our lives easier, although waiting in traffic behind someone who is texting instead of paying attention to the traffic signals, one may feel differently. Technology has given us cell phones, satellite navigation devices, laptop computers, Internet access, and complex security systems. The benefits in communication, transportation, medicine, and crime prevention have enabled us to have lifestyles only imagined by previous generations.

We travel with ease to other parts of the world; we have instantaneous communications anywhere on the globe; we have access to advanced medical care; and we have sophisticated capabilities for preventing and solving crimes. Unfortunately, technological advances come at a price. Cybercrimes, invasions of privacy, identity theft, and easy dissemination of child pornography are but a few of the crimes that have resulted from technological advances.

The impact of globalization. A rather ubiquitous bumper sticker reads, "Think globally. Act locally." That is an apt message for today's society. The world is a much smaller place than it was when the authors were undergraduates studying criminology. Thanks to the previously mentioned advances in science and technology, as well as media coverage, today references to community are as likely to mean the world community as our local community. As an example, in the Atlanta metropolitan area there are many thousands who are employed by more than 300 foreign-owned companies. One need only look around one's home to witness the impacts of international trade. We may witness positive events as they occur thousands of miles away from our location (as this was being written, millions around the world were watching the marriage of the UK's Prince William to Kate Middleton). Conversely, we may also witness the negative (the efforts by various leaders to suppress democratic uprisings across North Africa).

Unfortunately, advances in communication and transportation have also advanced the abilities of individuals and organizations to engage in transnational crime. Human trafficking organizations that enslave young women from less affluent nations and force them into prostitution are found within our metropolitan areas. Drug networks span the globe. Environmental crimes, cyber crimes, crimes against children, public corruption, weapons smuggling, and other organized crimes easily transcend national borders. And, as we are too aware, no community is safe from the threat of international terrorism.

The impact of media. The mass media have tremendous influence on our lives. The news media keep us informed of current events in politics, world affairs, economic issues, fashion trends, natural disasters, wars, terrorism, and crime. Nothing of consequence fails to be noted by local news outlets. Those activities and occurrences of more significance are immediately shared with national and international news organizations. While readership has declined substantially during recent years, newspapers such as *USA Today,* the *New York Times,* and the *Washington Post* are read by hundreds of thousands of people. They are supplemented by myriad newsmagazines such as *Time* and *Newsweek.* Telecasts by network television stations can be viewed during the traditional news hours as well as on cable stations such as CNN and Fox News that offer 24/7 coverage of national and international happenings. In addition to the electronic media's traditional coverage, we can now access news that we are personally interested in at times of our own choosing through the Internet.

Of greater importance to younger viewers are the numerous offerings provided on network, cable, and pay-for-view television. These are augmented by video rentals and theater presentations. For better or worse, the entertainment media shape how we look at ourselves and others, what we buy, what we think we need, and how we think we are supposed to act (Hunter and Barker, 2011). Unfortunately, celebrities like Lindsay Lohan and Paris Hilton are not the role models that we would wish our children and grandchildren to emulate.

The impact of politics. In Chapter 14, we will discuss the impacts of ideology and politics on the administration of justice. In this section, we touch on how political the criminal justice system is, how public policies are based upon political ideologies, as well as how political dissent may be manifest through criminal activities.

County sheriffs are elected in partisan elections. In some cities police chiefs are elected, although the majority are appointed by elected officials. At the state level, police commissioners, highway patrol directors, and the heads of investigative agencies are usually appointed by the governor, with many states requiring approval by the legislature. As a result, at both the local and state levels, those who receive such appointments are politically connected. The story is similar at the federal levels where US Marshals are appointed by the president and confirmed by the Senate. Likewise, the heads of other federal law enforcement agencies, such as the FBI director, are also appointed by the president.

Prosecutors are perhaps the most political of the actors within the criminal justice system. Local prosecutors, usually called district attorneys, are elected within partisan elections. Solicitors are usually appointed by city officials to serve as prosecutors in their courts of limited jurisdiction. At the state level, attorneys general are top elected officials who usually rank second in power and prestige behind the governor. Federal district attorneys are appointed by the president and confirmed by the Senate.

Judges at local and state levels are selected in a variety of processes ranging from partisan elections, nonpartisan elections, and merit selection to direct appointments by public officials. Federal district judges, appellate court judges, and Supreme Court justices are appointed for life by the president and require Senate approval. As with law enforcement administrators and prosecutors, those judges who are not directly elected must have political connections in order to be appointed and confirmed at their respective levels.

Politics is not limited to criminal justice practitioners. Protests of unpopular government policies, challenges to laws, and the manners in which they are enforced may be limited to peaceful demonstrations, or they may result in mob actions and riots that result in violence and the destruction of property. They may also lead to violent dissent by individuals and/or organized terrorism aimed at forcing change.

The impact of law. There are two phrases that are often heard regarding the impact of **law** within the United States. One is that we are a nation that is "governed by the rule of law." This refers to the checks and balances within our federalist system of government and the protections offered by our national and state constitutions. Indeed, our rights to due process, fair and equitable treatment, protection from procedural violations, as well as recourse for illegal actions by those in authority are cornerstones of our legal system.

The second phrase, that we in the United States have "too much legality and too little justice," is also accurate. This refers to the difficulties that the working class and lower middle class (who do not qualify as indigents) have in affording legal representation in criminal matters. It is even more applicable in civil matters. The poor may have excellent representation or mediocre representation depending upon their location. The affluent can afford to hire quality attorneys to protect their interests. This is a disparity that will exist until such time as legal services are provided for the working and lower class as well as the poor.

The impact of morality. When the issue of **morality** comes up, people usually become suspicious. This is due to a couple of factors. The first is that those who like to proclaim their own virtue usually have very little to talk about. Indeed, a common strategy of politicians and conmen (no, they are not necessarily the same!) is to stress their honesty and integrity. An old-time county commissioner once informed one of the authors that "the key to being a good politician is caring. Once you learn how to fake that, you've got it made!"

Another adage regarding **ethics** and moral standards says "You can't legislate morality!" Our response is "Of course you can; they are called laws." Violations may result in civil suits or even criminal prosecutions. As our society becomes more complex and congested, there will be an increase in those matters once thought to be personal that become public concerns. Sexual harassment and unethical business dealings are two such issues that exemplify these changes.

Morality is also worthy of discussion in that how an individual views right and wrong serves as the template for determining proper behavior. Pollack (2012) presents several **ethical systems** that are commonly followed. *Ethical formalism* is based upon the view that proper behavior is not based upon outcome but upon the goodwill of the actor. *Utilitarianism* is the concept that one should strive to achieve the greatest good for the greatest number of people. *Ethics of virtue* is basically living by the *golden rule*. The *ethics of caring* focuses on meeting the needs of others. The most difficult ethical system to promote is unfortunately one that is followed by many people, including some criminologists that we know. That system is *egoism,* in which practitioners feel that, if it is beneficial for them, it is moral.

The impact of self-image. We conclude this section by returning to the assertion that we made at the beginning of the chapter: that is, how we perceive justice is influenced by our personal identity. That identity or *self-image* is based upon a convoluted mixture of the influences that we have just discussed. This **self-view** determines our *philosophy of life,* the mechanism by which we judge ourselves and others. In essence, this shapes not only our self-image (our self-respect, as well as our respect for others), but our view of the world (including what we think is just).

The Meaning of Justice

How one defines justice is largely determined by how one views society. Each of these perspectives sees society and its laws in a different light. Furthermore, within these perspectives there are numerous disagreements on what constitutes crime and how society should respond to it. Indeed, criminologists are not immune from these disagreements: "Although science generally strives to be 'value free' criminology is heavily influenced by ideology. Liberal (left) criminologists tend to associate with the positive school of crime and focus on social causes of crime. Conservative (right) criminologists lean toward the classical school of crime and tend to focus on **deterrence**" (Vito and Holmes, 2007, p. 27).

Justice Defined

Hunter and Barker (2011, p. 7) define justice as *the fair and equitable application of the rule of law by agents of social control regardless of the socioeconomic status of the individuals concerned.* While they admit that this is a rather idyllic view, they argue that it is what a free society should strive for. They then state that to accomplish justice there are six components the administration of justice must contain. These components are:

1. Compliance with the rule of law (codified legal standards must exist and must be followed);
2. Equity (law enforcement must be applied in an equal manner to everyone subject to it);
3. Fairness (the laws, as well as their application, must be fair and not single out groups or individuals for arbitrary treatment);
4. Accessibility (there must be allowances for those individuals who do not have financial recourse to receive competent legal advice and support);
5. Effectiveness (the system must work for common citizens in actuality as well as on paper); and
6. Oversight (there must be remedies for failures or misapplications of justice to be corrected) (Hunter and Barker, 2011, pp. 7–8).

Types of Justice

There are several types of justice in addition to criminal justice. Using the criteria established by the lead author in *Police-Community Relations and the Administration of Justice,* they are as follows:

Social justice. Social justice is seen by its proponents as not just emphasizing equity and fairness in the application of jurisprudence but in regulating how a society's resources are allocated. Social justice seeks to see that people are treated both fairly and "morally" within all areas of society. Social justice may either be distributive or commutative.

Distributive justice. Distributive justice seeks to distribute rewards and punishments so needs are considered, but merit is rewarded. The United States' system of *welfare capitalism* is based upon distributive justice. Protections exist to ensure that the tenets of civil and human rights are provided but individual successes or failures are allowed.

Commutative justice. Commutative justice places a greater emphasis upon need rather than individual merit. Proponents of this perspective argue that biases due to class, ethnicity, gender or other distinctions make capitalist society inherently unfair. Therefore, greater efforts by government in the redistribution of wealth and enhancement of life for minorities and the lower class must be implemented to address social inequities.

Civil justice. Civil justice is the legal system that regulates the relationships between individuals. Redress for harm from another's actions is not by criminal prosecution but by seeking legal intervention to regain that which was lost due to another's improper actions and/or to prevent further harm. Due to the complexities and costs of successful litigation, it is in the areas of civil law that the poor and the middle classes are more likely to experience inequitable treatment.

Restorative justice. Yet another type of justice that may or may not involve the criminal justice system is the practice of restorative justice. Instead of seeking to punish based upon criminal sanctions or impose legal compensation, restorative justice seeks to avoid formal adjudication by using arbitration to resolve conflicts. Restorative justice may take place in lieu of civil litigation and it may also be used as an alternative to criminal prosecution.

Criminal justice. Criminal justice is the system that the readers of this text are interested in. As we have noted above, it is not truly separate from the other systems of justice and actually interacts with them. Please note that the *criminal justice system is concerned not only with the enforcement of laws, but with the protection of legal rights as well.* To ensure that laws are not arbitrarily imposed, the criminal justice system relies upon procedural law as well as substantive law. *Substantive law* defines behaviors (and in some cases, failures to act) that are deemed to be unlawful and establishes sanctions for their commission (or omission). *Procedural law* regulates how substantive law may be applied. The famous *exclusionary rule* is one mechanism by which American courts ensure that a defendant's due process rights are protected. (Hunter and Barker, 2011, pp. 8–9)

The Mission of a Criminal Justice System

The mission of a criminal justice system is "to apply the rule of law as a means of providing social stability" (Hunter and Barker, 2011, p. 10). In achieving its overall mission the criminal justice system must balance the rights of individuals with the rights of society. We have presented typologies on types of crimes and criminals. We will conclude this chapter by discussing the different types of rationales for our criminal justice system.

Rule of Law

The rule of law is the means by which a government protects society from crime and protects those accused of criminal behaviors from miscarriages of justice. Due process and crime control must be balanced in order to accomplish the following tasks on behalf of society and its citizens.

Vengeance/Retribution

People have a large capacity for forgiveness; however, we also have an innate need to seek retribution on behalf of ourselves and our loved ones against those who have harmed us. In order to keep citizens from "taking the law into their own hands," agents of social control must exact vengeance on behalf of those who have been harmed. This does not have to be specific in every case, but there must be a viable demonstration of governmental willingness to do so.

Atonement

As advocates for convicted felons who have returned to society may rightly attest, the stigma of conviction and incarceration is difficult to overcome. However, since tribal times, a basis of punishment has been that once offenders atone (pay their "debt to society"), they are allowed to reenter society.

Deterrence/Prevention

The fundamental premise of the classical system of justice is that the imposition of punishment deters further crime from occurring. **Specific deterrence** is the concept that by being punished an offender will decide that his criminal behavior was not worth the harm that he incurred. **General deterrence** is the concept that by seeing the offender punished for her criminal activity, others contemplating similar crimes will be dissuaded from doing so.

Treatment

Like deterrence, the outcomes of treatment are often disappointing. The premise of treatment is that offenders will be rehabilitated so that they may reenter society and live productive lives. Despite debate about the appropriateness and/or adequacy of various treatments, fundamental fairness requires that treatment remain an important component of our correctional system.

Incapacitation

When the term *incapacitation* is used, the most common application is that of **incarceration**. Proponents of incapacitation argue that while offenders may return to crime later, they are prevented from doing so while under correctional control. Critics argue that they may be impeded from committing crimes against the general public, but they usually return to society embittered and with less chance for success than prior to their confinement (*The Economist*, 2010). Others simply note the decline of crime rates as imprisonment of serious offenders has increased (Tremoglie, 2011; von Drehle, 2010; Zax, 2010).

Reparations

A more humane means of applying the rule of law is to focus on victims rather than on the offenders' debt to society. Instead of punishment based upon the harm that they committed, offenders are ordered to make reparations to the victims of their crimes. This restorative technique is seen as benefiting victims, offenders, and the community.

Social Stability

In providing for the rule of law, the criminal justice system also provides for social stability. Hunter and Barker define social stability as "the maintenance of order and the continuation of equitable social control by government" (2011, p. 11).

Maintenance of Order

Maintenance of order includes all those activities for which government exists. These include holding elections, collecting taxes, enforcing zoning regulations, garbage collection, public utilities, crowd control at public events, traffic enforcement, and emergency services.

Equitable Social Control

Addressing social inequities is one of the more controversial aspects of government. While we should be grudging in our tolerance of government intrusion, we must also acknowledge that these actions are necessary to allow "life, liberty, and property" for all. Progressive taxation, compulsory education, mandatory minimum wages, protection of minority rights, and health-care reform are examples of controversial government "intrusions" that are now seen as vital to public stability.

Symbolic Reassurance

Our last requirement for social stability is a concept that we introduced in the first edition of this book. **Symbolic reassurance** is covered in detail within Chapter 14. Basically, it is the view that the criminal justice system not only provides guidelines for society to follow, it also punishes evildoers to affirm law-abiding citizens' belief in the system. Universal conformity is not attained through threats of prosecution, but by reassuring law-abiding citizens that the system of justice is working. Taken to an extreme, this concept implies that as long as the public perceives that "something is being done," the public will, for the most part, remain supportive.

Reality Check: Religious Wars

The connection between religion and violence is long. Every religious movement in the world has been attacked by members of other religions who either felt threatened or saw opportunities to advance their causes. If one views a list of wars involving the three largest monotheistic religions during the past 2,000 years, one will see that Christians, Muslims, and Jews have been at war with others or themselves since their inception. During tribal times, Jews conquered or drove out non-Jewish peoples from the lands they occupied. Following the spread of Christianity, other religions, including Judaism, were suppressed by Christian adherents. After the establishment of Islam, followers conquered lands belonging to Christians, Jews, Hindus, as well as other religions.

At the end of the eleventh century, several efforts were made by European Crusaders to retake the Holy Land. During this same period, Jews in Europe were persecuted and massacred by Christians. During and after the Crusades, Christians began fighting among themselves as Protestants and Catholics each sought to impose their views upon others. Similarly, different sects of Muslims (Sunnis and Shiites) began sparring over who were the proper followers of the Prophet Mohammed.

Atheists take delight in pointing out "the many wars caused by religion." In actuality, religion was often the scapegoat used to justify wars to gain lands, conquer indigenous peoples, achieve political supremacy, and/or impose trade agreements. Perhaps one of the most blatant examples is England breaking away from the Catholic Church in 1534 and the dissolution of the monasteries from 1536 to 1541. The driving force behind these events was Henry VIII's determination to have a male heir and his desire to acquire the massive wealth contained within the monasteries of England, Wales, and Ireland.

Identify a conflict that may be considered a "holy war." Then examine the actual motives of the participants to determine whether religion was the cause of the war or an excuse for it.

Summary

We began this chapter by emphasizing how crime and criminality relate to the myriad of other important issues within our lives. To study crime and its derivatives (criminality, criminology, criminal justice, and crime science), we must first study human nature. Regardless of the approach that one takes to the study of human behavior, there are commonalities found within all: for example, the idea that humans have a need for acceptance.

We discussed two central wants that we as humans have. The first is self-worth. Whether consciously or subconsciously, most of our activities are geared to promoting our own self-image. The second vital need is that of justice. We cited the Reverend Rob Bell's statement, "The core of human existence is a longing for justice."

How individuals see the world is shaped by how they view themselves. These two perspectives, worldview and self-image, provide the means by which we evaluate all other aspects of life, particularly crime and justice. We then presented catalysts and impediments to justice. These include family, religion, gender, race and ethnicity, age, education, social class, ecological/geographical differences, culture, science, technology, globalization, media, politics, law, morality, and self-image. The various types of justice were then discussed. These include social justice, distributive justice, commutative justice, civil justice, restorative justice, and criminal justice.

The mission of a criminal justice system is "to apply the rule of law as a means of providing social stability." In achieving its overall mission, the criminal justice system must balance the rights of individuals with the rights of society. The rationales for our criminal justice system are rule of law, vengeance/retribution, atonement, deterrence/prevention, treatment, incapacitation, reparations, social stability, maintenance of order, equitable social control, and symbolic reassurance.

Discussion Questions

1. Discuss the central wants that human beings have. Explain why you agree or disagree as to whether these are indeed central wants.
2. Select the catalyst that you think has the most influence on human behavior. Select the catalyst that you think has the least influence.
3. Discuss the relationship between war and religion. Is it as strong as it appears to be?
4. Describe the other types of justice that complement criminal justice.
5. Identify the rationales for our criminal justice system.

2

The Problem of Crime

Crime is one of the most fascinating events or phenomena in every culture and society across the world. The mass media, in particular, seem to delight in regaling us with stories related to crime. For example, the cover of the April 21, 1997, issue of *US News and World Report* pictured a baby in a striped prison uniform with the large-type words "Born Bad?" to draw attention to its story on how certain factors, particularly biology, may influence criminality (Wray, 1997). A little over a year later in its May 25, 1998, issue, the same publication's cover displayed a pair of handcuffs and cited a special report inside entitled "Why Crime Is Down: The Real Story" (Witkin, 1998). The December 6, 1999, cover story was on crimes of the century.

Crime as Phenomenon

Thirteen years later, crime remains a focal topic within both the news and entertainment media. However, now the debate is whether we imprison too many people in the United States (*The Economist,* 2010) and what the impact of alternative sanctions would be (Tremoglie, 2011). Despite criticisms of imprisonment, crime rates continue to decline (Conklin, 2003; von Drehle, 2010; Zax, 2010).

The media perpetuate stories on crimes because the public is extremely interested in this subject. Among many citizens, crime is perceived as a major problem. For example, the Gallup Organization conducts numerous opinion surveys yearly. A consistent question in the surveys asks the respondent what he or she thinks is the most important problem facing this country today. The results from four surveys, taken in December 1997, April 1998, September 1998, and January 1999, show that crime was among the top three public concerns along with education and ethical issues (Gallup, 2000). Interestingly, ten years later, despite reports by both the FBI and the Bureau of Justice Statistics of drops in property and violent crime from 2008 to 2009, as well as of longer-term declines in both types of crime, results from an October 2010 Gallup survey indicate that two-thirds of Americans still perceive crime to be on the rise (Gallup, 2010).

There is little doubt that crime is an interesting subject. In addition to the criminal act itself and theories as to why crime occurs, interest exists in the characteristics of crime as well as in the characteristics of criminal behavior.

The Nature of Crime

What causes crime? Why does a person commit a crime? What is the best way to prevent crime? These are all important questions. However, to be able to truly answer these questions is a difficult task. Frank Hagan (2011) suggests that answering these types of questions is similar to asking, "What causes sickness?" (p. 92). It is difficult primarily because there are so few commonalities other than the fact that the criminal act is "a violation of criminal law" (p. 92).

Have you ever heard someone say, "That ought to be a crime" or "There should be a law against that," usually in conjunction with some type of behavior or action the individual has observed and of which he or she disapproved? While there are many unethical or immoral actions that might be considered criminal, not all are or can be. An interesting issue in the study of crime is the lack of consensus surrounding its development and why it occurs. This has led to the development of three differing views of crime.

It is probably safe to say that the majority of people in this country believe that the intentional taking of another's life is murder, whereas not everyone would agree that smoking marijuana should be illegal. It is clear that there are many different perspectives on what constitutes a crime and how to respond to criminal behavior. These differences provide us with the three major categories of views regarding crime: consensus, interactionist, and conflict (Bernard, Snipes, and Gerould, 2009).

The individual viewing crime from a **consensus perspective** views crimes as behaviors that are essentially harmful to the majority of citizens and agrees that these crimes should be controlled or prohibited by the existing criminal law. The consensus view looks at criminal law as a set of rules that express the **norms** of society, the will of the "majority," and that serve a social control function in restraining individuals who would take advantage of others for personal gain. The question with this view is whether those acts designated as criminal truly express the norms of the majority of society or of a select few (Roberson and Wallace, 1998).

The **interactionist perspective** accepts that criminal law defines the actions (or omissions) constituting a crime. However, the interactionist challenges the belief that the law represents the will of a majority of society. Instead, the interactionist views criminal law as being influenced by people who hold social power and use it to mold the law to reflect their interest. For example, the interactionist would say that the insurance industry has strongly influenced the creation of seat-belt and child car-seat laws (Bernard, Snipes, and Gerould, 2009).

From the **conflict perspective**, criminal law is a means of protecting the power of the upper class at the expense of the poor. The conflict view is based on the premise that society is a collection of diverse groups that are in constant conflict and that certain groups are able to assert their power and use the criminal law to advance their interests. Ultimately, social conflict theorists believe that criminal law protects the "haves" from the "have nots" (Hagan, 2011).

Defining Crime

Many definitions of crime are used by criminologists, attorneys, and laypersons. From them, we have developed the following definition, which will be used throughout this text (the reader should note that this definition is limited to crime within democratic societies): *Crime is that which a democratically selected legislative body has determined to be unlawful activity (commission) or inactivity (omission), for which there is a prescribed legal sanction.*

To be criminal, one must have committed an unlawful act or failed to act in a manner required by law. *Criminal behavior may be viewed as any action or failure to act as defined by criminal laws.* These actions do not have to be heinous crimes such as murder or rape. Indeed, many of the activities that an ordinary citizen may have engaged in (or failed to engage in) would qualify as criminal behaviors. Many of us have willingly or unknowingly participated in behaviors that were criminal. This does not necessarily mean that we are "bad people." However, it does demonstrate that defining criminal laws and enforcing them are a more complex issue than many realize.

Criminality is said to occur when "certain behaviors have been transformed by society into crimes and people engaging in those behaviors have been identified as criminals" (Barlow, 2000, p. 17). In other words, when crime and criminal behavior occur, a state of criminality exists. Whether a serious felony or a simple misdemeanor, crimes occur on a regular basis within our society and are committed by all types of people (often unknowingly). It is this constancy of criminality within all regions of our nation and the impacts of crime upon all levels of society that make the problem of crime such a fascinating topic. In order to understand the nature of crime, we must first understand the nature of **criminal law**, for it is the legal definition of crime that ultimately creates crime.

The Nature of Criminal Law

One of the most difficult questions in criminal justice is, why are certain behaviors criminal while others are not? As discussed earlier, based on the differing views of crime, no clear-cut answer to this question exists. However, at least one common theme determines what is criminal: moral behavior (Lilly, Cullen, and Ball, 2007). Since the beginning of time, societies have tried to regulate morality, initially drawing from their religions. Because of these moral imperatives, societies eventually legislated laws and sanctions against certain activities. The issue, as societies developed and modernized, was deciding what moral and acceptable behavior was.

While today many would argue that determining what is criminal is still deeply based in religious and moral imperatives, the reality is that the decisions of those who pass laws (state and federal legislators) determine what is criminal. Often their decisions are influenced by lobbyists and special-interest groups and are not necessarily a moral imperative but rather a desired behavior. Nonetheless, much of what is considered criminal behavior is based on either moral beliefs or social beliefs that the action in question is not acceptable. When such an action has been deemed unacceptable by a legislative body and made "criminal," those who still participate in that action must be sanctioned.

Characteristics of Criminal Law

Criminal law is the legal code that attempts to control public behavior by defining what constitutes a crime. Criminal law has the following features: *Criminal law is political in its origins* (because government is charged with creating and enforcing criminal laws and government is by nature political). *Criminal law is specific in its construction* (criminal laws are very clear and to the point about which behaviors are acceptable and which are not). *Criminal law is uniform in its application* (meaning that, theoretically, the law is applied equally to everyone). Finally, *criminal law contains provisions for penal sanctions* (it directs how a person who has committed a crime should be dealt with).

Ultimately, the reasons we have criminal law are to prevent society from degenerating into anarchy and chaos, to promote widely shared social values, and (according to conflict perspective proponents) to express the more narrow interests of the powerful segments of society. How law is imposed and enforced is based on two types of criminal law: substantive and procedural (Dantzker, 1998).

Substantive law explains what is criminal and what the sanctions for violations will be. Substantive laws are commonly called **felonies** (any offense punishable by more than one year of incarceration in a state or federal prison) and **misdemeanors** (offenses punishable by a fine or one year or less of incarceration in a city or county jail). The classification of a crime as well as the punishment is determined by statute. The substantive law spells out all the requisite information needed by governmental agents (police, prosecutors, and judges) to define a behavior as criminal and to provide sanctions for such behavior.

Procedural law regulates how to uphold or enforce substantive law. All states and the federal government have **codes of criminal procedure**. These codes delineate how government officials will enforce the substantive laws. The failure of government officials to follow procedural law can often result in the dismissal of a case. Within US society, citizens are protected by both state constitutions and the US Constitution.

Sources of Crime Statistics

Although a variety of sources of crime statistics exist, the best-known and most often used source is the Uniform Crime Reports (UCR) compiled and reported by the Federal Bureau of Investigation. Each month, local law enforcement agencies voluntarily submit the number of offenses reported by their agency to the FBI. However, since there are several hundred types of crimes due to the variety of laws from state to state, not all crimes can be included. Therefore, the UCR is primarily concerned with **index crimes**. These include murder and non-negligent manslaughter, forcible rape, robbery, aggravated assault, burglary, **larceny/theft**, arson, and auto theft. These crimes are reported even if there are no arrests and no recovery of property, and whether or not prosecution occurs.

Other data reported in the UCR are arrest rates, which include age, gender, and ethnicity/race of offender. Using the UCR, we can examine (albeit tentatively) a variety of crime trends in the United States. Although the UCR provides us with a variety of crime data, the following flaws must be acknowledged:

- Reporting practices by the police
- Lack of reporting by victims
- Improper classification
- Downgrading charges/plea bargaining
- Under- or overreporting by police
- Political manipulation
- Technical flaws (inaccurate volume of crime, population base)

Although the UCR is perhaps the most popular source of crime data, its potential inaccuracies have led to questions of its validity and an accusation that it leaves a "black hole" of criminality (Dantzker, 1998). In an attempt to offset that lack of knowledge, there are two other major sources of crime data: the National Crime Victimization Survey and self-reports.

The National Crime Victimization Survey

The shortcomings of the UCR led to the creation of a survey that bypasses the police and goes directly to victims. The **National Crime Victimization Survey** (NCVS) is believed by some (e.g., Doerner and Lab, 2012) to provide a more credible set of data on the type and frequency of criminal victimization than the UCR. The UCR relies on the collection and reporting of data to the FBI; the NCVS directly contacts a representative sample of people to determine whether they have been victims. From this information, data are extrapolated to fit the general population.

Unlike the UCR, the NCVS provides characteristics of victims (age, sex, race/ethnicity, marital status, annual family income, employment status, and occupational group). However, it is not a good source for characteristics of offenders. The NCVS is believed to provide a better indication of the incidence, seriousness, and cost of the types of crime that permits us to gauge fluctuations in the rates of these crimes over time and across geographical areas more precisely than the UCR.

Self-Report Surveys

Self-report surveys supplement the other two sources and provide an alternative to obtaining data that cannot be derived from official statistics. In these types of reports, individuals (often young people) are asked whether they have ever engaged in criminal behaviors. Advocates of self-report studies argue that they enable us to learn more about crimes not reported to official sources. The findings of self-report studies were instrumental in the development of **labeling theory**, an influential theory that will be described in Chapter 8. Flaws of these studies include the population (usually juveniles attending school who are coerced into participating), lack of honesty (resulting from distrust of the researchers and fears regarding anonymity), and incompleteness (inability to ask about all types of crimes).

National Incident-Based Reporting System

In 1982, a Bureau of Justice Statistics and FBI task force conducted a study on how to improve the UCR program. The results of the study led to the creation of a more comprehensive data collection system, the **National Incident-Based Reporting System (NIBRS)** (Reaves, 1993). Unlike the UCR, which primarily focuses on index crimes, the NIBRS looks at more categories of crimes, divided into two major groups of offenses (see Figure 2.1).

Figure 2.1   The NIBRS Offense Categories

Group A offenses

Arson
Assault offenses
  Aggravated assault
  Simple assault
  Intimidation
Bribery
Burglary/breaking and entering
Counterfeiting/forgery
Destruction damage/vandalism
Drug/narcotic offense
  Drug/narcotic violations
  Drug equipment violations
Embezzlement
Extortion/blackmail
Fraud offenses
  False pretenses/swindles
  Confidence games
  Credit card/ATM fraud
  Impersonation
  Welfare fraud
  Wire fraud
Gambling offenses
  Betting/wagering
  Operating/promoting
  Assisting gambling
  Gambling equipment violations
  Sports tampering

Homicide offenses
  Murder/non-negligent manslaughter
  Negligent manslaughter
  Justifiable homicide
Kidnapping/abduction
Larceny/theft offenses
  Pocketpicking
  Purse snatching
  Theft from building
  Theft from coin-op machines
  Theft from motor vehicle
  Theft of motor vehicle parts
  All other larceny
  Motor vehicle theft
Pornography/obscene materials
Prostitution offenses
  Prostitution
  Assisting/promoting prostitution
Robbery
Sex offense, forcible
  Forcible rape
  Forcible sodomy
  Sexual assault with an object
  Forcible fondling
Sex offenses, nonforcible
Stolen property offenses
Weapons law violations

Group B offenses

Bad checks
Curfew/loitering/vagrancy
Disorderly conduct
Driving under the influence
Drunkenness
Liquor law violations

Nonviolent family offense
Peeping Tom
Runaway
Trespassing
All other offenses

Source: Adapted from Reaves, 1993.

The Extent of Crime

As we saw in the previous section, several means are available to determine the incidences of crime. Despite these efforts, there is still a great deal of uncertainty among scholars as to the true extent of crime and the actual number of crime victims in the United States within any particular period of time. Fortunately, we can track trends by reviewing the changes within the various methods of data gathering. The good news at the time of this writing is that crime rates for both property offenses and violent crimes continue to decline.

According to the UCR (Federal Bureau of Investigation, 1999), 12,475,634 crimes were reported in 1998. Of these incidents, 12 percent were violent crimes and 88 percent were property crimes (Table 2.1). The National Crime Victimization Survey (Bureau of Justice Statistics, 2000) yielded a much higher finding of 31.3 million crimes that were said by victims to have occurred in 1998. Of these, 26 percent were reported to be violent crimes and 73 percent were said to be property offenses. While the numbers in themselves may appear impersonal, they represent individuals who have been harmed financially, physically, and/or emotionally as crime victims.

To put the incidence of crime in perspective, one should consider the UCR crime figures in Table 2.1. These figures reflect an increase in the US population of 57,542,154 over ten years, yet crimes reported to the police dropped by 4,180,758 in that time period, despite the nation having been in a severe recession for the last several years. Unfortunately, as indicated earlier, the US pub-

Table 2.1 UCR Crime Incidents for 1999 and 2009

	1999	2009
Population	249,464,396	307,006,550
Total number of crimes	14,475,613	10,639,369
Violent crime	1,820,127	1,318,398
Murder and non-negligent manslaughter	23,438	15,241
Forcible rape	102,555	88,097
Robbery	639,271	408,217
Aggravated assault	1,054,863	808,843
Property crime	12,655,486	9,320,971
Burglary	3,073,909	219,125
Larceny/theft	7,945,670	6,327,230
Motor-vehicle theft	1,635,907	794,616

Source: Crime in the United States (Federal Bureau of Investigation, 2010a).

lic thinks that crime is increasing, and despite the decline in criminal occurrences, it is obvious from these data that millions of Americans are victimized each year.

The Costs of Crime

Regardless of how it is reported, the fact is that crime is a problem and has dire consequences for society and citizens (Doerner and Lab, 2012). According to the Federal Bureau of Investigation (1999), the costs of criminal victimization in the United States exceeded $15.8 billion in 1998. Of this amount, only about 35 percent was recovered by law enforcement officials. These costs reflect only the value of property taken and do not reflect the costs of medical treatment for victims of violent crimes. Nor do they reflect the costs of property and injuries in incidents not reported to the police. It is not unreasonable to assume that the financial consequences of crime victimization in the United States could be several times higher. The cost of crime is high, and it is therefore imperative to restrict criminal behavior. Chapter 13 provides a more detailed discussion regarding the costs of crime.

Crime Typologies

While there is considerable agreement that certain behaviors should be termed *crimes,* there is even greater disagreement as to whether other behaviors should be termed *criminal.* Nor is there consensus on how society should respond to the various types of crime and criminal behaviors. In classifying crime and criminal behavior, it is helpful to make use of typologies. **Typologies** have been described as a "framework and theoretical construct used to describe and compare different forms of criminal behavior" (Vito and Holmes, 2007, p. 228). Hagan (2011) suggests that typologies can be used as (1) a scientific classificatory system or (2) a heuristic scheme (an educational tool). It is for the second purpose that we offer the use of typologies. An interesting issue is that except for classifying a crime as either a felony or misdemeanor, property or violent, little consensus exists as to how to classify crime. The purpose of the following sections is to acquaint the reader with the many types of crime and criminal behavior that exist within a democratic society.

In this text, we offer a broad typology of crimes adapted from Marshall Clinard and Richard Quinney's (1986) typology of criminal behaviors. The typology includes violent, property, public order, political, occupational, corporate, organized, and professional crimes. These crimes are known as *mala in se* **crimes** because most lawmakers and the public agree that these behaviors should be criminalized.

Violent Crimes

Violent crimes are viewed as any type of intentional action that causes some form of bodily injury or death to another. Murder is the leader in this area but is most certainly not the only violent crime (Doerner and Lab, 2012). Murder may range from a thoughtless blow struck while under emotional distress to a killing by a hired professional "hitman." Murders may be as simple as "crimes of passion" committed by angry lovers or complex serial killings by sexual sadists.

Probably the second best-known violent crime is **sexual assault.** Although many of today's statutes refer to rape as just one of various forms of sexual assault, forcible rape is the only one tracked in the FBI crime index. Sexual assault, in any form, is the uninvited touching of the genitals, the unwilling touching of the genitals of another, or the penetration of another in a sexual manner. Because it is against the victim's will and requires physical contact between the offender and victim, sexual assault is a violent crime regardless of the degree of injury sustained (Schmalleger, 2011). Sexual assault offenses may include sexual abuse of children, the elderly, the mentally incompetent, and the physically challenged. It may include the actions of serial rapists, pedophiles, and sexual sadists, who inflict severe physical harm or death on their victims. Sexual assault most definitely includes "date rape," whether committed by force or with the use of drugs to overcome the victim's resistance.

Another well-known violent crime is **assault.** While today much attention is paid to domestic assault, any unwanted, intentional contact made by one person against another is an assault. Because of the varying degrees of assault (simple unwanted touching to severe bodily injury), every state has its own assault typology (for example, in Texas an assault can range from a Class C misdemeanor to a first-degree felony).

Finally, the last violent crime we discuss is **robbery.** Many people find it difficult to think of a robbery as being violent, in comparison to, say, murder or assault. However, the act of robbery requires the physical taking of property from another either by threat of or by use of force. Even though it is done for economic motives, it is the use (or threat) of force that places robbery in the violent crime category.

Undoubtedly, some people might suggest that other crimes could be placed under the violent crime category. However, if one closely examines the four crimes listed here, one might conclude that each crime could be a typology in itself (i.e., assault).

Property Crimes

As with violent crimes, numerous **property crimes** exist. Regardless of their particular natures, property crimes are any crime in which one person has intentionally deprived another person of his or her right to that property by either destroying or taking the property. Many different crimes appear within this category, but three of the most common are arson, **burglary**, and larceny/ theft (Albanese, 2004).

Arson is the intentional destruction of property by flammable process (e.g., gasoline or dynamite). Arson is often committed for profit (e.g., insurance fraud) or for destroying evidence (of another crime previously committed). Burglary involves the unlawful entry into a building, vehicle, or machine with the intent to commit some type of criminal action, such as stealing property or assaulting someone. Larceny/theft is simply the unlawful taking of another's property in order to deprive that individual of the item. Some of the more commonly recognized types of theft are shoplifting, pickpocketing, embezzlement, passing bad checks, and motor-vehicle theft (Barlow, 2000).

Public Order Crimes

Although violent and property crimes are the two most prevalent categories of crime, a variety of other activities can be identified and classified. One such set of activities might be referred to as **public order crimes**. Public order crimes are those activities that would disrupt or interfere with socially acceptable behavior. Two of the best-known public order crimes are disorderly conduct and rioting. Both crimes can be committed in a variety of ways, but regardless of how they are committed, the question of criminality ultimately comes down to whether the activity is disturbing or interfering with acceptable behavior. Additionally, behavior or activity that could lead to harm to others may be included (e.g., yelling "fire" in a crowded movie theater) (Siegel, 2010).

Still another group of public order crimes includes victimless crimes. Victimless crimes do not have direct victims but are criminalized because they have been deemed to be socially unacceptable. Prostitution, drug use, and unauthorized gambling are the main victimless crimes. These crimes are also known as *mala prohibita* **crimes** in that they are crimes solely because of a ban imposed by a legislative body that felt such activities to be hazardous to society. They differ from *mala in se* crimes, such as the violent crimes discussed earlier, for which there is a consensus among the population that they are evil actions in and of themselves.

Political/State Crimes

In 1972, individuals broke into a room in the Watergate Hotel in Washington, DC, that housed information about the Democratic Party. That break-in eventually led to the resignation of then-president Richard M. Nixon. Although the act itself was a burglary (property crime), the purpose of the act had political ramifications, thus making it a **political/state crime**. A political crime involves any activity that violates the laws of government. The obtaining of information about one political party by another using illegal means could be viewed as a political crime (Schmalleger, 2011).

Social conflict theorists also argue that political crimes include the use of lawmaking and enforcement to maintain political power. Examples of these state-sponsored crimes could be the direct use of government assets (including criminal justice agencies) to suppress political opposition, as well as sponsoring terroristic behaviors against organizations or states to which a government is antagonistic.

Occupational Crimes

Occupational crimes are committed in the course of one's employment. Again, because almost all crimes can be either violent or property, they may carry the corresponding label (i.e., theft, burglary, assault), but because they are committed as part of one's work, the acts can be viewed as occupational crimes (Siegel, 2010). A postal worker throwing mail in the trash rather than delivering it and a police officer in response to a burglary call stealing items from the scene are both examples of occupational crimes. Embezzlement of a client's funds by an attorney or accountant would also be an occupational crime.

Corporate Crimes

Perhaps one of the most difficult of crimes to prosecute falls under the category of **corporate crimes**. Corporate crimes are criminal activities conducted during the course of doing business or that result from inappropriate business practices (Hagan, 2011). Corporate crimes differ from occupational crimes in that occupational crimes are committed by an individual or a group for self-gain, whereas corporate crimes are committed by groups of individuals on behalf of their company or organization. While corporate crimes are white-collar crimes (involving professionals or administrators), occupational crimes may be either white-collar or blue-collar crimes (involving lower-level employees).

The problem with corporate crimes is that prosecution of those responsible is often difficult because the crime was committed under the umbrella of the corporation. An example of this dilemma was that of the Ford Motor Company and the exploding Ford Pinto gas tank. The company was aware of the danger in how and where the gas tank was mounted and that a rear-end collision could cause a rupture of the tank and possibly fire, but it continued to manufacture the vehicle in that way. An accident did occur in which the occupant was killed because the car exploded into flames. Ford Motor Company was prosecuted and found guilty of negligent manslaughter, the penalty for which generally includes a term in prison. However, in this case no one did any jail time; instead Ford paid a hefty fine. Similar investigations have taken place in regard to recent deaths from faulty Firestone tires.

Organized Crimes

Organized crimes can be any criminal activity that is committed in an orderly and continuous fashion by a group or organization created to accomplish that purpose. The victimless crimes of prostitution, drug use, and gambling are three of the most common activities that can be a function of organized crime. Whereas the majority of crimes in the other categories are committed by individuals, organized crime is committed by several individuals acting in concert (Hagan, 2011). The majority of organized crimes involve the provision of goods or services to those desiring them despite their illegality. These types of crimes are deemed to be public order crimes.

Professional Crimes

Like corporate, occupational, and organized crimes, professional crimes may be found within the previous categories. Almost any crime found elsewhere can fit here; the qualifier is that the crime is committed as the primary means of financial support for the offender. An example would be burglaries in which only easily saleable or negotiable items (e.g., cash or jewelry) are taken by people who sell such goods to support themselves.

Hate Crimes

Hate crimes (also known as bias crimes) are criminal behaviors that may include either violent crimes or property crimes. The motivation for these crimes is prejudice based upon religion, sexual orientation (gay, lesbian, bisexual, or transgendered), race, ethnicity, national origin, or disability (FBI, 2010b). In response to a growing number of hate crimes occurring across the country, the *Matthew Shepard and James Byrd, Jr. Hate Crimes Prevention Act* was passed by Congress and signed into law by President Obama on October 28, 2009. This act was named for two men who were murdered in 1998 (see the Reality Check at the end of this chapter). This expanded the 1969 federal hate crime law to include crimes motivated by a victim's actual or perceived gender, sexual orientation, gender identity, or disability.

Stalking

Stalking is "a course of conduct directed at a specific person that involves repeated visual or physical proximity, nonconsensual communication or verbal, written or implied threats, or a combination thereof, that would cause a reasonable person fear" (Violence Against Women Grants Office, 1998, p. 6). While stalking has been a problem for centuries, it is only within recent times that legislation has been passed by the federal government and all fifty states to protect stalking victims. It is estimated that 3.4 million people, roughly 1 in 100, are stalking victims (Baum, Catalano, Rand, and Rose, 2009).

Bullying

Bullying is something that every one of us can remember from our childhood. To a degree it is an unpleasant but normal part of growing up. However, in recent years we have been inundated with stories of people who were bullied and harassed by others to the point of actually committing suicide. According to Olweus (1993), "A person is bullied when he or she is exposed, repeatedly and over time, to negative actions on the part of one or more other persons, and he or she has difficulty defending himself or herself." Bullying occurs more frequently in elementary, middle, and to a lesser degree high schools. However, it is not limited to children and may also be found in colleges, sports organizations, the military services, and other workplaces (Olweus Bullying Prevention Program, 2011).

Cybercrimes

The last category of crime that we will discuss is that of cybercrimes. As computer technology has improved and the use of the Internet has increased, so have criminal opportunities. Computer crime, or cybercrime, refers to any crime that involves a computer and a network. The computer may have been used in the commission of a crime, or it may be the target of criminal activities. Net crime refers, more precisely, to criminal exploitation of the Internet.

Types of cybercrimes include cracking (hacking into targeted networks), copyright infringement, child pornography, and child grooming (wooing children for sexual exploitation). Crimes that primarily target computer networks or devices would include computer viruses, denial-of-service attacks, and malware. Crimes that merely use computer networks or devices would include cyberstalking, fraud, identity theft, information warfare, phishing scams, and possibly spam. Computers and the Internet may also be used for harassment, cyberbullying, cyberstalking, drug trafficking, cyberextortion, cyberterrorism, and even cyberwarfare (Moore, 2011).

Terrorism

When we hear the word *terrorism* we tend to think of international terrorism committed by Al Qaida or other Islamic extremists. Or we think of domestic terrorists such as Timothy McVeigh and Eric Rudolph. However, terrorism has been utilized by a broad array of individuals and organizations to further their objectives. It has been practiced by right-wing and left-wing political parties, nationalistic groups, religious groups, revolutionaries, and ruling governments. An abiding characteristic of terrorism is "the indiscriminate use of violence against noncombatants for the purpose of gaining publicity for a group, cause, or individual" (Ruby, 2002).

There are several types of terrorism. *State terrorism* is the systematic use of terror by a government in order to control its population. Examples may be seen in the tactics used by autocratic rulers in North Africa and the Mideast in trying to suppress rebellions. *Religious terrorism* is motivated by religious ideologies and grievances against those deemed as threats. Religious terrorism is particularly dangerous due to the fanaticism of those who practice it and their willingness to sacrifice themselves for the cause. *Right-wing terrorism* seeks to combat liberal governments, preserve traditional social orders, and suppress minority groups. *Left-wing terrorism* seeks to overthrow capitalist democracies and establish socialist or communist governments in their place. *Pathological terrorism* is practiced by individuals who utilize such strategies for the sheer joy of terrorizing others rather than for well-defined political motives. The shootings at Columbine High School and of Congresswoman Gabby Giffords are examples of pathological terrorism. *Issue-oriented terrorism* is carried out for the purpose of advancing a specific issue and would include the environmental terrorism by Ted Kaczynski and the abortion clinic bombings by Eric Rudolph. *Separatist terrorism* is used by ethnic, religious, and political minorities within a nation-state who desire their own state, commonly due to discrimination from the majority group. *Narco-terrorism* is exemplified by the drug cartels in Mexico and South America who seek to intimidate their governments into not interfering with their drug trafficking. We will discuss terrorism in more detail within later chapters.

It should be evident from the crime categories discussed that many other typologies are possible. For most of us there is little need or desire to categorize crime beyond the misdemeanor/felony and violent/property dichotomies. However, typologies are useful for criminologists and criminal justice practitioners in understanding and responding to the myriad crimes found within our society.

Criminal Typologies

Earlier we noted that the interest in typologies extends more to criminal behavior than to crimes. In the preceding section, a typology of crimes was presented. Now we present a typology of criminal behaviors. As with our

crime typology, our criminal typology is adapted from Clinard and Quinney's (1986) typology.

Violent Personal Criminals

The violent personal criminal is someone who is unable to control hostility or allows anger toward others to erupt into violence. Although this person may have a long history of violent behaviors toward others, because crime is not a part of his or her career, the violent offender usually does not see him- or herself as a criminal. The violence is often viewed as a justifiable response to another's behavior. Thus, the violent offender frequently does not accept that what he or she has done is criminal. Domestic abusers blame their spouses for "provoking them." Mean drunks often engage in barroom brawls but "really didn't intend to hurt anyone." Pedophiles were "seduced" by their young victims. Racists who commit a "hate crime" did so because they have been "wronged by society." The list could go on ad nauseam, but the reader can see how a history of violent behavior is often rationalized by the offender.

Occasional Property Criminals

Occasional property criminals do not engage in theft or burglary on a regular basis. They commit their crimes as a means of obtaining thrills, to strike back against perceived wrongs done to them, to obtain desired items that they could not legitimately afford, or to augment their incomes. As with violent criminals, property criminals may also rationalize their behavior as necessary. Oftentimes the behavior is said to be committed as a means of survival, and as such, criminals do not identify or associate themselves with "real" criminals, that is, those who commit crime as a way of life or for the thrill.

Public Order Criminals

Public order criminals live in a state of ambiguity. They neither regard their behavior as criminal nor have a clearly defined criminal career. Public order criminals disagree with local, state, or national prohibitions against a specific victimless crime. They may be totally conformist in their other activities but frequently engage in what they believe should be legitimate behaviors. Purchasing drugs, soliciting prostitution, and participating in illegal gambling operations are but three of the more common public order crimes in which many otherwise "law-abiding citizens" participate. The problems that arise from such participation are that it supports organized crime organizations and creates disrespect for other legal prohibitions on the part of both those who participate and those who view the offenders as role models.

Political Criminals

Like violent, property, and public order criminals, political criminals do not identify with being a criminal or believe that they have committed any crime. Two types of political criminals exist. The first type is the person employed as a governmental official who abuses his or her position for personal benefit, to cause harm to those perceived to be enemies, or to provide undeserved aid or preferential treatment to associates. While such political criminals may fall within another category of offender (e.g., drug use in their private lives), they are criminal only when a violation of law regulating the government is committed. Your position in the debate about former president Bill Clinton's alleged behavior with several female accusers and his relationship with Monica Lewinsky was based on whether or not you thought his behaviors were private actions or violations of his office. A more readily identifiable type of criminal would be a politician or governmental official who uses state powers to harass or (as evident in the 2011 suppression of rebels in Libya by Muammar Gaddafi) kill political opponents.

The second type of political criminal believes that the government itself has acted in an unjust or illegal way, provoking his or her response. This person engages in opposition actions deemed to be criminal by the government, which may involve simple sit-ins or banned demonstrations, or may result in actual terrorist activities, such as the 1995 bombing of the Federal Building in Oklahoma City by domestic terrorist Timothy McVeigh and the destruction of the Twin Towers in New York by Muslim extremists. It is the perception of this offender that the criminal label is attached solely because of the perceived threat he or she may pose against the government.

Occupational Criminals

The occupational criminal may commit petty theft by stealing pens and paper from work. This individual can easily rationalize such behavior as inconsequential and will often consider it as a perk of the job. This type of occupational criminal (and there are many) usually accepts the conventional norms and values of society and has little or no self-conception of being criminal. Indeed, most would be enraged if they were accused of being criminals. On the opposite end of the spectrum are those people who use their position to obtain considerable fortunes by selling information and/or by granting favors to others for personal gain. Like the offender who "borrows" items from work, this occupational criminal may also see his or her actions as being merely perks of the job.

Corporate Criminals

As discussed in the previous section, corporate crimes are among the most difficult crimes to prosecute. Corporate criminals are generally white-collar criminals (professionals or administrators) who seek to advance their company or organization by engaging in illegal practices. These practices may involve such activities as bribing government officials to get lucrative grants, circumventing state or federal environmental regulations, conspiring to fix prices, or developing an illegal monopoly. Often these offenders are unrepentant; they consider what they did as merely "good business." In addition, the prosecutions that occur often nab only underlings who will or must "take the heat" on behalf of their superiors. Last, many such criminals may see the fines imposed as being worth the profits obtained through their illegal actions.

Organized Criminals

All of us have seen movies or television programs that depict organized criminals. These may range from the old Mafia movies—from *Some Like It Hot* to *The Godfather* to *Goodfellas*—to depictions of the violent world of contemporary drug lords. These depictions are distorted in that they tend to overstate the amount of violence used and the luxuriant lifestyles of organized criminals. However, they are accurate in that they demonstrate the difficulties law enforcement faces in thwarting the illegal behaviors demanded by the numerous public order criminals within our society.

Despite pretensions to the contrary ("I just provide a service for the public"), organized criminals generally accept their criminality. Crime is pursued as a way of life. The criminal activity may often begin as minor but usually progresses to major criminality. The progression aids in the development of isolation from mainstream society, and this isolation, along with the huge sums of money that can be made by those in the higher echelons of the organization, ensures continued involvement.

Professional Criminals

Other than the organized criminal, the professional criminal is probably the only criminal type who not only recognizes and accepts his or her status as a criminal, but actually takes pride in it. Generally this individual has a well-developed criminal career engaging in specialized crimes. The desired outcome of the criminality is primarily economic gain. Professional criminals include the romantic-sounding "cat burglars" who steal from the homes of the affluent despite the presence of high-tech security systems, as well as their less talented colleagues who burglarize small businesses in order to "earn" their living. Other professional criminals might include bank robbers, con artists, shoplifters, blackmailers, and any others who make a living from their criminal activities.

These typologies provide insights into the varieties of crimes and criminals found within US society. The first, crime typologies, offered brief insights

Reality Check: Hate Crimes

The Murder of Matthew Shepard

Perhaps the best-known case of hate-based crime was the murder of Matthew Shepard, a young gay man, in Wyoming in 1998. Shepard was offered a ride home from a lounge by Aaron McKinney and Russell Henderson, who had seemed to befriend him. Instead, they drove to a remote area where they robbed and tortured him, then tied him to a fence and left him to die. Although he was still alive when discovered, Matthew Shepard never regained consciousness.

Witnesses stated that McKinney and Henderson had previously talked about their plan to "rob a gay man." Henderson pleaded guilty on April 5, 1999, and agreed to testify against McKinney to avoid the death penalty; he received two consecutive life sentences. The jury in McKinney's trial found him guilty of felony murder. McKinney received two consecutive life terms without the possibility of parole (Black, 1999; Cart, 1999).

The Murder of James Byrd, Jr.

James Byrd, Jr., was an African American male who was murdered by three white supremacists in Jasper, Texas, on June 7, 1998. Byrd had accepted a ride from Shawn Allen Berry (whom he knew), Lawrence Russell Brewer, and John William King. Instead of taking him home, the three took him to a secluded area where they beat him unconscious, urinated on him, and tied his feet to their truck with a logging chain. They then dragged him behind the truck for two miles on a rough macadam road. Byrd was killed when his body hit the edge of a culvert, severing his right arm and head. The murderers drove for another mile, then dumped Byrd's torso in front of an African American cemetery (Stewart, 1999).

The driver of the truck, Shawn Allen Berry, was sentenced to life in prison. He has a parole eligibility date of June 7, 2038. Since 2003, he has been in protective custody where he is confined to a small cell for 23 hours a day. Lawrence Russell Brewer and John William King, white supremacists with prior prison records, were both sentenced to death. King is awaiting execution at the Polunsky Unit, which houses Texas's death row (*New York Times*, 1999). Brewer was executed in 2011.

The murders of these two men were the impetus for the *Matthew Shepard and James Byrd, Jr. Hate Crimes Prevention Act* discussed previously.

Critics argue that hate crime laws are unnecessary, discriminatory, and unconstitutional. They also point to the murder of Jesse William Dirkhising as an example of a hate crime by two gay men that has been ignored by the "liberal media." Do you think this case is a relevant comparison?

into what may influence specific types of crime. The second, criminal typologies, explored how certain types of criminals might perceive their criminality. From an applied perspective, neither is of much value unless we understand what originally led to the criminal behavior and what may be done in response to it. We explore these issues within the Reality Check and throughout the following chapters.

Summary

There is little doubt that crime is an interesting subject. In addition to the criminal act itself and theories as to why crime occurs, there is an interest in characteristics of crime and how crime can be labeled and classified. While there are some actions people might wish were criminal, not all are. Crime is formally defined as that which legislative bodies define as activities (commission) or failures to act (omission) that are unlawful. Participation in such an act or failure (to act) means an individual has committed a crime. An interesting issue in the study of crime is the lack of consensus surrounding its development and its causes. This has led to the development of three differing views on the nature of crime: consensus, interactionist, and conflict perspectives.

Regardless of the view, the reality is that when a criminal act has been committed, punishing or sanctioning the offender is a priority. However, determining what is criminal must be accomplished first. Much of what is considered criminal behavior is based on either moral or social beliefs that the action is not acceptable. When such an action has been deemed unacceptable and made "criminal," those who still participate in that action must be sanctioned.

Criminal offenders exist because of criminal law, which can be viewed as being political in its origins, specific in its construction, uniform in its application, and containing provisions for penal sanctions. Criminal law, with respect to policy and process, is divided into substantive and procedural law. Substantive law explains what is criminal. Procedural law explains how to uphold or enforce substantive law.

Because law is the basis of societal interaction, the occurrence of crimes creates public interest. Of particular interest is the extent of crime. We attempt to determine how much crime exists through crime statistics. The best-known and most frequently used source of crime statistics is the Uniform Crime Reports (UCR). The National Crime Victimization Survey (NCVS) and self-surveys are other means of gathering crime statistics. The newest attempt to collect crime data is the National Incident-Based Reporting System (NIBRS), which has been designed to collect more information than the UCR and will eventually replace it.

Last, we presented several examples of crime and criminal offenders based on our adaptations of Clinard and Quinney's typologies. The first included violent crimes, property crimes, public order crime, political crimes, corporate crimes, organized crimes, and professional crimes. The second provided a brief overview of the criminals who engage in those crimes.

Discussion Questions

1. Considering the three views of crime, which one seems to best represent current societal views? Which view seems the most prudent? Is there another way to view crime?
2. There are many reasons why society sanctions criminal behavior. Are these reasons valid? Are there other reasons? Do the reasons seem to truly reflect today's society?
3. Using only the index crimes, identify at least five characteristics you would use to describe crime.
4. Of what value are crime trends? What types of trends would you look for if the information was wanted by a police department? A prosecutor's office? The mayor?
5. How would you classify criminal behavior? What would be the focus of your typology?

3

The Study of Crime

In Chapter 1, we discussed how human nature impacts our existence. We then reviewed those important social institutions that shape who we are as human beings. We followed with the need for justice, the development of crime, as well as social responses to criminal behavior. We followed in Chapter 2 with a review of the problem of crime, the nature of criminal law, and the administration of justice.

Introduction to Criminology

Conceptually, criminology has existed for more than 200 years (Dantzker, 1998). Yet, as an academic field of study, it is still relatively new. For many years, criminology was a subfield within sociology. The majority of early criminologists were sociologists who studied crime and its place in and impact on society. Many of today's criminologists still acquire a sociological education, but because of a movement in the 1950s to separate criminology from sociology, there are existing academic programs that are "strictly criminology." What led to the beginning of the separation, perhaps a catalyst for this movement, was C. Ray Jeffery's (1956) critical analysis of criminology, "The Structure of American Criminological Thinking." Yet, "the truer emergence of criminology appears to have begun in the late 1960s as sociology and other social sciences were undergoing criticisms and change" (Dantzker, 1998, p. 8).

Defining Criminology

Providing a definition of *criminology* is easy; agreeing on one is not. All criminology textbooks and the majority of introductory criminal justice textbooks offer definitions of criminology. In the previous edition of this text, we used the definition of criminology offered by Dantzker (1998): "Criminology is the scientific approach to the study of crime as a social phenomenon, that is, the theoretical application involving the study of the nature and extent of criminal behavior" (p. 27). We now acknowledge the growth and development of the discipline by proposing a more holistic definition: *Criminology is the study of human behavior as it relates to crime, its causes, its consequences, and the search for suitable responses.*

With this definition, it can be said that a major objective of criminology is developing general and testable principles. These principles are intended to be used as building blocks of the body of knowledge relating to the process of law, justice, crime, punishment, and treatment.

The Interdisciplinary Nature of Criminology

We wish to make it very clear that to correctly address the issues raised within the two previous chapters, criminology as a discipline cannot be separated from the study of justice administration, justice studies, criminal justice, policing, courts, corrections, legal studies, or any of the myriad of names used by educators, scholars, and practitioners. Furthermore, its interdependence with the separate disciplines of anthropology, biology, chemistry, criminalistics, economics, forensic science, geography, law, medicine, philosophy, psychiatry, psychology, political science, religious studies, sociology, and victimology (to name but a few) must not be overlooked.

In his "Presidential Address: The Future of Justice Studies," Hunter (2011, pp. 11–12) made the following assertions regarding the nature of criminology:

> We have "Come of Age." While there will be ongoing debates as to whether criminology/criminal justice warrants being classified as a discipline and what our position is within academia, *we are too large and too influential to be ignored.* We are also too important to be a captive subfield within sociology.
>
> There is no criminology versus Criminal Justice. To overlook either the nature of crime or society's responses to crime is to fail to do either well. We as a discipline need to expand beyond criminology/criminal justice parameters to incorporate other categories of types of justice: social justice; distributive justice; commutative justice; and civil justice as legitimate areas of study.
>
> We do have theoretical foundations however; we have tended to ignore them in presenting ourselves to other professions. By complementing criminology and criminal justice with *Justice Studies,* we include the other explanations needed (political, economic, legal, administrative, etc.) to address the relevant issues within our discipline.
>
> We cannot ignore the linkage between theory and practice. Theory guides practice, which is then researched to refine theory and subsequently determine future practice. Therefore, *we must increase our interactions with practitioners and our influence on public policy.* In our research and our pol-

icy recommendations, we must ensure that we move beyond the myopic focus on responding to offenders and emphasize the following: victimology; primary and secondary crime prevention; globalization of crime and comparative studies; forensic sciences; the need for "security" (personal, public, private, and national); and, the use of technology in crime, crime prevention, criminal investigations, adjudication and corrections.

The Study of Criminology

Defining criminology takes us to the next step, the study of criminology. Because criminology encompasses the previously mentioned sciences and social sciences, it tends to project "a multidisciplinary persona" (Dantzker, 1998, p. 28). By studying criminology, one may explore a variety of issues that include:

1. The creation and use of laws in society,
2. Examination of the patterns of crime,
3. Causation of crime and criminality,
4. Societal response and reaction to criminality,
5. The administration of justice,
6. Custody and punishment of those accused and convicted of criminality,
7. Treatment or rehabilitation of those labeled criminal, and
8. Treatment and consideration for victims of crime.

Individuals who study criminology and criminal justice are generally called *criminologists* and may focus on one or all of five specialty areas of criminological study. These areas include:

1. *Sociology of law,* which is the understanding of how laws are created and enacted, modified, and applied;
2. *Criminological theory,* which focuses on the causes and consequences of crime and criminal behavior;
3. *Penology,* which is the study of punishment, treatment, and correctional techniques;
4. *Justice studies, aka justicology* (Myren, 1970), which is the study of the criminal justice system, its components, and processes; and
5. *Victimology,* which is the study of crime victims, the relationships with offenders, and how society responds to their needs.

The Five Models of Criminology

The study of criminology can be even more specialized by beginning with a **legal model** of criminology, the roots of which may best be found in the **classical school** of criminology. The main tenets of the classical school are that an individual is bound to society by mutual **social contract**, that individuals have **free will** to make their own choices to act, that decisions are rationally made based upon the seeking of pleasure and avoidance of pain, and that punishment should be used as a deterrent to criminal behavior, meting out identical punishments for identical crimes (Albanese, 2004).

Criminologists who take the legal approach to criminology accept that individuals freely choose to commit crimes. They are interested in how the legal system deals with violators, an approach much different from that of the medical approach to criminology. (The classical school of criminology is discussed in detail in Chapter 4.)

The **medical model** of criminology primarily centers on the **positive school** of criminology, which attributes criminal behavior to internal and external influences that limit or prohibit rational thinking and/or freedom of choice. The medical model focuses on biological elements that include physical structure, heredity, and genetic and biochemical explanations for criminal behavior. This approach could encompass psychological reasons for criminal behavior. This approach also offers one of the oldest explanations for crime and criminality. Rather than using punishment based upon the severity of the offense to deter criminals, the medical model emphasizes treatment based upon the needs of the offender. While biological explanations have been unpopular with sociologically trained criminologists, the concepts of limited choice and treatment for offenders have been widely accepted. The medical model is used to provide individualized treatment for offenders and has seen resurgence among theorists as biosocial explanations for criminal behavior have emerged. (This model is discussed later in Chapter 5.)

The **sociological model** is similar to the medical approach in that it focuses on reasons for criminal behavior, usually finding that such behaviors arise from some type of social error or problem (Schmalleger, 2011). This approach is probably the most popular among contemporary criminologists because it allows them to study a wide variety of possible causes for criminality, such as upbringing, environment, economics, peer socialization, social structure, and other societal issues. Numerous theories have been developed to help provide explanations for crime and criminal behavior within the sociological approach to criminology.

Within the sociological explanations there are two distinct theoretical categories. **Structural functionalism** holds that society as a whole is sound but there are anomalies that impact upon individuals and groups, leading to criminality. The emphasis of structural functionalism is to identify those conditions within society that may cause criminal behavior and seek to eliminate them.

A second perspective that evolved within the sociological model is known as the **social conflict theory** or **political model** of criminology. Social conflict theorists argue that crime is the product of conflicts among members of society. Rather than seeking to address social issues that might impact on individual and group criminality, social conflict theorists either see crime as the natural product of societal power struggles or call for the restructuring of society (such as the elimination of capitalism) in order to achieve a just and equitable social order.

Finally, many criminologists are interested in looking at a mixed group of reasons for criminality and how the legal system affects this behavior. This is an **interdisciplinary model** of criminology, where more than one possible area of inquiry is considered. This multifactor approach emphasizes the interaction of various individual and environmental influences on crime and criminality (Jeffery, 1990). The various models of criminology are displayed within Table 3.1.

Overall, regardless of which approach to the study of criminology is taken, all are steeped in theory. These theories have been formed based on research conducted by criminologists. More thorough explanations of the many theories are provided within the next several chapters. The theories that we discuss will be two competing schools of thought: the classical school of criminology and the positive school of criminology.

The Classical School of Criminology

As a separate field of study, criminology has only existed since the late 1950s. However, as a field of interest, it has existed much longer. Pelfry (1980) stated that "criminology as a social focus emerged with the publication of Cesare Beccaria's *Essay on Crimes and Punishment* in 1764" (p. 1).

The Contributions of Cesare Beccaria

Cesare Bonesana, the Marchese di Beccaria, was an eighteenth-century Italian philosopher and lawyer. In his *Essay on Crimes and Punishment,* Beccaria suggested that an individual had a "social contract" with society in which he or she was bound to society by consent and vice versa. A key aspect of this social contract was free will, one's ability to exercise choice. Beccaria believed that a human being was generally a rational being who sought pleasure and tried desperately to avoid pain (Beccaria, 1963). His writings were in response to the extreme and inequitable nature of punishment during this time. Torture, brandings, mutilation, banishment, and death were common sentences. In addition, punishment was meted out disproportionately, with the nobility receiving light, if any, punishment for offenses, while the poor were severely punished for the same offense.

Based upon Beccaria's writings, the first recognizable criminological approach to criminal behavior and society's response would emerge. Beccaria identified three types of crimes that warranted punishment: crimes that threat-

Table 3.1 The Five Models of Criminology

	Legal Model	Medical Model	Sociological Model	Political Model	Interdisciplinary Model
School	Classical	Positive	Positive	Positive	Mixture
Orientation	Legal	Biological/ psychological	Sociological	Sociological/ political	Integrated
View on reason	Rational thinking	Limited reason	Limited reason	Limited reason	Rationality varies with approach used
View on free will	Freedom of choice	Limited or no choice	Limited or no choice	Limited or no choice	Amount of choice varies
Solution to crime	Punishment based upon offense	Treament based upon offender need	Treatment based upon offender need	Social change based upon societal needs	Combination based upon approach used

ened the security of the state, crimes that injured citizens or their property, and crimes that ran contrary to the social order. In responding to these offenses, he argued that the punishment should fit the crime: property offenses warranted payment of monetary fines; crimes inflicting personal injuries demanded corporal punishment; serious crimes against the state might warrant the death penalty, but only in exceptional cases. Beccaria viewed excessive use of the death penalty as "war waged by society against its citizens" (Schmalleger, 2012, p. 60).

In addition to making punishment appropriate to the crime, Beccaria called for equal justice under the law, stressing that punishment for an offense should be the same regardless of a person's position in society. Furthermore, he called for the abolition of torture to elicit confessions (a common practice in the eighteenth century), and he argued that the accused's guilt or innocence should be determined by his or her peers.

Beccaria was the first to stress that punishment should not be for retribution but for the purpose of deterrence. The prevention of future crime was seen as being more important than exacting revenge. His views would have an impact on the criminal justice systems of several European nations, most notably France, Russia, Austria, and Prussia (Schmalleger, 2012).

The Contributions of Jeremy Bentham

Beccaria's ideas were refined by the English social philosopher Jeremy Bentham. Bentham was an advocate of utilitarianism (the social ideology that in their laws and actions governing bodies should seek to achieve the most utility or good for the greatest number of people). Bentham (1948) argued that people would choose pleasure and avoid pain. Thus, punishment for criminal behavior should be sufficient to negate any pleasure to be derived from criminal acts. Ultimately, the belief was that individuals make conscious decisions to commit criminal acts based upon their expected benefits from those acts. If society could impose more pain upon the individual than he or she could gain from commission of the criminal act, that person would be deterred from committing further crimes. This weighing of pain and pleasure came to be known as **hedonistic calculus** (Bernard, Snipes, and Gerould, 2009).

Bentham (1948) argued that in order for hedonistic or moral calculus to work, punishment should be severe enough to offset the benefits of the crime, but it should not be excessive. In addition, for the punishment to dissuade the offender and other individuals contemplating similar crimes, it had to be swift and certain. By "swift" he meant that punishment must take place within a reasonable period of time so that the reason for punishment was not forgotten by the offender or observers. By "certain" he meant that the potential for being caught and punished had to be reasonably high or, regardless of the severity of the sanction, there could be no deterrent effect.

Bentham's adaptations of Beccaria's earlier works would become the foundation for the classical school of criminology. Bentham's principles are still found within the justice systems of the world's democracies.

Tenets of the Classical School

The main premise of the classical school is that crime can be controlled by punishing identified offenders in a way that makes potential offenders fearful of the consequences of committing crime. Our adaptation of the primary tenets of the classical school is as follows:

1. The social contract—an individual is bound to society only by his or her own consent and, therefore, society is responsible to him or her.
2. Free will—individuals are free to make their own choices to act.
3. People seek pleasure and avoid pain.
4. Punishment should be used as a deterrent to criminal behavior.
5. Punishment should be based upon the seriousness of the crime.
6. Punishments for identical crimes should be identical.

The Concept of Deterrence

As the reader will have noted, classical criminology is based upon the concept of deterrence. This application of punishment to alter behavior or prevent misconduct is sometimes referred to as *deterrence theory*. The application of deterrence theory is thought to be both general and specific in nature. By *general deterrence* we mean that punishing an offender is done so that others in society who might be contemplating similar acts become aware that they risk suffering the same punishment. By *specific deterrence* we mean that the offender who has committed the criminal behavior realizes that the benefits received from the act were not worth the costs of the punishment for the crime.

As we noted in the previous section, in order for either general or specific deterrence to work, punishment must be severe enough to outweigh the benefits of the crime. In addition to severity, the punishment must be imposed as swiftly as possible after the crime has occurred in order to make an impression upon the offender and any would-be offenders considering a similar act. Last, the punishment should be certain so that offenders will have cause to fear that their crimes will be discovered, successfully prosecuted, and punished.

In the United States, swiftness (also known as celerity) and certainty are often lacking in our apprehension, adjudication, and punishment of criminals. Therefore the US justice system tends to overly rely on severity as a means of gaining compliance. Unfortunately, as pointed out by both Beccaria (1963) and Bentham (1948), severity alone cannot produce conformity.

The Concept of Justice

When criminologists discuss the classical school of criminology, they often tend to focus on the concept of deterrence and overlook other aspects of this legal model of justice. However, other important concepts should be emphasized. The first is the concept of the social contract, which was noted in the discussion of Beccaria's contributions and in the tenets of the classical school. It should be understood that there is a two-way commitment between the individual and society: the individual has an obligation to abide by the laws enacted by society's legislative bodies and enforced by appropriate agents of social control, and the state has the responsibility to provide fair and equitable treatment of that individual in exchange for his or her compliance. Failure on the part of the state to treat its citizens properly negates the social contract.

Another important concept of the classical school is **equity**. By equity we mean that the law is applied equally to every member of society regardless of social station. Issues such as race, class, religion, gender, and ideology are not to influence the administration of justice. Failure on the part of the state to provide for equitable treatment could result in dismissal of the charges against the accused. Chronic failure on the part of the state to provide for equitable treatment could result in distrust of the system and nullification of the social contract.

A third concept that must be considered is **due process**—every individual who is charged with violating a criminal law must be accorded the full protection of the law during the investigation, prosecution, and adjudication of his or her case. In addition, the imposition of any sanctions must be in accordance with legal proscriptions (Barlow, 2000). As with equity issues, failure to provide due process could result in acquittal. Chronic failures could seriously impair the state's ability to govern.

Current Status of the Classical School

Overall, the classical school insisted upon a clear-cut legal definition of acts punishable as criminal and fostered the idea of free will. The classical school of thought would maintain strength and prominence within academia until the early 1900s, when it began to decline because of a more treatment-oriented approach fostered by the positive school of criminology. It should be noted, however, that the **neoclassical school** remains the model by which the US criminal justice system operates in the prosecution and adjudication of adult offenders.

The Positive School of Criminology

Beginning in the late 1800s, a second school of thought emerged in criminology. It is popularly recognized as the positive school of criminology, and its humble beginnings are often attributed to an Italian physician, Cesare Lombroso. This school of thought is believed to have emerged "in opposition to the harshness of the classical school, as well as in response to the lack of concern for the causes of criminal behavior" (Pelfrey, 1980, p. 5).

Members of the positive school of thought believed that external forces—biological, psychological, and sociological—caused criminal behavior. They rejected the legal concept of crime recognized by the classical school. In search of differences between criminals and noncriminals, they focused on the individual instead of on the law and sought scientific status for criminology. A major shift from the classical school was the emphasis on treatment as opposed to punishment.

Determinism

The positive school is based upon the notion of **determinism**, which means that factors beyond a person's control determine behavior. This perspective also implies that a man or a woman is not a self-determining agent free to do as he or she wishes and as his or her intelligence directs (Vold, 1958). In other words, determinism is the opposite of free will. If a person acts of his or her free will to commit a crime, it means he or she made a rational decision to do so. Various forms of determinism are defined by biological or cultural factors. **Grim determinism** is the belief that God has ordained certain behaviors and nothing can prevent them from occurring. This perspective was prevalent during ancient and medieval times. **Hard determinism** is the view that behavior may be programmed at birth. It is mostly natural (e.g., biological) and allows for no or only limited free will. **Soft determinism** views behavior as having biological (nature) or sociological (nurture) characteristics (Gaines and Miller, 2010). In this perspective, an individual's freedom of choice may be limited by nature and/or nurture.

Darwin's Theory of Evolution

In 1859, Charles Darwin published *On the Origin of Species,* in which he outlined his theory of evolution. His work caused a sensation and was controversial because it attacked the biblical theory of creation and established a new area of **science** for understanding human behavior and other social and physical phenomena. Scientists were encouraged to explore a different approach in the study of criminal behavior. The debate over free will and determinism was a long-standing issue in philosophy and religion, and some thinkers believed that God determined, or predestined, an individual's fate.

In a similar way, the positivist approach raised questions of determinism, in this case scientific rather than religious. Though the positivists looked to worldly forces rather than to God, their ideas challenged everyday assumptions about free will. In essence, the positivists, in their quest for answers, were raising very basic philosophical questions in the social sciences (Hagan, 2011).

In his work, Darwin presented evidence that humans were animals, except that they were more highly evolved or developed than other animals. The ancestors of modern people were less highly evolved and were part of a continuous chain linking humans to the earliest and simplest forms of life. The idea that some individuals might be reversions to an earlier evolutionary stage was originally suggested by Darwin, who wrote, "With mankind some of the worst dispositions which occasionally without any assignable cause make their appearance in families, may perhaps be reversions to a savage state, from which we are not removed by many generations" (Darwin, 1871, p. 137). Darwin's work was also important because it formed the theoretical basis for the early biological explanations of crime.

Lombroso's Theory of Atavism

As previously noted, Cesare Lombroso is recognized as the father of the positive school. Darwin's theory of evolution heavily influenced much of his work. Lombroso was an Italian physician who was the first criminologist to employ the scientific method (measurement, observations, and the application of generalizations from one's research findings to other similar research) in his work. In 1876, he wrote and published *The Criminal Man,* in which he coined the term ***atavism***. The theory of atavism asserts that criminals are born—as opposed to made—and their criminal behavior is the result of primitive urges. Criminals were believed to be evolutionary accidents that were throwbacks to more primitive people. By nature they possessed a relatively underdeveloped brain, and this physical shortcoming made them incapable of conforming to the rules and expectations of a complex modern society. They exhibited a lack of guilt or remorse for any wrongdoing and were unable to learn the distinction between good and evil.

The characteristics that Lombroso linked to criminal behavior included deviations in the criminal's head size and shape, asymmetry of the face, large jaws and cheekbones, unusually large or small ears or ears that stood out from the head, fleshy lips, abnormal teeth, receding chin, abundant hair or wrinkles, long arms, extra fingers or toes, and an asymmetry of the brain (Lombroso-Ferrero, 1972). Since many of these characteristics supported his theory, he concluded that criminal offenders had physical characteristics that resembled those of lower animals, such as monkeys and chimpanzees.

Lombroso described the *born* criminal as one who was biologically predisposed to criminal behavior. However, other types of criminal offenders fell within six categories: the *habitual* or *professional* criminals, who engaged in crime as a trade or occupation; the *morally insane; criminoloids;* the *juridical criminal;* the *hysteric;* and those who violated the law in *crimes of passion.* Criminals who fell under the category of the morally insane were mental and moral degenerates, alcoholics, drug addicts, and other similar types of offenders. Criminoloids were described as occasional or situational offenders, whose participation in criminal behavior was determined by environmental factors.

Lombroso believed criminoloids exhibited some degree of atavism and differed from the born criminal in degree only, not in kind. Juridical criminals violated the law usually in an impulsive act. They lacked self-control, care, or any type of forethought. Criminals who engaged in passion crimes responded to intense emotions that may have been provoked by love, jealousy, hatred, or the need to seek vengefulness. The hysteric usually engaged in criminal behavior through some compulsive, neurotic, or schizoid act.

Lombroso's theory of atavism attracted international attention, but it was not long before he and his students began to soften his position. By the time of his death in 1909, he had modified his view of atavism. He decided that born criminals constituted only one-third of the total criminal population and the remaining two-thirds comprised two additional types—insane offenders, whose crimes were the result of any one of many complex mental disorders, and criminoloids, whose personalities were somehow warped by a host of environmental factors (Lombroso-Ferrero, 1972).

Lombroso's work did not escape criticism. It was suggested that many differences he found between his prisoners and control group subjects were too small to be statistically significant. It was also suggested that his findings were biased in that many of his subjects were Sicilians (who were at the bottom of Italy's socioeconomic order). Despite these criticisms, the arguments that Lombroso made regarding limited will, the use of scientific methods to study the causes of crime, and treatment rather than punishment of criminals would serve as the foundation for the positive school of criminology (Bernard, Snipes, and Gerould, 2009).

Tenets of the Positive School

Although Lombroso's biological approach was rejected by US criminologists, they did accept his positivist tenets (Reid, 2011). Instead of the medical model, however, they developed the sociological model mentioned earlier in the chapter. The positivist tenets are as follows:

1. Denial of the free will concept,
2. Multiple causes of criminal behavior,
3. Causes are biological and environmental,
4. Using scientific methods to look at causes, and
5. Actions toward the criminal should be to correct the behavior, not punish it.

Edwin Sutherland and the criminologists at the University of Chicago who pioneered the development of US criminology were instrumental in promoting the twentieth-century rehabilitative ideal. This perspective holds that the causes of crime can be identified and that changes (both social and individual) can be made to reduce the potential for criminality to occur and/or to minimize its impact upon society (Sutherland and Cressey, 1978).

Current Status of the Positive School

While the US system of justice was based upon the classical school of criminology, sentencing and correctional efforts have been based upon positivist tenets since the early part of the twentieth century. Positivist tenets have also been the basis of the juvenile justice system. We do not suggest that all sentencing considerations and correctional efforts were based upon positive school considerations. The focus on punishment has always been a part of US correctional efforts.

Today, positive school criminology dominates academic studies of crime and criminality. The following chapters demonstrate this influence in their explanations of crime and criminal behavior. Despite the resurgence of classical criminology with its current "get tough on crime" emphasis, positive school ideals continue to be practiced in both adult and juvenile corrections in the United States.

The Nature of Criminological Inquiry

In a primer that reviews the leading theories of crime causation, it is necessary that we discuss the nature of criminological inquiry and why it is so important for students of criminology and for criminal justice practitioners. While many students cringe at the requirements of theory and research methods, the truth is that they are not only necessary parts of the study of crime and justice, but also integral parts of life and learning. Scientific investigation is very similar to criminal investigation: the use of a logical order and established procedures to solve real-world problems.

Social Science Research and the "Real World"

As police officers, we (the authors) sought to determine whether a crime had been committed (what occurred and when it occurred), who had done it, how they had done it, and why they had done it. We then sought to use that investigatory knowledge to develop a successful prosecution of the offender. Our endeavors in the field taught us that the theory course that we had grudgingly endured had provided the rationale for human behavior that the strategies of policing, courts, and corrections were based upon. We also discovered that those theories were not developed in some esoteric vacuum. They were in fact the products of trial-and-error experiments, conducted in policing, the courts, and corrections, that had been refined and reapplied to their appropriate subject area. Today's police-deployment strategies, legal processes, and correctional techniques are all solidly based upon prior theory and research.

Scientific Method

The scientific method seeks to prevent the errors of casual inquiry by utilizing procedures that specify objectivity, logic, theoretical understanding, and knowledge of prior research in the development and use of a precise measurement instrument designed to accurately record observations (Bryman, 2008; Creswell, 2008; Gavin, 2008; McBurney and White, 2007). The result is a systematic search for the most accurate and complete description or explanation of the events or behaviors that are being studied. Just as a criminal investigation is a search for "the facts" and a criminal trial is a search for "the truth," the scientific method is a search for knowledge. The criminological researcher seeks to use the principles of empiricism, skepticism, relativism, objectivity, ethical neutrality, parsimony, accuracy, and precision to assess a particular theoretical explanation.

In the above formula, **empiricism** is defined as seeking answers to questions through direct observation. **Skepticism** is the search for disconfirming evidence and the process of continuing to question the conclusions and the evidence that are found. Objectivity mandates that conclusions are based upon careful observation that sees the world as it really is, free from personal feelings or prejudices. Criminological researchers often acknowledge that total objectivity is unattainable, but every reasonable effort is made to overcome any subjective interests that might influence the research outcomes. This is known as intersubjectivity. Ethical neutrality builds upon objectivity by stressing that the researcher's beliefs or preferences will not be allowed to influence the research process or its outcomes. Parsimony is the attempt to reduce the sum of possible explanations for an event or phenomenon to the smallest possible number. Accuracy requires that observations be recorded in a correct manner exactly as they occurred. Precision is specifying the number of subcategories of a concept that are available (Adler and Clark, 2007; Maxfield and Babbie, 2009; Vito, Kunselman, and Tewksbury, 2008).

The Relationship Between Theory and Research

As was discussed in a prior section, the practice of criminal justice is based upon theories about the causes of crime and how to respond to them. Criminology is an academic discipline that studies the nature of crime, its causes, its consequences, and society's response to it. Criminal justice as an academic discipline tends to focus more upon the creation, application, and enforcement of criminal laws to maintain social order. There is so much of an overlap between the two disciplines that within this text we shall deal with the two as one discipline (as indeed many criminologists and criminal justice experts consider them to be). Regardless of one's orientation, theory is integral in the development of research. Likewise, theory that has been validated by research is the basis for practice in the criminal justice system.

What theory is. Theory suggests how something should be. Personal ideologies are of no value in criminological theory unless they can be evaluated scientifically. We shall define theory as "an attempt to explain why a particular social activity or event occurs" (Dantzker and Hunter, 2012, p. 7). A theory is a generalization about the phenomenon that is being studied. From this broad theory, more precise statements (concepts) are developed.

Specific measurable statements are hypotheses. The method by which the hypothesis is observed and measured is research. The relationship between theory and research may be either inductive or deductive in nature. Inductive logic occurs when the researcher observes an event, makes empirical generalizations about the activity, and constructs a theory based upon them. Deductive logic begins with a theoretical orientation. The researcher then develops research hypotheses that are tested by observations.

What research is. Research is the conscientious study of an issue, problem, or subject. It is a useful form of inquiry designed to assist in discovering answers. It can also lead to the creation of new questions. Research creates questions, but ultimately, regardless of the subject under study, it is the goal of research to provide answers. "Research is the scientific investigation into or of a specifically identified phenomenon and is applicable to recognizable and undiscovered phenomena" (Dantzker and Hunter, 2012, p. 9).

Why research is necessary. There are a number of specific reasons for conducting criminal justice or criminological research. Three primary reasons are:

1. *Curiosity.* Wanting to know more about an existing problem, issue, policy, or outcome.
2. *Addressing social problems.* The most salient social problem related to criminal justice is crime. Who commits it? How do they do it?
3. *Development and testing of theories.* Striving to determine why criminal offenders act as they do. Developing and testing explanations that can be used to reduce criminality and/or prevent criminals from reoffending.

The third reason is the focus of this text.

Reality Check: International Terrorism

The motivations for international terrorism are to create fear among civilian populations in order to promote religious, political, or ideological goals. This is done by deliberately targeting noncombatants. Terror attacks are used to intimidate people from cooperating with their government and to provoke that government to adopt counterterrorism strategies that will be unpopular with its citizens.

Terrorism has been a commonly used technique for centuries. However, due to technological advances in communications and transportation, it has become more common since the mid-1900s. The Irish Republican Army used bombing campaigns; the Palestine Liberation Organization used airplane hijackings, attacks at airports, and hostage taking at the 1972 Olympics in Munich; and the South Moluccans in the Netherlands took hostages on trains to draw international attention to their political struggles. During this period, Americans were concerned about citizens who traveled abroad, but there was little fear of attacks from international organizations. This changed in 1993 when radical Muslims who opposed the US support of Israel exploded a bomb beneath the North Tower of the World Trade Center. The bomb did limited damage to the building, but killed seven people, including an unborn child. Four conspirators were convicted and imprisoned for this attack.

The World Trade Center bombing made Americans aware of international threats, but our greater concern was with our homegrown terrorists. Our vulnerability was exposed to the world with the airliner crashes that occurred on September 11, 2001. Two airplanes flown into the World Trade Center demolished both buildings and killed those inside as well as emergency responders. Another airplane was crashed into the Pentagon. A fourth plane was crashed when the passengers, having learned about the other attacks by cell phones, thwarted the hijackers' plan to crash into the US Capitol. A total of 2,996 people were killed (2,977 victims and 19 hijackers) because of the attacks.

The US government quickly determined that Al Qaida, headed by Osama bin Laden, bore responsibility for the attacks. It was discovered that bin Laden was operating out of Afghanistan with the support of the Taliban (a radical Islamist group dominated by the Pashtun tribe that had seized control of the Afghan government). When demands to turn bin Laden over were rebuffed on October 7, 2001, the United States and coalition allies invaded Afghanistan and drove the Taliban from power. The stated intent of military operations was to remove the Taliban from power and prevent the use of Afghanistan as a terrorist base of operations. Unfortunately, Osama bin Laden escaped and, despite several near misses, eluded capture for more than nine years.

The motivations for bin Laden, Al Qaida, and the Taliban are both religious and political. Bin Laden's stated goals for Al Qaida were to end US military presence in the Middle East and the Arabian Peninsula, overthrow

continues

Reality Check, *continued*

Arab regimes he considered corrupt and insufficiently religious, end US support for Israel, and return East Timor and Kashmir to Muslim rule. This message had great appeal to many Muslims who felt that Western society was not only decadent but hostile to Islam. Immoral secularism of the United States and Europe was seen as having led to evils such as pornography, immorality, secularism, homosexuality, feminism, gambling, and many other ideas that radical Islamists often oppose. Therefore, bin Laden was seen as a freedom fighter and defender of the true faith.

Due to his direct involvement in attacking the West, his encouragement of jihad, his personal example, and his financial support (he inherited US$80 million at the age of thirteen), bin Laden's message has been accepted by many thousands of radical Muslims. Resentment from the 2,000-year strife between Christians and Muslims, lingering bitterness from colonialism, hostility toward the West's policies and influence, and the fear that Islam's traditional beliefs are being threatened have provided devotees willing to take extreme actions (including suicide bombings) against Americans and their allies. Terrorist and guerrilla groups still operate in Afghanistan, Pakistan, Iraq, as well as other areas of Northern Africa and the Mideast. In addition, several countries either actively or covertly support his ideology.

On May 1, 2011, US Navy SEALS conducted a covert operation into Pakistan. During their forty-minute raid, Osama bin Laden was shot and killed, along with one of his sons and several of his followers.

Identify a non-Muslim-based terrorist organization. Describe the terrorist acts that they have committed and discuss what their motivations are.

Criminology Today

The study of criminal behavior today is as strong and vital as it ever has been. In many respects, it has become an even more important field of inquiry in light of violent episodes, such as the recent shootings at schools, in community centers, and in churches as well as the continuing threat of both domestic and international terrorism. Understanding why these events occur is vital, particularly for the future protection of life and property.

Summary

Criminology is defined as the scientific approach to the study of crime as a social phenomenon, that is, the theoretical application involving the study of the nature and extent of criminal behavior. The specialty areas within the study of criminology are sociology of law, the understanding of how laws are created and enacted, modified, and applied; criminological theory, the causes and consequences of crime and criminal behavior; penology, the study of punishment, treatment, and correctional techniques; justicology, the study of the criminal justice system, its components, and processes; and victimology, the study of crime victims, their relationships with offenders, and how society responds to their needs.

The five models of criminology were then presented. These include the *legal model,* which emphasizes how the legal system deals with violators; the *medical model,* which focuses on biological and psychological reasons for criminal behavior; the *sociological model,* which focuses on reasons for behavior as resulting from some type of social error or problem; the *political model,* which views crime as the product of conflicts among members of society; and the *interdisciplinary model,* which emphasizes the interaction of various individual and environmental influences on crime and criminality.

We then discussed what theory is and its relationship to research. We noted that scientific investigation is very similar to criminal investigation: the use of a logical order and established procedures to solve real-world problems. Theories provide the rationales for human behavior that the strategies of policing, courts, and corrections are based upon.

Just as a criminal investigation is a search for "the facts" and a criminal trial is a search for "the truth," the scientific method is a search for knowledge. The criminological researcher seeks to use the principles of empiricism, skepticism, relativism, objectivity, ethical neutrality, parsimony, accuracy, and precision to assess a particular theoretical explanation.

Criminology is an academic discipline that studies the nature of crime, its causes, its consequences, and society's response to it. Criminal justice as an academic discipline tends to focus more upon the creation, application, and enforcement of criminal laws to maintain social order. Regardless of one's orientation, theory is integral in the development of research. Likewise, theory that has been validated by research is the basis for practice in the criminal justice system.

Discussion Questions

1. Explain why crime is considered a phenomenon.
2. If you were to become a criminologist, what subfield would you study? Why?
3. The history of criminology is best explained through the various schools of thought. The classical school seems to be the most dominant. Why?

4. What is determinism? Identify and describe the types of determinism and what role they may play in today's criminal behavior.
5. Identify Lombroso's six types of criminals and discuss which types of criminal acts committed today might best match with each type.
6. What are the tenets of the positive school of criminological thought? Explain how they might apply in today's criminal justice system.
7. Explain the relationship between theory and research.

4

Deterrence and Opportunity Theories

The contributions of Cesare Beccaria and Jeremy Bentham led to the development of the classical school of criminology. The classical school was concerned with the application of law and punishment in order to deter criminal behavior. General deterrence is effective when those contemplating crimes see the severity of punishment that a similar offender received and are dissuaded. Specific deterrence was based upon the offenders deciding that the punishment received for committing the crime was greater than the benefits received from having done so. In order for deterrence to work, punishment had to be severe (greater than the benefits received), swift (occurring within a reasonable time after the crime so that both the offender and the public recalled the details), and certain (the likelihood of being caught and punished was thought to be high).

The necessary revisions of the neoclassical school made allowances for issues that might impact the rationality or the free will of offenders. These issues included aggravating and mitigating circumstances; immaturity; insanity; necessity or duress; and to a lesser degree, ignorance and chemical impairment.

The Neoclassical School of Criminology

The application of classical criminology during the eighteenth century quickly revealed flaws with the idea of identical punishment for identical crimes, as well as with the concepts of free will and rationality. It was discovered that aggravating or mitigating circumstances sometimes caused similar crimes to differ in significant ways. In addition, while the concept of free will was not abandoned, people recognized that there were sometimes circumstances in which freedom of choice was limited. Likewise, under certain conditions, people did not always act rationally. These issues quickly led nations that had been implementing classical criminology to revise their ideas (Bernard, Snipes, and Gerould, 2009). The changes in classical criminology resulting from these realizations developed into neoclassical criminology.

In their administration of justice, the nations that use classical tenets incorporate these neoclassical revisions: allowance for mitigating and aggravating circumstances, and consideration of youth, insanity, necessity, duress, self-defense, and, to lesser degrees, ignorance and intoxication (Lilly, Cullen, and Ball, 2007; Roberson and Wallace, 1998; Liska and Messner, 1999).

Rationales for Leniency

Saying that there are "aggravating" or "mitigating" circumstances is quite simply a way of acknowledging that other issues may have played a role in the commission of a crime. **Aggravating circumstances** are those that cause the offender to be punished more severely than he or she would normally be for a specific crime. For example, conviction for the rape of a child would warrant a more serious punishment than rape of an adult because our society views a child as more vulnerable and helpless. **Mitigating circumstances** are those that would result in a more lenient sentence than would normally be imposed for a similar crime. A first-time offender would normally receive a lesser sentence than someone who has an extensive criminal history.

Immaturity or youth is often a consideration for leniency under neoclassical criminology. The separate juvenile justice system and age limitations on the imposition of adult penalties are modern exemplars of these considerations. In most states, juveniles under the age of twelve cannot be adjudicated as adults. Nor can juveniles under the age of sixteen face the death penalty.

Insanity has traditionally been a defense in the US legal system. Offenders must not only have been sane when they committed their crimes, but must also be mentally competent to stand trial. The determination of what constitutes insanity and competence to stand trial varies considerably among states depending upon the legal criteria that are used. The various standards for insanity are discussed in a later chapter.

Necessity, duress or coercion, and self-defense are also considerations. If someone was forced by circumstances to behave in a manner that might ordinarily be considered criminal, he or she may be excused based upon the circumstances. For example, if you broke into a remote mountain cabin to escape a blizzard, the necessity of the act of breaking and entering would excuse your actions. However, if you engaged in additional unlawful behaviors that were not necessary, such as defacing the property, those would not be excused. Crimes committed under coercion from others are also excused, but the reasonableness of the coercion in regard to the crime committed would have to be considered. For example, a person who commits a less harmful offense because of physical threats or intimidation would most likely be held blameless, but one who commits a violent crime against others to avoid a similar or lesser injury would most likely be held accountable. In these incidents, the reasonableness of one's actions would have to be considered. Also, actions that would be considered unlawful may be excused if they were necessary to defend oneself or others from a greater harm.

Last, criminal acts committed due to ignorance or while under the influence of drugs or alcohol may receive consideration for leniency. Ignorance of the law is not an excuse for escaping prosecution, but it may be considered as a mitigating circumstance in sentencing. Intoxication or chemical impairment will not excuse criminal behavior but may also be used as a mitigating circumstance if it can be shown that the behaviors were not anticipated.

Nothing Works

Starting in the 1970s and into the new century, the classical school has seen resurgence in the areas of sentencing and corrections. This is because of the public's and justice system practitioners' disenchantment with the positive school of thought (primarily because the positive school's emphasis on rehabilitation did not seem to work). This view received support from Robert Martinson's (1974) survey of rehabilitation programs and his conclusions that nothing seemed to work.

Additional research regarding the failure of prisons to rehabilitate criminal offenders came from David Fogel (1975), who argued that criminal offenders deserve punishment because of the choices they made. In his *Justice Model for Corrections*, Fogel called for holding offenders responsible and accountable for their actions. This concept was further promoted by James Q. Wilson (1975) in *Thinking About Crime*. Wilson argued that crime was not the product of poverty or social conditions and could not be reduced by social programs. Instead he called for lengthy prison sentences and the elimination of criminal opportunity. This perspective is supportive of the two theoretical perspectives found within the new classical criminology: deterrence and opportunity.

Continuing increases in criminal behavior also contributed to a "get tough on crime mentality" that emphasized punishment. The "war on drugs" and habitual offender laws that emphasize "three strikes and you're out" are products of this reliance on punishment. The result is that the number of offenders incarcerated in US prisons and the number of individuals sentenced to death have risen significantly. However, as discussed in Chapter 2, supporters note that crime rates have continued to decline.

The Nouveau Classical School of Criminology

For descriptive purposes we shall refer to this resurgence of the neoclassical school's precepts as the nouveau classical school. The return of deterrence and "**just deserts**" was supported by the development of new theories using classical concepts but utilizing scientific principles in their application. We have categorized these newer theories as either *deterrence theories* or *opportunity theories*. (See Figure 4.1.)

Deterrence Theories

In recent years, advocates of the neoclassical school have revisited the importance of the social contract in applying punishment. As a result of the perceived failure of rehabilitation, some scholars have argued that criminals should be punished because their actions demand that criminal sanctions be applied. The culpability of the offender and the seriousness of the crime require that punishment be administered (Adler, Mueller, and Laufer, 1998). While critics argue that this is nothing but a return to retribution, advocates insist that the social contract must be enforced for the benefit of both the offender and society (Schmalleger, 2012).

Just Deserts

The modern concept of "just deserts" is seen by proponents as being the needed application of punishment to promote general deterrence. The basic

---

Figure 4.1   Nouveau Classical Theories

Deterrence Theories	Opportunity Theories	Crime Science
Just deserts perspective	Environmental criminology	Crime science
Nothing works doctrine	Defensible space	
Criminal personality theory	Broken windows theory	
Social crutch hypothesis	Routine activities	
Rational choice theory	Criminology of place	
Rotten apples	Crime pattern theory	
	Situational choice theory	
	Crime prevention through environmental design	

premise of the just deserts argument is that even if specific deterrence is not accomplished, society needs to see that criminals receive the punishment they deserve. Such punishments are seen by advocates as effective general deterrents. They insist that failure to exact punishment would be a violation of the social contract and would erode respect for the law. In recent years, those in the United States who have wearied of stories of criminals going unpunished tend to be drawn to this argument. Some people view such punishments as symbolic reassurance (discussed in later chapters) for the law abiding rather than punishment in the name of general deterrence.

Criminal Personality Theory

While just deserts is a strategy more than a true theory, **criminal personality theory** qualifies as such. Samuel Yochelson and Stanten B. Samenow (1976) base this theory on the belief that the social environment has little impact on the development of criminal behavior. Instead, criminals are said to freely choose their actions. Sociological, psychological, and economic theories are seen as mere excuses offenders use to rationalize their behavior. In a return to early biological theories, offenders are seen as being born with criminal personalities. These individuals are innately selfish, untrusting, and untrustworthy. Instead of being victims of society, they are victimizers of society. Therefore, in order to change their behavior patterns, criminals must be forced to accept their own responsibility for their actions.

Critiques of this theory (e.g., Hagan, 2011) argue that it is not a true theory but a rehashing of old biological precepts of born criminals. However, the argument that criminals are self-serving antisocials who knowingly refuse to conform to societal standards is appealing to "get tough on crime" advocates.

Seductions of Crime Theory

Earlier in this chapter and in Chapter 2, we discussed the concepts of specific and general deterrence. The focus of deterrence is to try to outweigh the pleasure from committing a crime using pain (punishment, usually in the form of incarceration) that will dissuade the offender from committing that crime again. Katz (1988) introduces another element to the hedonistic calculus that is the basis of deterrence theory. He addresses the pleasure obtained from the crime in a different manner than other deterrence theories do. He argues that "the causes of crime are constructed by the offenders themselves" in ways that are compellingly seductive (p. 24). In other words, offenders not only enjoy the fruits of their crimes, they enjoy committing them.

Seductions of crime theory is particularly appropriate for explaining crimes such as rape and pedophilia, in which the offenders enjoy the feeling of power from dominating and degrading their victims. It also complicates the traditional thoughts about using punishment to deter crime. That is because according to Katz (1988), we must not only deal with the fruits of the crime and the pleasure that an offender experiences while committing a crime, but also deal with the seductive appeal that certain crimes may have. As an example, an affluent middle-aged woman may find that the sensual excitement of having a forbidden affair with a younger man is actually more thrilling than the pleasures from the sexual experiences. Therefore, focusing on factors such as age, gender, and material conditions may have far less relevance than situational factors that precipitate actions or reflect a crime's seductive appeal.

Social Crutch Hypothesis

Dantzker has coined the term *social crutch hypothesis* to explain how crime may have an appeal in yet another manner than seductiveness of the criminal act. Instead, he argues that offenders may develop a learned dependency on excuses provided by well-intentioned people that enable them to deny their own responsibility for their actions. Dantzker offers the analogy that when an individual breaks a leg or injures a knee, hip, or foot, one of the most common aids used for mobility is crutches. Initially, these may be a useful tool, but as one heals, the crutches generally are needed less and less. There are some individuals who would rather continue to use the crutches, however, than take a chance to proceed on their own strength and determination. It is being offered here that criminological theories could be viewed as a crutch for criminal behavior.

When one examines the many theories addressed in this text, an argument could be made for how many offer more of an excuse for behavior than an explanation of why those behaviors occur and what may be done to prevent them. Dantzker sees these theories as crutches that deny accountability rather than forcing offenders to take responsibility for their own actions. Many of these excuses include blaming society for such things as poverty, discrimination, racism, misogyny, and so on, when more times than not it appears to have been one's choice to act in the manner displayed. Because various "theories" are available, it allows individuals to use them as crutches, something to lean on and help explain their behavior rather than placing the blame where it may belong, on the individual.

Rotten Apples Theory

Rotten apples theory was developed to explain police deviance but is applicable to explain corrupt and/or unlawful behaviors within any organization. The rotten apples theory argues that rotten apples are corrupt individuals who have slipped through the screening process or deviant individuals who continue their deviance in an environment that gives them more opportunity. The basis of the rotten apples theory is that a few morally weak individuals corrupt everyone else.

The rotten apples theory is popular with police officers and administrators because it blames the corrupt activities on one or a few highly unethical people who contaminate others. It appears that this theory may be more of an excuse than an explanation, but it is popular with organizations who wish to protect their image by blaming one or a few individuals for behaviors rather than acknowledging that it may be a systemic problem.

This theory was recently used by Pope Benedict XVI, who expressed great sadness about revelations of widespread abuse of children by Roman Catholic priests and religious. He stressed that "authorities in the church have not been vigilant enough" in combating the problem. In other words, they did not remove the few rotten apples in time to avoid what became a major scandal (Greenleaf, 2010). We include it under deterrence theories because its focus is to correct bad behaviors through individual accountability.

Opportunity Theories

Opportunity theories merge classical and positivist approaches to crime prevention based on the individual's rationality and freedom of choice as expressed within classical theory. This ability to choose is merged with positive theory's use of empiricism to understand how choices are influenced by situational factors. Situational influences are then altered or adjusted to deter or prevent crime from occurring. These findings are then used to develop appropriate crime-prevention strategies. While this is known as opportunity theory, it is also referred to as environmental criminology and situational crime prevention.

Environmental Criminology

The basic premise of environmental criminology is that there are environmental influences that impact both vulnerability to crime and propensity to commit specific crimes. This premise can be traced to the works of the Chicago School in the social ecology of crime. Their research studied the effects of social pathology and **social disorganization** on urban areas. These earlier studies are discussed in Chapter 7. Their use of cartography and areal research has been adapted by modern criminologists in their crime-prevention efforts.

The Crime Equation

Cohen and Felson (1979) introduced the following crime equation in their pioneering work on routine activities theory. It has since become the basis of opportunity/situational theories. They stated that crime occurred when a motivated offender and an attractive target came together in the absence of capable guardians. We have borrowed from Brantingham and Brantingham (1991) to add "in space and time" to the formula. This allows for strategies that make temporal or areal adjustments to potential crime targets. The equation would look like this:

$$C = MO + AT - CG / S + T$$

  C = Crime
  MO = Motivated Offender
  AT = Attractive Target
  CG = Capable Guardians
  S = Space
  T = Time

Defensible Space

In 1972, Oscar Newman published the concept of defensible space. The concept was based upon his studies of crime rates at high-rise public housing in New York. Newman (1972) presented four dimensions that were necessary for space to be defended:

1. *Territoriality*—creating zones of influence through the use of physical and symbolic barriers to restrict entry to private or nonpublic areas. This not only limited access, but also promoted feelings of ownership by residents.
2. *Natural surveillance*—using the physical layout of buildings and green space to enable residents, workers, and clients to carry out surveillance of the area in which they live, work, shop, or play.
3. *Image*—designing the property in such a manner as to promote feelings of pride and possession among occupants.
4. *Milieu*—creating areas that are perceived by residents as being secure and nonthreatening.

Newman's model was utilized in the design of numerous public buildings across the United States.

Crime Prevention Through Environmental Design

C. Ray Jeffery published his opportunity theory in 1971. He coined the term *crime prevention through environmental design* (CPTED) to emphasize **crime prevention** based upon the physical nature of the crime site. The premise was that the proper physical design of private and public buildings and spaces would impact the perception of societal "defenders" as well as potential "offenders." CPTED stress a micro- (individual crime site) through macro-level (metropolitan, state, or national) integration of crime prevention efforts such as laws, training, and education, along with physical design features of homes, businesses, and public institutions.

Routine Activities Theory

The concept of **routine activities theory** was developed by Lawrence F. Cohen and Marcus Felson (1979), who believed that changes in the routine activities of everyday life could lead to criminality. Cohen and Felson contended that the disruption of daily activities influences criminal opportunity and therefore affects trends in a class of crimes that they label as direct-contact predatory violations: illegal acts in which an individual definitively and intentionally takes or damages the person or property of another. Their argument rests on the belief that structural changes in routine activity patterns can influence crime rates by affecting the convergence in space and time of the three minimal elements of direct-contact predatory violations: motivated offenders, suitable targets, and the absence of capable guardians against a violation (Cohen and Felson, 1979).

Cohen and Felson's ultimate conclusion is that criminality is a given. For whatever reason (social learning, social conflict, etc.), there will always be motivated offenders. Rather than worrying about the nature of criminality, they focus on preventing or deterring crime. For classical theory's use of punishment as deterrence to work, strategies that reduce the opportunity for crime to succeed must be employed. Rather than relying on punishment, the attractiveness of and/or accessibility to the target needs to be reduced. While some crimes will be displaced to other areas, times, or targets, many will be prevented from occurring.

Broken Windows Theory

Broken windows theory was first introduced by James Q. Wilson and George L. Kelling in the March 1982 edition of the *Atlantic Monthly*. They introduced the idea that when buildings are abandoned or are allowed to become deteriorated, they become vulnerable to vandalism. Initially, a window might be broken. Soon more windows will be broken. If the windows are not repaired, the tendency is for vandals to eventually break into the building and, if it's unoccupied, perhaps become squatters or light fires inside. The same could be said for neighborhoods. If streets and sidewalks are neglected, litter will begin to accumulate. Soon, more litter accumulates. As the decline continues, crimes such as vandalism to cars and buildings occur, followed by burglaries and other crimes.

According to Wilson and Kelling (1982), to contain or eliminate crime from urban neighborhoods, residents and public officials should fix the problems when they are small. Repair the broken windows within a short time, say a day or a week, and the tendency is that vandals will be much less likely to break more windows or do further damage. Clean up the sidewalk every day, and the tendency is for litter not to accumulate (or for the rate of littering to be much lower). Problems do not escalate and thus respectable residents do not flee a neighborhood. They further contend that such actions deter petty crimes from occurring, which helps in preventing major crimes from developing.

To a degree, this theory is similar to the social disorganization theory that will be discussed in Chapter 7. It does differ in its explanation regarding how the condition of the urban environment may affect crime. Three influential factors are seen as occurring when buildings and neighborhoods are not allowed to run down:

1. *Social norms and conformity*—appropriate behavior is being defined in that area.
2. *The presence or lack of monitoring*—humans monitor others to determine what the appropriate behaviors are and monitor others to ensure their conformity.
3. *Social signaling*—an ordered and clean environment sends the signal that this is a place that is monitored, and people here conform to the common norms of noncriminal behavior. A disordered environment that is littered, vandalized, and not maintained sends the opposite signal. Since people tend to act the way they think others act, they are more likely to act "disorderly" in the disordered environment (Wilson and Kelling, 1982).

Rational Choice Theory

Another theory that emphasizes situational aspects was proposed by Derek B. Cornish and Ronald V. Clarke (1986). Rational choice theory (also known as choice theory, situational theory and situational factors theory) argues that crime prevention can be accomplished by focusing on those situational aspects that influence the commission of particular types of crimes. Criminals do not randomly select their targets. Instead, they rationally choose both the crime that they will commit and the target of that crime. This assumption of rationality and choice led many criminologists (e.g., Akers and Sellers, 2009; Schmalleger, 2011; Shoemaker, 2009; Siegel, 2010) to categorize rational choice as a neoclassical theory. However, one could argue that with its focus on empirical techniques to assess and reduce vulnerability to crime, rather than on the process of dispensing justice, routine activities theory can easily fit within the domain of positive theory.

Rational choice theory, like routine activities theory, focuses on opportunity. The social control aspect of deterrence is left to others. Situational factors are emphasized. Clarke (1997, pp. 17–27) identified sixteen factors that influence vulnerability to crime. These situational factors or crime-prevention techniques are presented in Figure 4.2.

Crime Pattern Theory

The concept of activity spaces is central to crime pattern theory, which was developed by the Canadian environmental criminologists Pat and Paul Brantingham (2008). They use the concept to describe how offenders find targets in the course of their daily routines. Basically, the premise is that as offenders go from home to work, recreation, and shopping, they consciously or unconsciously apply a search template by which they evaluate potential crime targets. These search patterns may be simple travel along two or three regular

---

Figure 4.2   Clarke's Situational Factors

A. Increasing Perceived Effort
   1. Target hardening
   2. Access control
   3. Deflecting offenders
   4. Controlling facilitators

B. Increasing Perceived Risks
   5. Entry/exit screening
   6. Formal surveillance
   7. Surveillance by employees
   8. Natural surveillance

C. Reducing Anticipated Awards
   9. Target removal
   10. Identifying property
   11. Reducing temptation
   12. Denying benefits

D. Inducing Guilt or Shame
   13. Rule setting
   14. Strengthening moral condemnation
   15. Controlling disinhibitors
   16. Facilitating compliance

Source: Adapted from Clarke (1997, chapter 1).

Reality Check: Serial Killers

Serial killers are murderers who kill three or more people over a period of time. The time frame between murders may be lengthy, with a few murders over several years, or short, with new murders following within a few days. The murders are usually planned in advance, and specific victims or types of victims are selected. Serial murder differs from *spree murder* in that there is usually a cooling-off period between killings and the motivations are usually different. Serial killers are often loners who target vulnerable victims such as children and young women in order to satisfy their needs for power or to act out their hostility toward a type of victim. Spree killers often kill several people at one or more locations after some sort of triggering event sets them off. Occasionally serial killers may engage in spree killings, such as Ted Bundy did at the Chi Omega sorority at Florida State University.

Theodore "Ted" Bundy: Serial Killer and Spree Killer

Ted Bundy murdered at least thirty young women, and possibly many more, in the states of Washington, Oregon, California, Utah, Idaho, Colorado, and Florida from 1974 to 1978. Bundy was handsome, charming, and charismatic. His victims were usually attractive young women and girls who had long dark hair. He would use his charm and guile to lure his victims into his control. He was also an escape artist, having managed to escape twice while in custody on murder charges in Glenwood Springs, Colorado.

In the early morning hours of January 15, 1978, Bundy became a spree killer as well as a serial killer. He gained entry to the Chi Omega sorority house in Tallahassee, Florida, where he engaged in a sadistic binge that left two women dead and two others with horrific injuries. After leaving Chi Omega, Bundy broke into an apartment building several blocks away and attacked another student and left her for dead. A few days later, he abducted and murdered a young girl from a junior high school in Lake City, Florida. Bundy was caught in Pensacola, Florida, while driving a stolen van. He resisted arrest, actually struggling with the officer over his handgun. Bundy was tried and convicted on the Florida murders. He was executed in the electric chair at the Florida State Prison at Starke in January 1989.

John Wayne Gacy, Jr.: The Killer Clown

John Wayne Gacy raped and murdered thirty-three teenage boys and young men from 1972 to 1978. Twenty-six of his victims were found buried beneath the crawl space of his Chicago home. Gacy became known as the "Killer Clown" due to his charitable performances where he would dress as "Pogo the Clown" at fundraising events, parades, and children's parties.

continues

Reality Check, *continued*

Gacy was married with a wife and children and was a pillar of the community in Waterloo, Iowa. However, he became involved in sexual swinging, prostitution, pornography, and drugs. He began abusing young men who worked for him and blackmailing them into having sex. After being convicted of sodomy charges, Gacy was sentenced to ten years in prison. Gacy was released on parole after serving less than two years of his prison sentence.

Gacy then relocated to Chicago in 1971, where he promptly sexually assaulted a teenage boy. Unfortunately, the young man did not show up in court and the charges against Gacy were dropped. In 1972, Gacy forced another young man to perform oral sex on him, but those charges were also dropped. In 1972, Gacy celebrated his engagement to his second wife by molesting a young man in his home. When the victim resisted, Gacy stabbed him to death. This began his practice of raping young men, then killing them to keep them quiet. Thirty-two more young men and boys were murdered before a victim whom Gacy had chloroformed and molested but dumped alive was able to locate Gacy and lead police to him. During that investigation, the murders were discovered. On March 13, 1977, Gacy was sentenced to death for thirty-three of his murders. He was executed on May 10, 1994, at Stateville Correctional Center in Joliet, Illinois.

Ted Bundy and John Wayne Gacy both exemplify individuals who are not awed by the threat of severe punishment. They each had several close calls in which they were arrested and managed to avoid prosecution. Gacy only served twenty-one months for his rape charges in Iowa. He avoided prosecution in two rape cases in Chicago before his murders were discovered. Bundy managed to escape from custody while being tried for murder and had many narrow misses in his travels around the country. It is suspected that both had been killing for longer than they admitted. It is obvious that neither of them were deterred by the possibility of facing the death penalty. We suspect this was more from arrogant confidence that they could continue to beat the system rather than a lack of fear.

Discuss the Beltway Sniper attacks of Lee Boyd Malvo and John Allen Muhammad. Why would they be classified as spree killers rather than serial killers?

routes with occasional movements off their path, or they may be extremely complex events that take offenders to the edges of their activity areas.

You may see that crime pattern theory is routine activities theory with the concepts of mobility and perception added to the original concepts of opportunity and motivation. Offenders, like law-abiding citizens, are creatures of habit; they usually do not stray far from the area they know. This is because it is easier to commit crimes in the course of their daily routine than to make a special journey to do so. As a result, crimes will appear in patterns along their travel paths within their activity areas or clustered along the edges of their activity areas. Offenders are said to be attracted to affluent or target-rich areas that are convenient to them, but they do not usually travel too far into unfamiliar territory where they may be more vulnerable to being caught. In addition to tracking offenders, crime pattern theorists track the activity areas of potential victims. By mapping their nodes of travel, they may track patterns of victimization as well as offending.

Situational Choice Theory

Situational choice theory is a combination of environmental criminology, routines activities theory, and rational choice theory. Criminal behavior is viewed as a function of choices and decisions made within a complex context of situational constraints and opportunities. Crime happens when an offender and a victim come together at a particular place and time. That potential occurrence is influenced by the daily activities and movements of victims and offenders.

Criminals think about their decisions before they commit crimes. Crime occurs when benefits of committing that crime are greater than the benefits of not committing it. This approach focuses on crime incidents rather than on offenders and looks at how everyday life and lifestyles lead to crime. The concepts are discussed in detail within Felson's (2002) publication, *Crime in Everyday Life*.

Criminology of Place

Criminology of place incorporates the environmental issues described above with the social ecology of the Chicago School. The concepts of defensible space and broken windows theory are used to examine and help explain the impacts of social disorganization on communities (Schmalleger, 2012). Therefore, this theory may logically be located here or in Chapter 7. This approach is particularly useful in that it uses crime mapping to track "hot spots of crime." It differs from the previous theories in that it is concerned with both the physical and social environments and their relationships with offenders, victimization, and crime.

Crime Science

Crime science may be said to incorporate all of the previously discussed deterrence and opportunity theories. Proponents of crime science see it as a radical departure from the usual ways of thinking about and responding to the problem of crime and security in society. According to information provided by the University College of London/Jill Dando Institute of Security and Crime Science (2011), crime science differs from other criminological approaches because it is about crime. Traditional criminology emphasizes criminality, focusing on distant causes such as poverty, social disadvantage, parenting practices, and school performance. In contrast, crime scientists are concerned with near causes of *crime*—why, where, when, by whom, and how a particular offense is committed.

Crime science is seen by its proponents as being practical in its orientation and multidisciplinary in its foundations. Crime scientists work with criminal justice practitioners to reduce crime by making it more difficult for individuals to offend, and making it more likely that they will be detected if they do offend. Crime science is also interdisciplinary, drawing from criminology, sociology, psychology, geography, architecture, industrial design, epidemiology, computer science, mathematics, engineering, and biology.

Crime science may not be as unusual as its advocates feel it to be, as incorporating an interdisciplinary approach to solve current crimes and prevent future crimes is consistent with the direction that criminal justice/criminology is currently taking. However, crime scientists' emphasis on application is exciting.

Summary

The classical school was concerned with the application of law and punishment in order to deter criminal behavior. The neoclassical school made allowances for issues that might impact the rationality or the free will of offenders. There are "aggravating" or "mitigating" circumstances that acknowledge other issues that may have played a role in the commission of a crime.

Starting in the 1970s and into the new century, the classical school has seen resurgence in the areas of sentencing and corrections. This is because of the public's and justice system practitioners' disenchantment with the positive school of thought (primarily because the positive school's emphasis on rehabilitation did not seem to work). The return of deterrence and "just deserts" was supported by the development of new theories using classical concepts but utilizing scientific principles in their application. We referred to this resurgence of the neoclassical school's precepts as the nouveau classical school.

Deterrence theories have revisited the importance of the social contract in applying punishment. The concept of "just deserts" is seen by proponents as being the needed application of punishment to promote general deterrence. The basic premise of the just deserts argument is that even if specific deterrence is not accomplished, society needs to see that criminals receive the punishment they deserve. Criminal personality theory is based on the belief that the social environment has little impact on the development of criminal behavior. Instead, criminals are said to freely choose their actions. Seductions of crime theory introduced another element to the hedonistic calculus that is the basis of deterrence theory. It addresses the pleasure obtained from the crime in a different manner than other deterrence theories do. Offenders are seen as not only enjoying the fruits of their crimes, but also enjoying committing them.

Dantzker coined the term *social crutch hypothesis* to explain how crime may have an appeal in yet another manner than seductiveness of the criminal act. He argues that offenders may develop a learned dependency on excuses provided by well-intentioned people that enable them to deny their own responsibility for their actions. The rotten apples theory argues that rotten apples are corrupt individuals who have slipped through the screening process or deviant individuals who continue their deviance in an environment that gives them more opportunity.

The basic premise of environmental criminology is that crime occurs when a motivated offender and an attractive target come together in the absence of capable guardians. We borrowed from Brantingham and Brantingham to add "in space and time" to the formula. This allows for strategies that make temporal or areal adjustments to potential crime targets. Defensible space and crime prevention through environmental design both emphasize crime prevention based upon the physical nature of the crime site. The premise is that proper physical design of private and public buildings and spaces will impact the perceptions of societal "defenders" as well as potential "offenders."

Routine activities theory argues that structural change in routine activity patterns can influence crime rates by affecting the convergence in space and time of the three minimal elements of motivated offenders, suitable targets, and the absence of capable guardians. Rational choice theory argues that crime prevention can be accomplished by focusing on those situational aspects that influence the commission of particular types of crimes. Criminals do not randomly select their targets. Instead, they rationally choose both the crime that they will commit and the target of that crime.

Crime pattern theory describes how offenders find targets in the course of their daily routines. As offenders go from home to work, recreation, and shopping, they consciously or unconsciously apply a search template by which they evaluate potential crime targets. As a result, crimes will appear in patterns along their travel paths within their activity areas or clustered along the edges of their activity areas. Broken windows theory seeks to contain or eliminate crime from urban neighborhoods, residents, and public officials by repairing neglected and deteriorated buildings and neighborhoods. Such actions deter petty crimes from occurring, which helps in preventing major crimes from developing.

Situational choice theory views criminal behavior as a function of choices and decisions made within a complex context of situational constraints and opportunities. This approach focuses on crime incidents rather than on offenders and looks at how everyday life and lifestyles lead to crime. Criminology of place incorporates the environmental issues described above with the social ecology of the Chicago School. The concepts of *defensible space* and *broken windows theory* are also used to examine and help explain the impacts of social disorganization on communities.

Last, proponents of crime science see it as a radical departure from the usual ways of thinking about and responding to the problem of crime and security in society. Crime science is said to differ from other criminological approaches because it is solely about crime.

Discussion Questions

1. Describe how neoclassical criminology addressed the deficits of classical criminology.
2. Describe how deterrence is an integral component of classical and neoclassical theories.
3. Explain why there was a return to correctional practices based upon deterrence and "just deserts."
4. Select two of the nouveau classical deterrence theories and explain how they may be applied to criminal offenders.
5. Describe how the crime equation serves as the basis for opportunity theories.
6. Which of the opportunity theories do you feel best explains crime? Why?

5

Biological and Biosocial Theories

In Chapter 3 we discussed the positive school of criminology and the contributions of the Italian physician Cesare Lombroso. While the primary focus of this school has been sociological explanations of crime and criminality, early positive school theories revolved around biology and began with the concept of determinism. Because of racial stereotyping and dissatisfaction with hard determinism, these theories fell into disfavor with contemporary criminologists. Today, criminologists favor "nurture" (sociological and psychological factors) over "nature" (biological factors), although modern biological explanations have gained some status among criminologists who allow for the influences that nature may have upon nurture in producing crime and criminality. The concept of determinism and its challenges to the assumptions of free will and rationality were developed in the works of Darwin and Lombroso. While the biological explanations offered by Lombroso have long since been discredited, his arguments were instrumental in development of the positive school of criminology. The positive school called for scientific analysis rather than legal actions. Rather than punishment based upon the severity of the crime, the positive school called for treatment based upon the needs of the offender. The use of science to determine the causes of crime, to reduce the potential for crime by addressing social ills, and to provide appropriate treatment for offenders became the basis for academic criminology.

Biological Explanations

Within the remainder of this chapter we shall discuss the leading biological and biosocial explanations of crime, beginning with early theories that were influenced by Lombroso and Darwin. The focuses of these biological explanations of crime are displayed in Figure 5.1.

79

Figure 5.1   Biological Theories

Early Theories	Transitional Theories	Contemporary Theories
Physical features	Body types	Nutrition
Heredity	Genetics	Chemical imbalances
Feeblemindedness	Chromosomal abnormalities	Allergies
Gender	Intelligence	Environmental contaminants
		Substance abuse
		Neurophysiological factors
		Hormones

Early Biological Explanations

Charles Goring, a student of Lombroso's, measured the degree of correlation between physiological features and the criminal history of his subjects. In 1913, he published the results of his research in *The English Convict*. Goring's data showed that the criminals in his study were shorter and weighed less than the noncriminal control group subjects. The finding was taken as support of Goring's general thesis that criminal behavior, like other physical traits and features, could be inherited.

Goring's work was criticized by others who argued that his findings were flawed because he failed to account for the effect of environment. Despite the questions raised about his methodology, Goring's work was significant because he was the first to claim that criminal behavior might be the result of the interaction between heredity and environment, a view now held by many criminologists. He did not reject the influence of the environment as the cause of crime, but maintained that empirical evidence, evidence not found in his study, was required to support this view (Driver, 1972).

Physical Features and Criminal Behavior

In 1939, Earnest A. Hooten conducted research similar to Lombroso's and Goring's. The findings of his research were published in *Crime and the Man*. Hooten evaluated 13,873 inmates from ten states, comparing them along 107 physiological dimensions with 3,203 individuals who were not incarcerated and who formed the control group. He found that prisoners tended to have certain physiological characteristics (such as low foreheads, crooked noses, narrow jaws, small ears, long necks, and stooped shoulders) not found in the control group. Hooten labeled these criminals *organically inferior* and concluded that the primary cause of their criminal behavior was their biological inferiority.

Hooten (1939) also believed there was a relationship between criminals' body shape and the types of crimes they committed. He found that murderers tended to be tall and thin, while rapists were short and heavy. Men with average builds did not specialize in any particular crime because they, like their physical shape, had no specific orientation. Hooten's research was heavily criticized because it suffered from the same methodological flaws as Goring's work. Hooten's work also failed to gain recognition because it was published at the onset of World War II when theories of biological inferiority had come under attack by opponents of Nazism and fascism.

Heredity and Crime

Criminal behavior as an inherited trait received attention after biologists and medical researchers accepted the belief that behavior could be passed from generation to generation. The most famous of these studies were those of the dukes and the Kalhikaks. In 1877, Richard L. Dugdale published a study entitled *The Jukes: A Study in Crime, Pauperism, Disease, and Heredity.* After learning that six members of the Jukes family were incarcerated in rural New York, Dugdale traced the genealogy of the family back 200 years and found a history of pauperism, prostitution, exhaustion, disease, fornication, and illegitimacy. He attributed these findings to the "degenerate" nature of the family. His research was criticized because it was based on unreliable, incomplete, and obscure information and was filled with value judgments and unsupported conclusions. His work was also criticized because he had no control group to determine whether the level of criminality of the Jukes family was higher than that of other families with similar histories.

In 1912, Henry H. Goddard published *The Kallikak Family: A Study in the Heredity of Feeblemindedness.* He attempted to address the shortcomings of the Jukes study by placing the study of deviant families within an acceptable scientific framework that included a control group. For comparison purposes, he studied two branches of the same family. Martin Kallikak, a soldier in the Revolutionary War, had fathered two children with two different women. The first child was illegitimate and the result of a sexual liaison between Kallikak and a barmaid. After he returned home from the war, Kallikak married a "righteous" Quaker girl, and a second lineage was formed. Goddard found a higher proportion of crime and other problems in Kallikak and the barmaid's descendants (Goddard, 1912). Critics of Goddard's findings argue that educational and **environmental factors** explain his findings better than hereditary ones in that the "deviant" set of Kallikak descendants lived in poverty, while the "normal" set lived in wealth. They also argued that the claimed differences between the two groups were not as obvious as Goddard claimed (Hagan, 2006).

Feeblemindedness

During the early twentieth century, studies by Goddard (1914) and others (Goring, 1913; Zeleny, 1933) found low IQs (intelligence quotients) among prisoners and juveniles in reform schools. This research was later criticized by sociologists because of the small, unrepresentative samples of subjects and because the tests were unreliable. As a result, studies on intelligence and crime lost their popularity by the 1930s (Gould, 1981). Goddard (1914), of the New Jersey Training School for the Feebleminded, popularized IQ tests in the United States, beginning with his study of the Kallikak family. In the Kallikak study, he assumed that low intelligence or "feeblemindedness" was passed on biologically from one generation to the next. Although in his study of the Kallikak family Goddard employed a subjective definition of feeblemindedness, the later investigation identified feeblemindedness based on IQ distribution among those in institutions for the feebleminded, a somewhat more objective standard. These distributions yielded an IQ of 75 or less, or a mental age of twelve or below, as the cutoff point for classifying feeblemindedness.

The initial wave of research that followed Goddard's earlier studies reported that feebleminded prisoners constituted 25 to 90 percent of prison populations (Fink, 1938). The validity of this research, however, came into question when the US Army began to administer IQ tests to army draftees during World War I. These tests indicated that roughly one-third of the draftees were feebleminded, according to Goddard's definition of feeblemindedness (Zeleny, 1933). Clearly, this was an unsettling proposition. Consequently, the definition of feeblemindedness was revised downward to an IQ of 50, or a mental age of eight or below. This readjustment cast doubt on the earlier work of Goddard and others that had so often linked low intelligence and feeblemindedness with delinquency.

Gender

In addition to his earlier research on atavism, Cesare Lombroso (1920) was one of the first criminologists to study female criminals. In his book *The Female Offender,* he attributed the differences between males and females to variations in evolutionary development. He believed females were more primitive than males and that they possessed many traits common in children, that is, women were more likely to be vengeful, jealous, insensitive to pain, and lacking any sense of morality. According to Lombroso, women had lower rates of criminal behavior than men only because their natural deficiencies were "neutralized by piety, maternity, want of passion, sexual coldness, weakness, and an undeveloped intelligence" (Lombroso-Ferrero, 1972, pp. 150–152). Women committed crimes only when they inherited male characteristics— "virile" craniums, excessive body hair, moles, and other gross features. Lombroso's (1920) theory became known as the *masculinity hypothesis*. With the exception of prostitutes (who were thought to act out of atavistic yearnings), he believed, a few masculine females were responsible for the majority of crimes committed by women.

Lombroso (1920) also believed that masculinity among women itself was an anomaly. Conversely, women who were born with feminine features would be protected from crime by their innate physiological limitations and would be predisposed to unimaginative, dull, and conformist lives. Lombroso reasoned that, like male criminals, the majority of female criminals could be classified as occasional criminals whose physical features contained no signs of degeneration and whose moral character would be similar to that of their "normal sisters" (Lombroso-Ferrero, 1972, pp. 193–195). In addition, Lombroso argued that female occasional criminals might be encouraged to commit crime because of the increased frustrations they would meet in life as their educational opportunities increased. Lombroso, therefore, recognized the influences of female criminality that have gained popularity in recent decades. Although Lombroso's philosophy on female criminality was built on sexist and outdated notions of women's biological makeup, it remained influential for many years. Like his concept of atavism, it remains noteworthy more for the later studies it generated than for its own theoretical contributions (Chesney-Lind and Sheldon, 2004).

Transitional Biological Explanations

Early biological theories in criminology took the view that nature exerted influences on human beings that overcame socialization (nurture). This perspective assumed that offenders behaved differently because they were physically different from nonoffenders. These views followed the lead of Lombroso and were compatible with hard determinism. Later studies conducted in the 1940s through the 1970s made allowances for psychological and sociological influences. They were believed to be more in line with the soft determinism perspective that came to dominate criminology during the twentieth century. However, many of these later theories remained unpopular with criminologists because they still emphasized biological and psychological factors with little regard for sociological influences. In addition, some studies revisited issues such as race, class, and intelligence, resulting in opposition from both within and without criminology. These studies, however, mark the beginning of the transition in understanding crime and criminality from "nature versus nurture" to "nature *and* nurture."

Body Types

The body-build, or somatotype, school was developed by William Sheldon, who theorized that criminals had distinct physiques that made them susceptible to particular types of criminal behavior. Sheldon (1949) maintained that elements of three basic body types could be found in all people: *Endomorphs* are heavy persons with short arms and legs; they tend to be relaxed and extroverted and relatively noncriminal. *Mesomorphs* are athletic and muscular; they tend to be aggressive and particularly likely to commit violent crimes and other crimes requiring strength and speed. *Ectomorphs* are thin, introverted, and overly sensitive.

Sheldon (1949) compared 200 male delinquents in an institution with a control group of some 4,000 male college students. He found that compared to the students, delinquents tended to be mesomorphic. Sheldon theorized that people with athletic bodies were particularly apt to engage in adventurous and aggressive behaviors. As a result, muscular boys were more likely to join juvenile gangs and to be bullies.

Sheldon's work was followed by that of Sheldon Glueck and Eleanor Glueck (1950), who examined the relationship between body type and delinquency in 500 institutionalized delinquents who had persistent brushes with the law. These delinquents were matched with a control sample of nondelinquents. After measuring body types through photographs, they found more than 60 percent of the delinquents were mesomorphic compared with 31 percent of nondelinquents.

In 1956, the Gluecks conducted another study of somatotypes and delinquency. They found that mesomorphs who became delinquent were also characterized by a number of personality traits not normally found in mesomorphs. These included susceptibility to contagious diseases of childhood, destructiveness, feelings of inadequacy, emotional instability, and emotional conflicts (Glueck and Glueck, 1956). In addition, three sociocultural factors—careless household routine, lack of family group recreation, and meagerness of recreational facilities in the home—were strongly associated with delinquency in mesomorphs. Whether the mesomorphic body structure determines these characteristics or the personality traits are generated from environmental factors, including being labeled a "delinquent," was addressed by the Gluecks. They concluded that delinquency was caused by a combination of environmental, biological, and psychological factors and that there was no such thing as a "delinquent personality" among mesomorphs (Glueck and Glueck, 1956).

Both Sheldon's and the Gluecks' work was criticized. Sheldon's work was found to suffer from the same methodological flaws as the work of Lombroso, Goring, Hooten, and other early biologists (Bernard, Snipes, and Gerould, 2009). Critics argued that even if Sheldon's delinquent subjects were more mesomorphic, he could not rule out the possibility that their muscular, athletic bodies made it more probable that juvenile justice officials would view them as a threat and hence were more likely to institutionalize them. Criticism of the Gluecks stemmed from their not having a control group for the rapid body changes that occur in adolescence. They were also criticized because their method of somatotyping relied on visual assessments, not precise measurements. Finally, they were criticized because the delinquent population they studied included only institutionalized youths (Hagan, 2011).

Genetics and Crime: Twin and Adoption Studies

Early studies at the beginning of the twentieth century attempting to address the hereditary bases of criminality by examining traditional families, such as the Jukes and Kallikaks, were eventually abandoned because it was essentially impossible to disentangle the effects of nature (such as genes) from those of nurture (environment). Half a century later, researchers found that one way to determine the role of **genetics** was to compare the incidence and types of criminal convictions of identical and fraternal twins. Theoretically, twin research assumes that the environment exerts similar influences on each member of a twin set. Therefore, any differences between the twins would presumably be due to genetic factors. Therefore, the hereditary versus environmental influences on behavior can be accurately determined by comparing concordance rates between identical and fraternal twins. **Concordance** is a key concept in twin study research and is the term used in genetics for the degree to which related pairs of subjects both show a particular behavior or condition.

In the earlier studies conducted on the behavior of twins, researchers generally found greater similarities of criminal behavior between identical twins than between fraternal twins. A review of relevant studies conducted between 1929 and 1961 found that 60 percent of identical twins shared criminal behavior patterns (if one twin was criminal, so was the other), while only 30 percent of fraternal twins were similarly related (Mednick and Christiansen, 1971). This evidence was widely interpreted as supporting a genetic basis for crime.

In another study of twins, Christiansen studied 3,586 male twin pairs and found a 52 percent concordance for identical pairs and 22 percent concordance for fraternal pairs. This result suggests that identical twins may share a genetic characteristic that increases the risk of their engaging in criminality (Christiansen, 1974). Similarly, D. Rowe and D. W. Osgood have analyzed the factors that influence self-reported delinquency in a sample of twin pairs and concluded that genetic influences actually have explanatory power (Rowe and Osgood, 1984).

Critics have argued that other reasons may account for the concordance. Compared to siblings, identical twins spend more time together, tend to have the same friends, are more attached to each other, and tend to think of themselves as alike. They are also more likely than other siblings or even fraternal twins to be treated the same by their parents, friends, and teachers. All these likenesses produce similar attitudes and behaviors between identical twins, including delinquency and crime (Dalgaard and Kringlen, 1976).

Adoption studies yield findings similar to those of twin studies. It would seem logical that if the behavior of adopted children is more similar to that of their biological parents than to that of their adoptive parents, the idea of a genetic basis for criminality would be supported. If, however, adoptees are more similar to their adoptive parents than to their biological parents, an environmental basis for crime would seem more valid. Several studies indicate that some relationship exists between biological parents' behavior and the behavior of their children, even when their contact has been infrequent or nonexistent (Mednick and Christiansen, 1971).

One of the most significant adoption studies was conducted by Barry Hutchings and Sarnoff Mednick (1977), who analyzed 1,145 male adoptees born in Denmark between 1927 and 1941; of these, 185 had criminal records. After following up on 143 of the criminal adoptees and matching them with a control group of 143 noncriminal adoptees, Hutchings and Mednick found that the criminality of the biological father was a strong predictor of the child's criminal behavior. When both the biological and adoptive fathers were criminal, the probability that the youth would engage in criminal behavior greatly expanded. Twenty-five percent of the boys whose adoptive and biological fathers were criminals had been convicted of a criminal law violation compared with only 14 percent of those whose biological and adoptive fathers were not criminals (Hutchings and Mednick, 1977).

Chromosomal Abnormalities

Chromosomal theory has also been used to explain criminal behavior. Within this theory, aggressive behavior is linked with a genetic abnormality wherein a sperm or ovum contains more than one sex chromosome. When conception occurs, the resulting embryo will have an extra sex chromosome.

In 1965, the first well-known study that linked criminal behavior to an abnormal sex chromosome was made by British researchers who examined 197 Scottish prisoners for chromosomal abnormalities through a relatively simple blood test (Jacobs, Brunton, and Melville, 1965). Twelve of the group displayed chromosomes that were unusual, and seven were found to have an XYY chromosome. "Normal" males possess an XY chromosome structure, while "normal" females are XX. The XYY male, whose incidence in the prison population was placed at around 3.5 percent by Patricia Jacobs, was identified as potentially violent and termed a "supermale." The extra Y chromosome was thought to be the cause of violent behavior.

The supermale concept became popular after a number of offenders attempted to use it as a criminal defense for the crimes they committed. For example, in 1969, Lawrence Hannell, who was declared to be a supermale, was acquitted of murder in Australia on the grounds of insanity (Jones, 1986). The XYY defense, however, did not work for Richard Speck, who was convicted of killing eight Chicago nursing students in 1966. It was later learned that Speck did not carry the extra Y chromosome. Speck's case drew much attention after the public became concerned that all XYYs were potential killers and should be closely controlled. As it became clear that most violent offenders actually did not possess the extra Y chromosome, interest in the XYY theory dissipated.

Intelligence and Crime

Intelligence and crime were revisited by Travis Hirschi and Michael Hinde-lang (1977) when they reviewed many studies using both self-report and official data and found that delinquents' IQ scores were significantly lower than nondelinquents' scores. The authors concluded that low IQ was an important predictor of delinquency.

Subsequent studies also linked criminal behavior or delinquency to low IQ. Most of this research focused on delinquency in adolescents with low IQs. First, it was believed that youths with low intelligence did poorly in school. Students with poor performance felt more alienated from school; therefore, poor school performance was thought to contribute to delinquent behavior. Second, it was believed that a lower ability to engage in moral reasoning and to delay gratification increased the likelihood of offending. Finally, adolescents with low intelligence were thought to be less able to fully realize the consequences of their actions; therefore, they were susceptible to the influence of their delinquent friends (Lynam, Moffitt, and Stouthamer-Loeber, 1993).

Other controversial issues stemmed from research on IQ, race, and crime. On average, African Americans score about 15 percent lower than European Americans on intelligence tests. These findings led some researchers to conclude that low IQ scores were more prevalent among African Americans. This finding was thought to explain why, as a portion of the population, African Americans are arrested more often than whites (Hermstein and Murray, 1994; Wilson and Herrnstein, 1985).

The intelligence controversy began with a 1967 speech before the National Academy of Sciences by William Shockley, a winner of the Nobel Prize in Physics. Shockley maintained that the differences in IQ between African Americans and European Americans might be solely the result of genetic differences, and these genetic differences might also explain the differences in poverty and crime rates between these two groups (Shockley, 1967).

Arthur Jensen (1969) wrote a lengthy article in which he asserted some of the same points Shockley had made. Jensen argued that there was a strong possibility that African Americans were endowed with less intellectual capacity than were whites. From his review of the research on IQ, he found that approximately 80 percent of IQ was inherited, while the remaining 20 percent could be attributed to the influence of environmental factors. Jensen hypothesized that because African Americans differ significantly from whites in achievement on IQ tests and in school, the sources of these differences were genetic as well as environmental.

Richard Herrnstein (1973) agreed with Jensen that intelligence is largely inherited. He argued that intelligence influenced the formation of heredity castes. According to Herrnstein, social stratification is due to inborn differences in mental ability. Therefore, one's success in society is influenced by one's mental ability. In 1994, Herrnstein and Charles Murray wrote the controversial book *The Bell Curve*. *The Bell Curve* was an update of Herrnstein's earlier assertion that economic and social hierarchies reflect cognitive and intellectual abilities, as measured by IQ tests.

Studies such as those by Jensen, Herrnstein, and Murray came under fire because of alleged methodological flaws and were also severely criticized as racist and reflective of the ethnocentric views of European whites toward other cultures. Other critics argued that low intellectual abilities could be associated with the contribution of social class to achievement on IQ tests. This oversight was crucial because critics of IQ tests believe that they are biased in favor of those from middle- and upper-class environments, as such people do better on IQ tests than those who are less fortunate. The most obvious criticism was whether IQ tests were a legitimate measure of intelligence at all, since IQ tests attempt to measure innate potential, a feat some believe is impossible. For the most part, intelligence tests measure educability. But the problem of such a measure is that achievement in school is also associated with a cluster of other social and motivational factors that IQ tests may not be able to measure (Ryan, 1972).

The above studies show how intelligence can be misused when incorrectly applied to race, ethnicity, and social class. However, an argument could be made that intelligence does matter. Individuals who are not capable of critical thinking may turn to crime to compensate for their inability to achieve higher education or better jobs. Those same limitations may cause them to be caught more easily than other offenders.

Contemporary Biological Explanations

Modern biological theories in criminology differ from previous theories in that they examine the entire range of biological characteristics, including those that result from genetic defects (those that are inherited) and those that are environmentally induced. In addition, theories developed since the 1980s do not suggest that biological characteristics directly "cause" crime. Instead, they argue that certain biological conditions increase the likelihood that an individual will engage in some antisocial behavior that can be defined as criminal (Fishbein, 1990). Modern theories increasingly focus on the interaction between biological characteristics and the social environment, rather than looking solely at the effects of biology. Because these explanations stress the interrelationships of nature and nurture, they are more accurately called *biosocial theories* of crime.

Biochemical Conditions

Biochemical conditions, including those that are genetically predetermined and those acquired through diet and environment, are believed to influence criminal behavior. Biochemical theories received national attention in 1979 after they were used in the criminal trial of Dan White, who was tried and convicted in the murder of the former mayor of San Francisco, Harvey Milk. White was found guilty of a lesser offense and charged with diminished-capacity manslaughter, rather than first-degree murder, based upon the now-infamous "Twinkie Defense." The jury accepted his defense attorney's argument that White's behavior was precipitated by his addiction to sugar-laden junk foods (*Time*, 1979). Such explanations have gained cautious acceptance by biocriminologists and are being used to help understand criminal behavior from a different perspective. Biochemical theories see criminal behavior as a function of diet, vitamin intake, hormonal imbalance, environmental contaminants, or food allergies.

Nutrition

Biocriminologists maintain that minimum levels of vitamins and minerals are needed for normal brain functioning and growth, especially in the early years of life. If people with normal needs do not receive the appropriate nutrition, they will suffer from vitamin deficiency. People with vitamin deficiency can manifest many physical, mental, and behavioral problems, including lower intelligence test scores (Neisser et al., 1996). Therefore, diet and nutrition play a role in aggression and crime (Schoenthaler and Doraz, 1983).

More recent studies have revealed that an insufficiency of certain chemicals and minerals, including sodium, potassium, calcium, amino acids, and other vitamins or minerals, can lead to depression, mania, cognitive problems, memory loss, or abnormal sexual activity (Krassner, 1986). For example, some studies have examined the relationship between crime and vitamin deficiency and found that antisocial behavior could be caused by insufficient quantities of some B vitamins and vitamin C. Others have discovered that the behavior of schizophrenics and of children with learning and behavior disorders is affected by lack of some B-complex vitamins (B_3 and B_6). It was found that the addition of these vitamins to the diets of children who were deficient in them could control unruly behavior and improve school performance (Hippchen, 1978).

Hypoglycemia, Hyperglycemia, and Crime

One of the first studies that focused on chemical imbalances in the body as the cause of crime was published in a British medical journal. This study linked murder to hypoglycemia, or low blood sugar (Hill and Sargent, 1943). Low blood sugar can occur when there is too much insulin in the blood or because of near-starvation diets. It occurs when glucose (sugar) in the blood falls below levels necessary for normal and efficient brain functioning. When deprived of blood sugar, the brain's capacity to properly function is reduced. Symptoms of this chemical imbalance include irritability, anxiety, depression, crying spells, headaches, and confusion.

More recent studies have linked excess consumption of refined white sugar to hyperactivity and aggressiveness. Diets that are high in carbohydrates and sugar have been associated with deficiencies in attention span and students' scores on tests measuring reasoning power (Kershner and Hawke, 1979). Another study, however, published in 1994, seemed to contradict the notion that sugar may lead to hyperactivity. S. Schoenthaler and W. Doraz (1983) conducted an experiment on 276 incarcerated youths to determine whether a change in the amount of sugar in their diet would have an influence on their behavior within the institutional setting. They found that after several dietary changes were made, there was a significant reduction in disciplinary actions within the institution. Other studies have failed to produce the same results. One study of twenty-five preschool children and twenty-three school-age children who were sensitive to sugar involved following a different diet for three consecutive weeks. The first group of children was placed on a diet high in sugar, the second group on a diet using NutraSweet (aspartame), and the third group on saccharin. The findings revealed little evidence of cognitive or behavioral differences that could be linked to diet. Ironically, the sugar diets seemed to have a calming effect on the children (Wolraich et al., 1994).

Allergies

Some foods are believed to cause allergic reactions in humans that can lead to violence and even murder. Allergies are defined as unusual or excessive reactions of the body to foreign substances. Cerebral allergies cause an excessive reaction of the brain, whereas neuroallergies affect the nervous system. Both forms of allergic reactions are believed to cause the allergic person to produce enzymes that attack wholesome foods as if they were dangerous to the body (Wunderlich, 1978). Some foods commonly known to produce these allergic reactions are milk, citrus fruit, chocolate, corn, wheat, and eggs, all of which have been found to cause swelling of the brain and the brain stem. Allergic reactions have also been linked to mental, emotional, and behavioral problems, such as hyperactivity in children who may consequently be mislabeled as potential delinquents.

Environmental Contaminants

Pollution or environmental contaminants are believed to contribute to criminal behavior. Lead, copper, cadmium, mercury, and inorganic gases, such as chlorine and nitrogen dioxide, are sometimes found at dangerous levels. At high levels, these substances can cause severe illness or death; at more moderate levels, they have been linked to emotional and behavioral disorders (Schauss, 1980). Lead poisoning has also been found to contribute to hyperactivity in children and to antisocial behavior (David et al., 1976).

Deborah Denno (1993) investigated the behavior of more than 900 African American youths and found that lead poisoning was one of the most significant predictors of male delinquency and persistent adult criminality. Herbert Needleman and his colleagues (Needleman et al., 1996) tracked 300 boys from ages seven to eleven and found that those who had high lead concentrations in their bones were much more likely to report attention problems, delinquency, and aggressiveness. High lead ingestion has also been reported as contributing to lower IQ scores, which is in turn linked to aggressive behavior (Neisser et al., 1996).

Substance Abuse

In addition to the previous influences, the inappropriate use of alcohol and drugs is a major factor in crime and criminality. Goldstein (1995) describes three forms in which alcohol and drugs interact with violent crimes: *psychopharmacological use,* in which alcohol and/or drug use lowers inhibitions and elevates aggressive tendencies; *economic compulsion,* in which alcoholics and drug addicts commit crimes to support their addictions; and *systemic violence,* in which drug traffickers commit violent crimes against other drug dealers as well as law enforcement and civilians who may get in their way. Our focus within this section will be the first two factors.

Of state prisoners serving time for a violent offense in 2004, 37 percent said they were under the influence of alcohol at the time of the offense (Bureau of Justice Statistics, 2011). An estimated 86 percent of homicide offenders were found to have been drinking at the time of their offense. In addition, 60 percent of sex offenders, 37 percent of assault offenders, 57 percent of males in marital violence, and 13 percent of child abusers were drinking when they committed violence (Roizen, 1997).

The effects of alcohol abuse are even more widespread than the violence described above. Drunken driving, alcohol poisoning, foolish accidents, and unsafe sex are but a few products of binge drinking. The products of alcoholism may include those behaviors as well as the inability to hold a job, complete one's education, perform family duties, or function within society. Furthermore, alcohol dependency may lead to robbery, theft, burglary, fraud, prostitution, and other crimes to support that dependency.

Drug abuse, while not as prevalent as alcohol abuse, creates a serious problem for our society. This is disconcerting, especially given the following: "Illicit drug use in the United States has risen to its highest level in 8 years, according to the 2009 National Survey on Drug Use and Health. Last year, 8.7 percent of Americans aged 12 and older—an estimated 21.8 million people— said they used illicit drugs in the month prior to the survey, which represents a 9 percent increase over the 2008 rate" (National Institute on Drug Abuse, 2010).

Drug abuse leads to the same problems found with alcohol abuse. However, drug abuse is further complicated in that the possession and use of illicit drugs are crimes. The leading drugs that are abused in the United States (besides alcohol and tobacco) are club drugs, cocaine, heroin, inhalants, LSD (acid), marijuana, MDMA (ecstasy), methamphetamine, PCP/Phencyclidine, prescription medications, and anabolic steroids. While their impacts vary considerably, all can lead to bizarre behaviors, chemical addiction, and psychological dependency. Overdoses of the harder drugs can also result in serious health problems and in many cases death.

Neurophysiological Factors

Neurophysiology is the study of brain activity. Criminologists began to focus on this area of study after Charles Whitman barricaded himself in a tower at the University of Texas and killed fourteen people and wounded twenty-four others with a high-powered rifle (see the Reality Check at the end of this chapter).

Whitman's fatal ordeal led researchers to theorize that there might be an association between neurological impairment and crime. One such impairment is minimum brain dysfunction, or MBD. MBD can result from a head injury or it can be inherited. In its most serious form, MBD is said to cause an imbalance in the urge-control mechanism, dyslexia, visual perception problems, hyperactivity, poor attention span, and/or explosive behavior. Some studies have found that up to 60 percent of criminal offenders exhibit some brain dysfunction when subjected to psychological tests. Others have found some form of dysfunction in the dominant hemisphere of the brain (Bartol and Bartol, 2011).

Attention deficit hyperactivity disorder (ADHD) has also been linked to neurological factors. ADHD is most often found in children who exhibit poor school performance, bullying, stubbornness, and lack of response to discipline (Bartol and Bartol, 2011).

While numerous attempts have been made to link neurophysiological factors with crime, the majority of the theories remain unsubstantiated. However, that does not mean that a link does not exist; it just still needs to be proven.

Hormones

Some criminologists link criminal behavior to hormonal imbalances in the body, arguing that the male sex hormone, testosterone, accounts for aggressive behavior. Several studies have found that male adolescents and adults with records of violent and other crimes have higher testosterone levels than males without criminal records (Dabbs and Morris, 1990; Udry, Talbert, and Morris, 1986).

Olweus (2009) reported that boys aged fifteen to seventeen showed levels of verbal and physical aggression that correlated with the level of testosterone found in their blood. Boys with higher levels tended to be habitually impatient and more irritable than boys with lower levels of testosterone. Olweus concluded that high levels of testosterone contributed to this pattern of behavior.

Alan Booth and D. Wayne Osgood (1993) concluded there was a moderately strong relationship between testosterone and adult deviance. They also believed, however, that mediating factors, or an interaction between testosterone and other social factors, increased the chances of juvenile and adult crime. For example, higher testosterone levels were thought to increase the probability of criminal behavior in those persons who were risk-takers and exhibited impulsive behavior. Higher levels were also thought to diminish the interpersonal bonds that inhibit persons from committing deviant or criminal acts.

Although most research on hormones and crime has focused on males, some work has examined the role hormones play in female crime, especially in connection with the menstrual cycle. In some women, hormonal changes in the days prior to menstruation appear to be linked to increased stress, tension, lethargy, and other problems; this condition has been called premenstrual syndrome (PMS). Hormonal changes following ovulation have been linked to irritability and aggression, but research on the strength of this linkage has been inconclusive (Trunnell, Turner, and Keye, 1988).

Katharina Dalton (1961), a leading researcher, collected data from female prisoners to determine whether there was a link between PMS and female criminality. These prisoners were asked to think back to the time they committed their offense and to remember the dates of their menstruation. From this information, Dalton hoped to determine whether offenses occurred randomly

---

Reality Check: Brain Damage and Mass Murder

Charles Joseph Whitman was a student at the University of Texas at Austin and a former marine. On August 1, 1966, he murdered his wife and mother in their homes. He then went to the university's 307-foot tower armed with a small arsenal of weapons. While on the observation floor of the tower, Whitman killed thirteen people and wounded thirty-two others during a shooting rampage that lasted ninety-seven minutes. He was finally killed by Austin police officers who had dared to go into the tower after him. At that time, it was the worst mass murder in US history.

During Whitman's autopsy, the pathologist found a glioblastoma, which is a highly aggressive brain tumor. It is believed that this tumor, along with his abuse of amphetamines and mental instability from his dysfunctional family, contributed to Whitman's violent behavior. Investigators also found that he had sought psychiatric help. Whitman had kept a meticulous diary in which he described his uncontrollable urges to kill. Whitman willed his estate to any mental institution that would study mental problems such as his own (Johnson, 1972; Time, 1966; Lavergne, 1997).

The questions raised by Whitman's spree murders have led some researchers to theorize that spree and serial killers may have brain damage or other biological abnormalities that contribute to their actions. While killers like Ted Bundy were not found to suffer from such damage, others, like Henry Lee Lucas and Arthur Shawcross, were found to have severe brain injuries. Damage to areas like the frontal lobe, the hypothalamus, and the limbic system can contribute to extreme aggression, loss of control, loss of judgment, and violence (Scott, 2011).

If future studies find clear linkages between brain damage from injury or disease and mass murder, do you think this will influence how the US criminal justice system deals with mass murderers?

---

throughout the women's cycles or if the offenses occurred during their premenstrual phase. She found that almost half of the prisoners she studied reported they committed their offenses in the eight-day period immediately preceding and during menstruation.

There are some cases in which women have used PMS as a criminal defense. One 1980 case involved a woman in Great Britain who was exonerated of murdering her live-in boyfriend. The English defense attorney based the defense on the fact that the woman was suffering from premenstrual syndrome at the time of the homicide. The expert witness in this case testified that PMS caused the defendant to be "irritable, aggressive, and confused, with a loss of self-control" (Udry, Talbert, and Morris, 1986). In 1991, another case linking PMS to violent or criminal behavior was decided in favor of a woman by a Virginia judge. The judge dismissed drunken driving charges against the woman, who had allegedly kicked and cursed a state trooper, after her gynecologist testified on her behalf. The doctor claimed the woman's behavior was likely to have been due primarily to premenstrual syndrome (*Fayetteville Observer-Times*, 1991).

The PMS explanation is not without its critics. Some believe the research on this subject is methodologically flawed. For example, critics argue it assumes that women can accurately remember when menstruation occurred, since even a few days' error can place their crime outside their premenstrual phase. Dalton's work has also been criticized because stress and other factors, such as diet, can disrupt women's cycles, so menstruation may occur irregularly. If the stress of committing crime, or the stress leading up to the crime, hastens menstruation, it may appear that the crime was committed in a woman's premenstrual phase only because menstruation occurred sooner than normal (Katz and Chambliss, 1995). These arguments are supported by Diana Fishbein's (1992) study of women incarcerated for crimes of violence. Her findings revealed that for a significant number of women, the crimes were committed during the premenstrual period. Fishbein concluded that these women experienced cyclical hormonal changes that heightened their feelings of anxiety and hostility. However, the fact that the vast majority of women do not commit crimes during PMS appears to make this argument more of a mitigating circumstance than an explanation for criminal behavior.

Summary

The concept of determinism and its challenges to the assumptions of free will and rationality were developed in the works of Darwin and Lombroso. While the atavistic explanations offered by Lombroso have long since been discredited, his arguments were instrumental in development of the positive school of criminology. The positive school called for scientific analysis rather than legal actions. Rather than punishment based upon the severity of the crime, the positive school called for treatment based upon the needs of the offender. The use of science to determine the causes of crime, to reduce the potential for crime by addressing social ills, and to provide appropriate treatments for offenders became the basis for academic criminology.

Following in the footsteps of Lombroso were Goring and Hooten, who believed that heredity was linked to criminal behavior, and Dugdale and Goddard, who took heredity one step further and looked at family history as a possible factor in criminality. Sheldon examined the effect of body types, which was reinforced by the Gluecks' research. More recent research has included theories involving twins, chromosomal abnormalities, gender, and intelligence. Contemporary biological research has examined environment, nutrition, allergies, hormones, and neurophysiological factors.

The early biological theories emphasized hard determinism with little regard for the social environment. Later theories stressed soft determinism, in which nature was seen to be the primary influence, with nurture having some impact. Modern **biocriminology** proposes explanations based on the interaction of nature *and* nurture rather than nature *versus* nurture. Nature is seen as providing the predisposition for behaviors, with nurture creating the situations for behaviors to occur.

Biological explanations of crime and criminality have historically been ignored by US criminologists because most received their initial training in sociology. The potential of early and transitional biological theories for racial and class stereotyping has also created opposition both within the social sciences and in society at large. However, as we learn more about physiological influences on human behavior, we must consider the interaction of biosocial factors when studying crime and criminality.

Discussion Questions

1. Describe how the early biological theories exemplified hard determinism.
2. Why did the early studies of physical features and crime receive such strong criticism?
3. How did the transitional theories differ from the early theories? Why did they remain so controversial?
4. How have contemporary theories evolved beyond the limitations of previous theories?
5. Why do you think that even the new biosocial theories do not receive full support or attention?

6

Psychological and Psychosocial Theories

Chapter 5 introduced biological theories of crime causation. Psychological theories are also viewed as part of the positive school of criminology. As with the biological theories, the psychological theories have a rich background but are often not popular with sociologically trained criminologists. These theories, however, like those in Chapter 5, warrant discussion in order to understand the complexities of human (and subsequently criminal) behavior. As with biology, determinism plays a major fundamental role in the psychological theories.

Psychology and Determinism

Psychological and psychiatric theories explain criminal behavior primarily in terms of the personality attributes of the offender. These theories also consider biological and environmental factors in their explanations of criminal behavior. Much of the biological research done by psychologists and psychiatrists considered the impact of the environment on the offender. It also explained behavior by examining the relationship between the offender's biological and psychological characteristics to determine what may have caused the criminal behavior.

Psychological theories argue that criminal behavior originates in the personalities of the offenders rather than in their biology or their situation (i.e., environmental factors). Psychological theories have been generally classified into three areas: psychodynamic or psychoanalytic, behavioral, and cognitive theories. Psychological or **psychodynamic theories** examine unconscious behaviors that are believed to cause criminal behavior; **behavioral theories** examine the learning processes that lead to criminal behavior; and **cognitive theories** look at how thought processes, such as thinking and morals, affect one's behavior. Figure 6.1 shows the various psychological theories described within this chapter. Perhaps the best known, and the first of the psychological theories, is found in the works of Sigmund Freud, or **Freudian psychology**.

Freudian Psychology (Psychodynamic Theory)

Psychodynamic, or psychoanalytic, theory was developed by Sigmund Freud (1856–1939), a Viennese physician who was concerned with the medical treatment of a variety of functional disorders that seemed to be unrelated to any organic causes (Martin, Mutchnick, and Austin, 1990). Freud adopted the idea of the unconscious, an idea used by other psychiatrists, and argued that some behaviors could be explained by traumatic experiences in early childhood. He believed these early childhood experiences left a mark on the individual that was buried in the unconscious. In other words, the individual was not consciously aware of those experiences.

To explain his theory, Freud argued that there were three levels of the mind: conscious, preconscious, and unconscious. The **conscious** mind is the aspect of the mind that people are most aware of, such as their daily thoughts. The **preconscious** mind is said to contain elements of experiences that are outside our awareness but can be brought back to consciousness at any time, such as memories and experiences. The **unconscious** part of the mind contains biological desires and urges that cannot readily be experienced as thoughts. Part

Figure 6.1 Psychological Theories

Freudian Psychology	Behavioral Psychology	Social Learning	Cognitive Theory	Mental Disorders
Psychodynamic Psychoanalytic	Classical conditioning Operant conditioning	Imitation	Moral development Cognitive scripts Hostile attribution Expectancy Frustration-induced behavior Situational instigators	Psychometry Psychopathology Other personality disorders Mental illness Physiological factors

of the unconscious contains feelings about sex and hostility, which people keep below the surface of consciousness by a process called "repression" (Martin, Mutchnick, and Austin, 1990).

As a way to uncover these unconscious events, Freud developed the technique he called *psychoanalysis*. Psychoanalysis was premised on "free association." The patient would be put in a relaxed position and allowed to talk freely about whatever came to his or her mind. By exploring the associations among the issues the patient raised, Freud believed the individual would be able to reconstruct the earlier events and bring them to consciousness. Once the patient was conscious of these events, Freud argued, the events would lose their power and the patient would gain conscious control and freedom in his or her life (Bernard, Snipes, and Gerould, 2009). Freud later categorized his conceptions of the conscious and unconscious into three categories—the **id**, **ego**, and **superego**. The conscious state was called the ego, while the id and superego were the two unconscious states.

The id is the great reservoir of biological and psychological drives, the urges and impulses that underlie all behavior. This includes the libido, the full force of sexual energy in the individual. The id is a permanent unconscious state and responds to what Freud called the "pleasure principle," which causes a person to seek and maintain his or her own pleasure regardless of the expense to others. The superego is the force of self-criticism and conscience. It is the moral aspect of people's personalities and is used to judge one's behavior. The ego is the conscious state of the personality, and it operates on the "reality principle," which orients the person toward the real world in which he or she lives. It attempts to mediate the conflict between the demands of the id and the prohibitions of the superego.

Freud explored how the ego handles the conflict between the id and superego and found that the basic conflict stems from guilt. The individual experiences all sorts of drives and urges coming from the id and feels guilty about them because of the prohibitions of the superego. Freud offered some explanations of how the individual might deal with this conflict. One way was through **sublimation**, in which negative drives are diverted to activities approved by the superego. An example would be to work off aggressive feelings in athletic competition.

A less positive way is to repress the behavior. In **repression**, the drives are pushed back into the unconscious state in an effort to deny that they exist. Repression can result in **reaction formation**, in which the person acts out in extreme ways regarding certain issues. Prudish behavior by seeking to repress intense sexual desires would be an example of reaction formation (Bartol and Bartol, 2011). **Projection**, in which individuals with repressed desires attribute those desires or behaviors to others, is also a response to repression according to Freud (1948).

Freud was also interested in the early experiences of childhood. He developed a theory of how children evolve through a series of phases in which the basic human drives become oriented. The most basic human drive at birth is called *eros*. Eros is the instinct to preserve and create life and is expressed sexually. Early in their development, humans experience sexuality, which is expressed in the seeking of pleasure through various parts of the body. According to Freud, the series of phases in which the basic human drives are oriented are the oral stage, the anal stage, and the genital stage. During the oral stage, or first year of the infant's life, the child attains pleasure by sucking and biting. During the second and third years of life, the anal stage, the focus of sexual attention is on the elimination of bodily wastes. In the phallic stage, which occurs around ages four and five, the child focuses attention on his or her genitals. Males begin to have sexual feelings for their mothers, a phenomenon Freud called the **Oedipus complex**. Girls develop feelings for their father, and this is called the **Electra complex**.

The latency stage occurs at age six, and during this period feelings of sexuality are repressed until the genital stage, which begins at puberty and marks the beginning of adult sexuality. If conflicts are encountered during any of these stages, the child can become fixated at that point and later, as an adult, will exhibit behavior traits characteristic of those encountered during infantile sexual development. For example, those who are fixated on or who did not receive the attention they needed in the oral stage may become smokers or alcoholics. Freud's contention was that the root of adult behavioral problems could be traced back to the early years of life.

These descriptions have been used to develop psychological explanations for criminal behavior. The psychological perspective on ego development attributes criminal behavior to disturbances or malfunctions in the ego or superego. The id, unlike the other two, is viewed as a constant biological source of drives and urges, and it is similar in all individuals. Freud's theory, although not criminologically based, has been used to explain why some individuals are criminals. Freudians would argue that criminals possess underdeveloped superegos that lead them to have constant feelings of guilt and anxiety (Martin, Mutchnick, and Austin, 1990).

Freudians would most likely deal with criminal behaviors in the same manner as they would other psychological disorders, through *transference*. Transference is the healing process in which the analysts attempt to get patients to replay the earlier events in their lives that are thought to generate the problems. Within this process, the patients are led to learn to cope with those earlier issues in order to correct current behavioral problems. One of the most common criticisms of this psychoanalytic theory is that it is untestable (Martin, Mutchnick, and Austin, 1990). Proponents of psychoanalysis disagree. They argue that Freud's ideas can be expressed in testable hypotheses and that there is sufficient empirical evidence to support the theory. Despite these arguments, Freud's theory is given little weight in current explanations of criminal behavior (Dantzker, 1998).

Behavioral Psychology

Behavioral theories maintain that human behavior is developed through learning experiences. Whereas Freudian theories focus on unconscious behavior or biological factors, behavior theories focus on the actual behaviors people engage in during the course of their daily lives. These theories argue that our behaviors are shaped by other people's reactions to us. Behaviors are constantly being shaped by life experiences and can be reinforced by **rewards** or eradicated through **punishment**.

One of the oldest formulations about the nature of learning is that we learn by association (Anderson and Bower, 1973). This reliance on association is a basic tenet of behavioral psychology. Behavioral theories were founded in the work of Ivan Pavlov (1849–1936), a Russian physiologist. Pavlov's work with dogs won him the Nobel Prize in physiology and medicine in 1904. The dogs salivated whenever food was presented to them. They were always fed in the presence of a ringing bell. Soon Pavlov found the dogs would salivate every time they heard the bell ring, even when no food was present. Pavlov concluded that the dogs' salivation was an automatic response to the presence of food, and they could be conditioned to respond to other stimuli. This activity became known as **classical conditioning**, the process by which a learned reaction becomes automatic and internalized. Pavlov's finding was significant because it demonstrated that animal behavior could be modified by manipulating associations with external changes in the environment.

In classical conditioning, the subject is passive and learns what to expect from the environment. A more refined version of behavioral conditioning is **operant conditioning**. In operant conditioning, the subject is active and learns how to get what it wants from the environment. Operant conditioning is associated with John B. Watson (1878–1958) and B. F. Skinner (1904–1990) and is now the dominant behavioral theory in psychology. Operant learning uses rewards and punishment to reinforce or curtail certain behaviors. For example, rats may be taught to press a lever by rewarding that behavior with a food pellet or by punishing them with an electric shock for failing to push the lever. The rat learns to influence its environment by associating rewards and punishments with its own behaviors. Thus operant conditioning is another method of learning by association (Bernard, Snipes, and Gerould, 2009). As to its application to criminal behavior, the argument is that a person may become criminal based on associations with the act. For example, an adolescent who steals something because of prompting by the taunts of friends eventually will steal without the taunting.

Not all behaviorists follow the teachings of Watson and Skinner. Some hold that a person's learning and social experiences, coupled with his or her values and expectations, determine behavior. While classical and operant conditioning are associated with the behaviorist school of learning, a third theory describing how people learn by association attempts to combine them with elements of cognitive psychology.

Social Learning Theory

Social learning theorists believe behavior is learned through a process called *behavior modeling* or **imitation**, and all behavior is thought to be learned, including criminal behavior. In modern Western society, there are three principal models for behavior. The most prominent models are parents. Since children are in close contact with their parents, they model, or imitate, what they see their parents do. If children grow up in a home where violence is a way of life, they may learn to believe that such behavior is acceptable and rewarding. Even if parents tell children not to be violent and punish them if they are, the children will still model the violent behavior of the parents. Rather than altering the child's behavior, the inconsistencies of the parents' actions and statements, coupled with seemingly unfair punishment, exacerbate the child's frustration. Albert Bandura described this process as resulting in adolescent aggression resulting from disrupted dependency relations with the parents. Parents who are poor role models, yet hold back affection and nurturing to "teach" their children proper behavior, tend to create frustration and anger within those children (Bandura and Walters, 1959).

Social learning theories are also known as social psychological explanations. Several social learning theories have been proposed by criminologists. Because they are more commonly associated with sociological explanations of crime and criminality, these theories are discussed in Chapter 7.

Cognitive Theory

Cognitive theory is another area of psychology that has received increased recognition in recent years. Psychologists with a cognitive perspective focus on the mental process—the way people perceive and mentally represent the world around them and how they solve problems. The pioneers of this perspective were Wilhelm Wundt (1832–1920), Edward Titchener (1867–1927), and William James (1842–1920). **Moral development theory** and intellectual development theory are the perspectives that are used to explain the behavior of criminals. Jean Piaget (1896–1980), the founder of this approach, hypothesized that people's reasoning processes develop in an orderly fashion, beginning at birth and continuing until they are twelve or older (Piaget, 1932). At first, during the sensorimotor stage, children respond to the environment in a simple manner, seeking interesting objects and developing their reflexes. By the fourth and final stage, the formal operations stage, they have developed into mature adults who can use logic and abstract thought.

Lawrence Kohlberg (1969) applied the concept of moral development to issues in criminology. He maintained that people move through stages of moral development during which their decisions and judgments on issues of right and wrong are made for different reasons. It is possible that serious offenders have a moral orientation that differs from that of law-abiding citizens. Kohlberg's stages of development are as follows:

Stage 1: Right is obedience to power and avoidance of punishment.

Stage 2: Right is taking responsibility for oneself, meeting one's own needs, and leaving to others the responsibility for themselves.

Stage 3: Right is being good in the sense of having good motives, concern for others, and "putting yourself in the other person's shoes."

Stage 4: Right is maintaining the rules of a society and serving the welfare of the group or society.

Stage 5: Right is based on recognized individual rights within a society with agreed-upon rules, such as a social contract.

Stage 6: Right is an assumed obligation to principles applying to all humankind, such as principles of justice, equality, and respect for human personality.

Kohlberg classified people according to the point on this scale at which their moral development ceased to grow. In studies conducted by Kohlberg and his associates, criminals were found to be significantly lower than noncriminals of the same social background in their moral judgment development (Kohlberg, Kauffman, Scharf, and Hickey, 1973).

The majority of noncriminals were classified in stages 3 and 4, while the majority of criminals were in stages 1 and 2. Moral development theory, then, suggests that people who obey the law simply to avoid punishment or who have outlooks mainly characterized by self-interest are more likely to commit crimes than those who view the law as something that benefits all of society and who honor the rights of others. Research using delinquent youths has found that a significant number were in the first two moral development categories, while nondelinquents were ranked higher. In addition, higher stages of moral reasoning are associated with such behaviors as honesty, generosity, and nonviolence, which are considered incompatible with delinquency (Henggeler, 1989).

Cognitive Scripts

Another cognitive theory is the **cognitive scripts model** proposed by L. Row-ell Huesmann (1997). In this model, individuals are said to apply cognitive scripts developed from past experiences to deal with new situations. New experiences are interpreted in light of the closest cognitive script that can be applied from memories of past behaviors. Behaviors that have been deemed as most appropriate in previous circumstances are then applied. Sometimes these behaviors are appropriate, sometimes not.

Feedback from the current experience is used to develop new scripts. Whether a script becomes encoded in memory depends upon how others respond and how consistent it is with the individual's other views of him- or herself. Like the previously discussed behavioral reinforcement, a variety of competing influences (both internal and external) may determine whether the behaviors selected are criminal or noncriminal.

Hostile Attribution

Kenneth Dodge (1993) uses a model similar to cognitive scripts to explain how children develop hostile attitudes. According to the **hostile attribution model**, previous influences on mental development cause some people to interpret ambiguous actions as hostile and threatening. The result is that these individuals, because of their flawed perceptions of hostility, respond aggressively to situations that do not warrant aggression. This model not only attempts to explain why some people typically act aggressively, but could also account for other criminal acts that might result from biased personal perceptions of society or specific social situations. This model has the potential to be expanded to social groups as well in that classes of people might develop feelings of hostility toward society or social events or other social groups. For example, hostile attribution could be said to occur among members of ethnic minorities who come to perceive all of society as being biased against them. It might also be applied to working-class whites who may believe that they, rather than ethnic minorities, are the recipients of societal biases.

Expectancy Theory

Julian Rotter (Bartol and Bartol, 2011) has done extensive research on the importance of expectations (**cognitions**) about consequences (outcomes) of behaviors, including the reinforcement that will be gained from them. People think about the consequences or outcome of their actions before they involve themselves in an act. Rotter argues that whether an act or specific behavior occurs depends on one's expectations and how much one values the outcome of that act. To predict whether someone will behave a certain way, we must estimate that person's expectancies and the importance he or she places on the rewards gained by the behavior. Often, the person will develop "generalized expectancies" that are stable and consistent across relatively similar situations (Mischel, 1986).

The hypothesis that people enter situations with generalized expectancies about the outcomes of their behavior is an important one for criminologists. Applying Rotter's theory to criminal behavior, one could hypothesize that when people engage in unlawful behavior, they expect to gain something in the form of status, power, security, affection, material goods, or living conditions. The violent person, for example, elects to behave that way in the belief that something will be gained. A serial murderer might be on a mission to kill prostitutes because he wants to cleanse the world of these women, believing that is God's will, and that he will be rewarded with a place in heaven for a job well done (Bartol and Bartol, 2011).

According to **expectancy theory**, to simply label a violent person impulsive, crazy, or lacking in ego control fails to include other essential ingredients in the act. Although self-regulation and moral development are involved, people who act unlawfully interpret situations and select what they consider to be the most effective behavior under the circumstances. When people act violently, they usually do so because that approach has been successful in the past. Less frequently, they may have simply observed someone else gain by employing a violent approach and decide to try it for themselves.

Frustration-Induced Criminality

Leonard Berkowitz (1962) introduced a cognitive model that can be used to explain behaviors that do not appear to reflect previous behaviors as the earlier cognitive theories do. Whereas cognitive scripts or expectations of reward usually reinforce certain behaviors, **frustration-induced criminality** is said to occur when the rewards that individuals or groups have come to accept as normal responses to their behaviors do not occur. According to Berkowitz, the higher the expectation of reward a person has, the more frustrated he or she will become if that reward is not forthcoming. In addition, if the failure of rewards becomes more frequent, the person may become more sensitized to the lack, resulting in increasing levels of frustration.

Unlike the hostile attribution model in which individuals or groups react with hostility due to an ongoing perception of threat or injustice, in frustration-induced criminality the opposite occurs. Individuals or groups react in a criminal manner because their expectations of reward have not been met. This model could be used to explain how a good-looking "ladies' man" might react violently toward a woman when his advances are rebuffed. His reaction might be amplified if he felt that the woman rejecting him was somehow inferior to others with whom he had been successful.

Situational Instigators

We conclude our discussion of cognitive theories by examining the influence of **situational instigators**. Bartol and Bartol (2011) provide support for the view that behavior may be situational and that the circumstances of the situation may override previously developed prohibitions. Stanley Milgram's (1963) classic study of authority as an instigator of deviant behavior exemplifies this cognitive model. In this experiment, students were led to believe that they were administering electrical shocks to test subjects. The subjects were actually accomplices of the researcher who "reacted to the pain" of being shocked.

Milgram found that despite personal concerns for the safety of the subject, the majority of students followed the orders of the "experimenter," even when the voltage applied was thought to be life-threatening. He concluded that for many students the close proximity of an "authority figure" tended to overcome personal inhibitions about causing harm to others. This is actually not a new discovery. Many of the Nazis prosecuted by the Allies after World War II cited the fact that they were following the orders of their superiors as a defense for their behaviors.

Philip Zimbardo's **deindividuation** experiments were a series of studies that demonstrated the effects of situational instigators. In one study, Zimbardo (1970) found that residents of New York City looted an abandoned automobile within twenty-four hours while residents of Palo Alto, California, left a similarly abandoned vehicle untouched for seven days except, as an act of kindness rather than vandalism, to lower the hood during a rainstorm. He concluded that the anonymity that New Yorkers felt because of population density contributed to their higher potential for criminal behavior.

In a later study, Zimbardo (1973) conducted a prison experiment at Stanford University. College students were paid to assume roles as prisoners or prison guards. The personal identities of both prisoners and guards became secondary to their assigned roles. The situation became so intense with the "guards" becoming abusive and the "prisoners" becoming desperate for release that Zimbardo was forced to complete the experiment early rather than risk causing psychological trauma to his subjects. The deindividuation of the students as they assumed their group personas led Zimbardo to conclude that when placed in "psychologically compelling situations" many people can be made to do almost anything (Zimbardo, 1973, p. 164).

Studies of situational instigators demonstrate that the circumstances in which people find themselves can indeed cause their behaviors to be altered. The loss of individual inhibitions in a mob or riot is all too real for those who have seen it. Likewise, the bad behavior of ordinarily conforming people when they think that their behavior is anonymous has been well documented by the police as well as by a multitude of divorce lawyers. Unfortunately, situational theories do not explain why some individuals are able to resist the pull of group associations while others very easily shed their normal identities.

Psychometry

Psychometry attempts to identify psychological and/or mental differences that might exist between criminals and the law abiding. The feeblemindedness studies of Goddard (1914) and the delinquency studies of the Gluecks (Glueck and Glueck, 1956) discussed in Chapter 5 are examples of psychometric research. More recently, Hans Eysenck (Eysenck and Eysenck, 1996) has postulated that male hormones in reaction with other chemical imbalances may produce psychosis. However, with the possible exception of the research on the abnormal need for stimulation on the part of psychopaths, psychometric explanations do not appear to have conclusive support. Perhaps the best known of the psychometric explanations are the **personality studies**.

Personality can be defined as the reasonably stable pattern of behavior, including thoughts and emotions, that distinguishes one person from another (Mischel, 1986). One's personality reflects a characteristic way of adapting to life's demands and problems. The way people behave is a function of how their personalities enable them to interpret life events and make appropriate behavioral choices. Some researchers believe personality can be linked to criminal behavior. In their early work, Eleanor and Sheldon Glueck (1956) administered Rorschach (inkblot) tests to 500 delinquents and a control group of 500 nondelinquents. They found greater personality problems in the delinquent group. The Gluecks' findings are suspect because the problems could be the result of delinquent classification as much as distinct personality differences.

Several other research efforts have attempted to identify criminal personality traits. For example, Eysenck (1977) identified two personality traits that he associated with antisocial behavior: extroversion/introversion and stability/instability. Extreme introverts are overaroused and avoid sources of stimulation, while extreme extroverts are unaroused and seek sensation. Introverts are slow to learn and be conditioned; extroverts are impulsive individuals who lack the ability to examine their own motives and behaviors. Those who are unstable, a condition that Eysenck calls "neuroticism," are anxious, tense, and emotionally unstable (Eysenck and Eysenck, 1985). People who are both neurotic and extroverted lack self-insight and are impulsive and emotionally unstable; they are unlikely to have reasoned judgments of life events. While extrovert neurotics may act self-destructively, for example by abusing drugs, more stable people will be able to reason that such behavior is ultimately harmful and life-threatening. Eysenck believes that the direction of the personality is controlled by genetic factors and heredity. According to Eysenck, these findings do not mean that individuals having these traits will become criminals (in fact, many leaders in business and government exhibit such traits) but that they have a greater potential to do so.

A number of other personality deficits have been identified in the criminal population. A common theme is that criminals are hyperactive, impulsive individuals with short attention spans (attention deficit disorder), conduct disorders, anxiety disorders, and depression (Farrington, 1988). These traits make them prone to problems ranging from **psychopathology** to drug abuse, sexual promiscuity, and violence (Frost, Moffitt, and McGee, 1989). As a group, people who share these traits are believed to have a character defect referred to as the antisocial, sociopathic, or psychopathic personality. Although these terms are often used interchangeably, some psychologists do distinguish between sociopaths and psychopaths by suggesting that the former are a product of a destructive home environment, while the latter are a product of a defect or aberration within themselves (Lykken, 1996).

Psychopathology

It has been suggested that criminal behavior may result from a personality pattern or syndrome commonly referred to as the *psychopathic* or *sociopathic* personality; these terms are often used interchangeably. Robert Hare (1970) proposed a useful scheme to outline three categories of psychopaths: the primary, the secondary or neurotic, and the dyssocial. Only the primary psychopath is the "true" psychopath. Hare classifies the criminal psychopath in this category. The other two categories meld a heterogeneous group of antisocial individuals who comprise a large segment of the criminal population. Secondary psychopaths commit antisocial or violent acts because of severe emotional problems or inner conflicts. They are sometimes called acting-out neurotics, neurotic delinquents, symptomatic psychopaths, or simply neurotic characters. The third group, dyssocial psychopaths, displays aggressive, antisocial behavior they have learned from their subculture, for example from gangs or families. In both cases, the label "psychopath" is misleading, because the behaviors and backgrounds have little if any similarity to those of primary psychopaths. Yet both secondary and dyssocial psychopaths are often incorrectly called psychopaths because of their high **recidivism** rates.

In recent years, the term *sociopath* has often been used by criminologists and sociologists to refer to the repetitive offender who does not respond appropriately to treatment, **rehabilitation**, or incarceration. Psychiatrists use the phrase "antisocial personality disorder" (ASP), and many psychologists refer to those offenders who demonstrate a "failure to conform to social norms with respect to lawful behaviors as indicated by repeatedly performing acts that are grounds for arrest" (American Psychiatric Association, 1994, p. T-4). However, ASP is narrower than primary psychopathy because it restricts its definition to behavioral indicators. Hare's definition of primary psychopathy includes emotional elements and in the future is likely to include cognitive aspects. However, with each new publication of the *Diagnostic and Statistical Manual of Mental Disorders (DSM)*, the definitions used to describe antisocial personality disorder are increasingly similar to Hare's primary psychopathy.

One respected authority on the behavioral characteristics of the psychopath is Hervey Cleckley. In *The Mask of Sanity,* Cleckley (1976) describes the major behaviors demonstrated by the full-fledged psychopath as distinct from the other psychopathic types referred to previously. Superficial behavior and average to above-average intelligence are two of the psychopath's main features. These characteristics are said to be apparent during initial contacts. Psychopaths usually impress others as friendly, outgoing, likable, and alert. They often appear well educated and knowledgeable, and they display many interests. They are verbally skilled and can talk themselves out of trouble. In fact, their vocabulary is often so extensive that they can talk at length about anything (Hare, 1991). Studies show, however, that they often jump "from one topic to another and that much of their speech is empty of real substance, tending to be filled with phrases, repetitions of the same ideas, word approximations, . . . and half-formed sentences" (Hare, 1991, p. 57).

Psychometric studies indicate that psychopaths usually score higher on intelligence tests than the general population, particularly on individual tests (Hare, 1970). They do not seem to be plagued with **mental disorders**, either mild or severe, and they lack any symptoms of excessive worry and anxiety, irrational thinking, delusions, severe depressions, or hallucinations. Even under high pressure, psychopaths can remain cool and calm. Not everyone agrees with the view that psychopaths do not suffer from some mental disorder. Some clinicians argue that psychopathy and schizophrenia are part of the same spectrum of disorders (Hare, 1996). Some forensic clinicians maintain that they occasionally see offenders who qualify as both psychopathic and schizophrenic (Hare, 1996). Some evidence suggests that it is not uncommon to find psychopaths who seem to have mental disorders in maximum-security psychiatric units for highly violent or dangerous patients.

Other principal traits of the psychopath are selfishness and an inability to love or give affection to others. According to Cleckley, egocentricity is always present in the psychopath and is essentially unmodifiable. The psychopath's inability to feel genuine, meaningful affection for another is absolute. Psychopaths may be likable, but they are seldom able to keep close friends, and they have difficulty understanding love in others. They may be highly skilled at feigning deep affection, and they may effectively mimic appropriate emotions, but true loyalty, warmth, and compassion are foreign to them. They have a remarkable disregard for truth and are often called "pathological liars." They seem to have no internalized moral or ethical sense and cannot understand the purpose of being honest, especially if dishonesty will bring some personal gain. They are unreliable, irresponsible, and unpredictable, regardless of the importance of the event or the consequences of their impulsive actions. Impulsivity appears to be a central or cardinal feature of psychopathy (Hart and Dempster, 1997).

In the 1960s, notorious psychopath or sociopath Charles Manson exhibited an uncanny ability to attract a devout cluster of unresisting followers. Ted Bundy, a charming and physically attractive law student, murdered the women he charmed with his wit and intelligence. Although some psychopaths have little contact with the criminal justice system, many others do because of persistent offending. Many of the murders and serious assaults committed by nonpsychopaths occurred during domestic disputes or extreme emotional arousal. On the other hand, this pattern of violence is rarely observed in criminal psychopaths (Hare, Hart, and Harpur, 1991). Criminal psychopaths frequently engage in violence as a form of revenge or retribution or during a bout of drinking. Nonpsychopaths tend to attack women they know well, whereas psychopaths attack men who are strangers. Crimes committed by psychopaths are described as cold-blooded, "without the emotions that accompany the violence of nonpsychopaths" (Hare, 1991, p. 395). Hare's research supports the conclusion that psychopaths are not treatable because of their callous attitudes and behaviors (1996, p. 41).

Other Personality Disorders

Psychopathology (antisocial personality disorder) is the best known of the personality disorders, but it is not the only one that can lead to inappropriate or criminal behaviors. Anyone can display these behaviors, not just criminals. *Paranoid personality disorder* is exemplified by distrust of others, finding hidden meanings in benign remarks or actions, and maintaining grudges against those who they feel have harmed them. *Schizoid personality disorder* is demonstrated by feelings of detachment from others and the desire to be alone. *Schizotypal personality disorder* may result in odd and eccentric behaviors accompanied by excessive social anxiety.

Borderline personality disorder may be exhibited through unstable and intense personal relationships, impulsiveness, excessive spending, obsession with sex, substance abuse, risk taking, as well as intense, inappropriate anger including physical fighting. *Histrionic personality disorder* is often displayed by divas (both male and female) who have to be the center of attention, who engage in provocative or sexually seductive behavior, who exaggerate their emotions, and who feel that their relationships are more intimate than they actually are.

Narcissistic personality disorder results in a grandiose sense of self-importance, the view that one is special and is entitled to preferential treatment, exploitation of others, lack of empathy, envy of others who may have what one thinks one should have, and arrogant and haughty behaviors.

Avoidant personality disorder is the near opposite of narcissistic personality disorder in that individuals feel inadequate and avoid social situations due to fear of rejection. They are more likely to be victims rather than offenders. *Dependent personality disorder* may be seen as learned helplessness in which there is a constant need for others to take care of them.

Obsessive-compulsive personality disorder is characterized by preoccupation with details, rules, or order, as well as excessive devotion to work. Sufferers have a need to achieve perfection, which causes them to be overconscientious, scrupulous, and inflexible about morality and ethical issues. They are reluctant to delegate work to others, are often hoarders, are miserly spenders, and demonstrate rigidity and stubbornness in their dealings with others.

Mental and Physiological Disorders

Mental illnesses range from mild emotional distress to outright insanity. Most of us experience periods of depression and frustration at times in our lives that cause us to think or act irrationally. Such irrational behavior, although notable to friends and family members, may not be severe and may not have lingering consequences. When such behavior does interfere with our ability to function within our work or social situations, some sort of intervention may be necessary. If the behaviors could be harmful to us or others, compulsory intervention may be needed.

There are numerous stories of violent mentally ill people who pose harm to themselves or others. While the police do on occasion have to deal with people who are depressed, schizophrenic, paranoid, or suicidal, these contacts are not frequent. Police contacts with people who are totally out of touch with reality are even less frequent, and rarely will the police officers have to deal with a deranged person who is committing acts of mayhem against others. When such incidents do occur, however, they catch the attention of the media and public alike.

Most acts of violence by mentally ill people are assaults on family members within their home (Monohan, 1996). They are usually the result of mentally disturbed individuals' inability to cope with what is to them an adverse situation. When these situations become explosive and weapons are available, such people can be extremely dangerous. Fortunately, the vast majority of these situations are dealt with through counseling or medical intervention before they escalate to violence.

Physiological disorders would more appropriately be classified as biological influences on human behavior. However, we are discussing them

Reality Check: Pathological Terrorism

In previous chapters, we discussed international and domestic terrorism. Within the domestic terrorism discussion, we talked about "lone wolf" terrorists. We have also discussed serial killers and spree (or mass) murderers. Pathological terrorism is in the gray area between spree killing and lone wolf domestic terrorism. The motivation of lone wolf terrorists is criminal rather than political. In pathological terrorism, the actors commit their acts for the pleasure of terrorizing others.

Pathological terrorists frequently operate alone rather than in groups and often are not true "terrorists," as they lack any well-defined political motive. The shootings at Columbine High School, at Virginia Tech, and at Congresswoman Gabby Giffords's town meeting serve as examples of pathological terrorism since those who carried them out sought to use violence to terrorize for their own enjoyment.

The Columbine High School Shootings

The Columbine High School massacre occurred on Tuesday, April 20, 1999, at Columbine High School in Littleton, Colorado. Two students, Eric Harris and Dylan Klebold, entered the school wearing trench coats to conceal their weapons. They then began a shooting spree in which they killed twelve students and a teacher. They also wounded twenty-one other students. After police arrived on the scene, the two boys committed suicide. Investigations into their motives revealed that the two felt that they were outcasts and wanted to punish those whom they hated (which included basically everyone). Their plan had been developed over several months. It was their intention to kill hundreds of their fellow students and then commit suicide. While the outcome was not as gruesome as they had hoped it would be, it is one of the deadliest school massacres within the United States.

The Virginia Tech Massacre

The Virginia Tech massacre occurred on April 16, 2007, on the campus of Virginia Polytechnic Institute and State University in Blacksburg, Virginia. In two separate attacks that were approximately two hours apart, Seung-Hui Cho, a senior English major, killed thirty-two people and wounded many others before committing suicide. Cho had previously been diagnosed with a severe anxiety disorder for which he had been treated while in middle school and high school. Due to federal privacy laws, Virginia Tech was not informed of Cho's previous diagnosis or the accommodations he had been granted at school.

Cho shot his first victims around 7:15 a.m. in West Ambler Johnston Hall. He initially shot and killed a female student and a male resident assistant who came to her aid. Cho left the scene and returned to his dormitory room, where he changed out of his bloodstained clothes, logged on to his computer to delete his e-mail, and then removed the hard drive. He then went to an off-campus post office and mailed a package of writings and video recordings to NBC News.

continues

Reality Check, *continued*

After returning to the Virginia Tech campus, Cho walked to Norris Hall with a small arsenal of weapons and ammunition. More than two hours after his initial murders, Cho began an attack in which he entered various classrooms, killing thirty people and wounding seventeen more. After ten to twelve minutes of shooting others, Cho shot himself in the head. The massacre is the deadliest shooting incident by a single gunman in US history, on or off a school campus.

The Tucson Massacre

On January 8, 2011, Jared Lee Loughner killed six people, including Chief US District Court Judge John Roll and a young girl, at a Safeway supermarket in Tucson, Arizona. He wounded fourteen others, including US Representative Gabrielle Giffords, who was critically injured by a gunshot wound to the head. Congresswoman Giffords was holding a "congress on your corner" meeting, where she was meeting publicly with constituents, when Loughner attacked.

Initially, it was thought that the attack was politically motivated. Later it became obvious that Loughner had serious behavioral problems. According to friends, Loughner abused alcohol and drugs after dropping out of high school in 2006. He also became remote, distancing himself from former friends. His bizarre behavior caused him to be fired from his job and ordered to obtain mental health clearance if he wished to return to Pima Community College. Instead, he withdrew from the college.

Loughner allegedly developed an intense hatred for Congresswoman Giffords after attending an earlier constituent meeting in which she had not satisfactorily answered a peculiar question that he had asked. Loughner kept Giffords's form letter, which thanked him for attending the 2007 event. An envelope in the same box as the letter was scrawled with phrases like "die bitch" and "assassination plans have been made."

Loughner had researched the punishments for murder and had e-mailed a friend an incoherent diatribe, which he ended by saying, "Plead the Fifth!" He purchased a Glock 9mm pistol as part of his plan to assassinate Congresswoman Giffords. At the constituent meeting, Loughner shot Giffords, then began shooting people in the crowd, until he was subdued by bystanders. When he was arrested by police, he said, "I plead the Fifth," as he was taken into custody. A photograph taken of a smirking Loughner by the forensic unit of the Pima County Sheriff's Office was released to the media and published on front pages nationwide. Loughner has been indicted on forty-nine counts by federal grand juries in Arizona. He has pled not guilty.

Congresswoman Giffords is slowly recovering from her severe wound. As this was written she was able to travel to Cape Canaveral to witness her astronaut husband take off in the space shuttle.

What theories from this chapter do you think apply to these killers? Do you think Loughner should be allowed to plead insanity? Why or why not?

within this chapter because of their psychological impacts on those who suffer from them as well as the responses they evoke from others. There are currently forty types of muscular diseases affecting more than 1 million Americans (Muscular Dystrophy Association, 2011). Neurological disorders such as multiple sclerosis and cerebral palsy make life difficult for those with these disorders. Epilepsy, although not a continuously debilitating condition, can also create problems for those who experience periodic seizures. Tourette's syndrome, autism, and Down syndrome are other physiological disorders that can cause serious difficulties for those individuals whose actions are misinterpreted by others.

Attention-deficit hyperactivity is another disability that affects many Americans. Inattention difficulties, hyperactivity, and impulsiveness exemplify this disorder. School failure and emotional difficulties are frequent byproducts of this disorder when it is not properly treated. Other physiological disorders include dyslexia, letter reversal that makes reading difficult; dyscalculia, which makes understanding math difficult; and dysgraphia, which is difficulty with written work or handwriting. Last, auditory processing difficulties can make comprehension of auditory information problematic. The effects of physiological disorders may lead to truancy and juvenile delinquency resulting from frustration with school failures and may also lead to severe emotional difficulties if left untreated.

Summary

The psychological theories of criminality follow a deterministic path, similar to the biological theories discussed in Chapter 5. The early psychological theorists focused on personality development and its link to criminality. Beginning with Freud, this argument was that criminal behavior resulted from arrested development at a particular stage of adolescence.

Behavioral theorists such as Pavlov suggested that conditioning plays a role in criminal behavior. This conditioning may be either classical (which is passive and expectant) or operant (which is active and solicitous). Operant conditioning, associated with John B. Watson and B. F. Skinner, uses rewards and punishment to reinforce certain behaviors. It is probably the dominant learning theory in psychology.

Social learning theories are exemplified by Rotter's expectancy theory, in which expectations about consequences and reinforcement of the behavior play major roles. This is substantiated by social learning theory, which states that learning and social experiences, values, and expectations determine behavior.

Cognitive theory focuses on the mental process of perception and problem solving. Cognitive theories combine components of the previous theories.

A key cognitive theory is Kohlberg's moral development theory, which offers seven stages of moral development. Other cognitive theories include cognitive scripts, hostile attribution, expectancy theory, frustration-induced criminality, and situational instigators.

We also discussed mental disorders, including psychometry, which examines personality and how one adapts to life's demands and problems. We also discussed the impacts of psychopathology, physiological disorders, and mental illness on behavior.

Psychological theories have garnered minimal support among criminologists as explanations of criminal behavior. This is due to the sociological training of most US criminologists and the limited application of most psychological explanations to individual offenders. As was the case with biological theories, psychological explanations warrant consideration in an interdisciplinary approach to the problems of crime and criminality.

Discussion Questions

1. What is the relationship between determinism and psychology? How does it differ from that of biology?
2. Why do you think that Freud's psychoanalytic theory is not a highly recognized or acceptable theory in criminal justice?
3. Compare and contrast psychoanalytic theory with behavioral theory.
4. Does social learning theory address the issue of the formation of gangs and gang behavior? In what way?
5. Which of the cognitive theories do you believe best explains criminal behavior? Justify your selection.

7

Social Structure Theories

In the previous two chapters, we introduced theories associated with the human mind and body. Perhaps to many criminologists the next set of theories examined, the social theories, "might best be considered the 'heart and soul' of criminological thought" (Dantzker 1998, p. 45). It is within the social theories that a majority of the explanations of criminal behavior are found. As Mark L. Dantzker (1998) points out, there are a number of theories or explanations and no common consensus on how they should be divided. In this text, we have opted to divide the social theories into three main categories: social structure, social interaction, and social conflict. This chapter and the next two deal separately with these three social perspectives. This chapter addresses the social structure theories, that is, the theories that examine criminality as a result of social structure.

Structural Functionalism

To begin, social structure and social interaction theories are considered structural functionalist theories. Structural functionalism is based on the view that the overall structure of society is sound (functional) and there is a great deal of consensus among members of society as to what is appropriate behavior. However, imbalances may occur that cause individuals or groups to become deviant. These social imbalances may be due to the structure of society or they may be due to social interactions. While the overall social structure does not require drastic overhaul, over time it may require "tweaking" in order to correct inequities or injustices that occasionally arise as social changes take place. The theories to be discussed are shown in Figure 7.1.

117

Figure 7.1 Social Structure Theories		
Social Disorganization	Strain	Cultural Deviance

Concentric zone theory
Social ecology theory
Deviant places theory
Race, crime, and
    urban inequality theory
	Strain theory
	Anomie theory
	Institutional
	    anomie theory
	Relative deprivation
	    theory
	Integrated theory
	General strain
	    theory
		Culture conflict theory
		Middle-class
		    measuring rod theory
		Focal concerns theory
		Differential opportunity
		    theory
		Subculture of violence
		Code of the street

Social Structure Theories

The primary premise of **social structure theories** is that the lower classes engage in criminal and deviant behavior to a higher degree than does the middle class. A special note of interest is that the majority of the theories to be discussed were built upon the study of youth. Several theories are identified and offered in this section within the broad categories of social disorganization, strain theory, and cultural deviance theory.

Social Disorganization

Clifford Shaw and Henry McKay's (1942) ecology of crime theory attempted to explain crime and delinquency as a product of transition or change in the urban environment. They contended that transitional communities manifest social disorganization and maintain conflicting values and social systems. Shaw and McKay determined that environment strongly influenced criminal behavior. It was their belief that delinquency was produced by deteriorated neighborhoods rather than by the individuals who lived there. Their model included evidence of deterioration and disorganization that led to a loss of control over youth and encouraged gangs. The gangs then perpetuated delinquency, leading to higher crime rates (see Figure 7.2).

Concentric zone theory. To support their social disorganization model, Shaw and McKay offered what became recognized as **concentric zone theory**. This model divided the city of Chicago into five zones, starting with the innermost circle and moving away (see Figure 7.3). According to Shaw and McKay (1942), the highest crime was in Zone II, the area in transition. Those individuals who lived in this area experienced a lack of community cohesion and

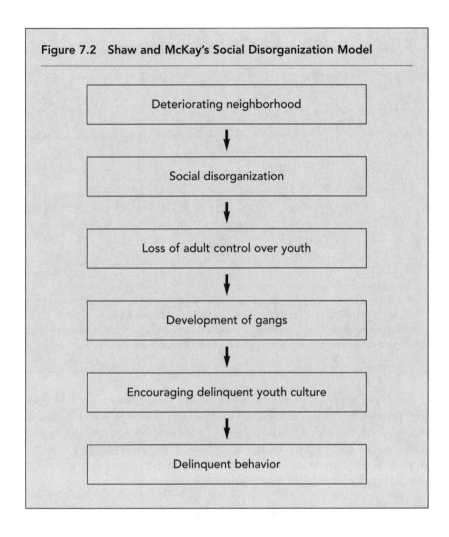

Figure 7.2   Shaw and McKay's Social Disorganization Model

Deteriorating neighborhood

↓

Social disorganization

↓

Loss of adult control over youth

↓

Development of gangs

↓

Encouraging delinquent youth culture

↓

Delinquent behavior

severe social disorganization. However, as they became able to afford better housing in Zone III, they left this chaos behind. Unfortunately, those moving into Zone II inherited the same confusion.

All theories have their strengths and weaknesses. The strengths of this theory are that it identifies why crime rates are highest in slum areas and points out factors that produce crime, still a relatively solid explanation for high crime rates in poor neighborhoods today. It is also interesting that it demonstrated that ethnicity's impact on crime was largely due to the areas that certain ethnic groups were forced to reside in rather than any inherent lawlessness.

The weaknesses of Shaw and McKay's theory are that it does not answer the following questions: Why does middle-class crime occur? Why are some youths insulated from a delinquent career? What causes some gang members

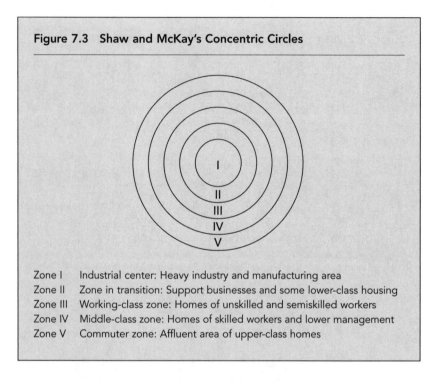

Figure 7.3   Shaw and McKay's Concentric Circles

Zone I   Industrial center: Heavy industry and manufacturing area
Zone II   Zone in transition: Support businesses and some lower-class housing
Zone III   Working-class zone: Homes of unskilled and semiskilled workers
Zone IV   Middle-class zone: Homes of skilled workers and lower management
Zone V   Commuter zone: Affluent area of upper-class homes

to forgo criminality as adults? And why are most lower-class people **law abiding**? Overall, this theory seemed to create as many questions as it answered. It did, however, become the basis for many of the urban programs used by federal and state governments to deal with urban problems. The effort to eliminate social disorganization continues to receive support from many social scientists, social advocates, and governmental leaders today.

Social ecology theory. **Social ecology theory** is the successor to Shaw and McKay's social disorganization model. While abandoning the concentric zones, later social ecologists focused on the social ills that plagued certain areas of large cities. These "areal studies" emphasized community factors such as community deterioration, high unemployment, concentrated poverty, fear, resentment, and social isolation. Social ecologists argued that the social environments within these depressed urban areas inevitably led to high crime rates.

Bernard Lander's (1954) study of census data in Baltimore led him to conclude that anomic (which we will discuss later in this chapter) and socioeconomic factors created social instability that resulted in crime. D. J. Bordua (1958) found support for socioeconomic factors in his areal research in Detroit. Other studies (i.e., Chilton, 1964; Polk, 1957; Quinney, 1964; Shevky and Bell, 1955) also used social area analysis to study the impact of social disorganization on crime. The mixed results from these studies have resurrected interest in social disorganization theories, but provide limited empirical support. Today's social ecologists use computer mapping to contrast crime "hot spots" with areas of concentrated poverty, community deterioration, and rapid population changes. These efforts are often used in conjunction with environmental and/or situational crime-prevention strategies.

Deviant places theory. Rodney Stark (1987) built upon social ecology theory by seeking to understand what it was about disorganized neighborhoods that sustained crime. In his **deviant places hypothesis**, Stark utilized ecological explanations, along with other environmental explanations (such as the physical features discussed within Chapter 4), to develop thirty propositions about high-crime neighborhoods. Those propositions explain how neighborhoods, rather than people, are different. His major premise is that urban congestion brings "good kids" into contact with "bad kids," which promotes delinquency. Family crowding within homes pushes young people out onto the street, where they associate with delinquent peers. Therefore, normal people can be drawn into structural conditions that lead to crime and delinquency (Barkan, 2012).

Race, crime, and urban inequality theory. Robert J. Sampson and William Julius Wilson (2003) apply the concepts of social disorganization theory and **culture conflict theory** in their examination of urban crime. They seek to overcome the shortcomings that they see in these two theories by including race and social inequality within their explication of urban crime. As one would expect, they take the conservative promotion of values to task as well.

They stress the harsh lives that inner-city residents live as being the root cause of lawlessness. Instead of emphasizing poverty, inadequate health care, disrupted families, schools in shambles, and the depletion of economic resources as factors that lead to "bad culture," they argue that the emphasis of criminologists should be "bad structures" that create "cognitive landscapes" in which violence and crime are the products of social inequality.

The inequitable ecology that African Americans living within inner cities experience is seen as creating "concentration effects." They posit that "the most important determinant of the relationship between race and crime is the differential distribution of blacks in communities characterized by (1) structured social disorganization and (2) cultural social isolation, both of which stem from the concentration of poverty, family disruption, and residential instability" (Sampson and Wilson, 2003, p. 113).

They suggest that macro-social forces (e.g., segregation, migration, housing discrimination, structural transformation of the economy) interact with local community-level factors (e.g., residential turnover, concentrated poverty, family disruption) to impede social organization (Sampson and Wilson, 2003, p. 114). In addition, ecological segregation is seen to create "cultural disorganization" that weakens efforts to oppose delinquent values. Urban violence and crime are seen as products of the socialization of children who grow up within the social isolation and ecological landscapes of large US cities.

Strain Theories

The next category of social structure theories are the strain theories. Like social disorganization theories, **strain theory** focuses on the problems of the lower class within society. Strain theories differ from social disorganization theories in that they emphasize an individual's inability to reach higher goals or values because of his or her economic placement in society. When goals are blocked or unattainable, strain occurs that may lead individuals or groups to reject social norms and standards of behavior.

Strain theory. The prominent theorist in the development of strain theory was Emile Durkheim, a preeminent sociologist and criminologist. The basic assumptions of Durkheim's (1933) theory are:

1. An explanation of personal behavior must take into account the various social forces surrounding the individual.
2. Social facts, such as customs, obligations, laws, morality, and religious beliefs, are quantifiable and measurable things and may compromise the ingredients of scientific analysis.
3. As societies develop from simple, homogeneous populations to advanced states of division of labor, any explanation of deviance must also change.
4. A most logical and fruitful method for understanding and explaining social features would involve historical and comparative analysis.
5. The application of theory to effect planned change is a justifiable function of social science and specifically of sociology (Martin, Mutchnick, and Austin, 1990, pp. 50–51).

More simply, Durkheim believed that crime (1) is normal and necessary behavior that is inevitable and linked to the differences within society; (2) can be useful and even occasionally considered healthy because the existence of crime implies that there is a way for social change to occur, and social structure is therefore not rigid or inflexible; and (3) calls attention to society's ills. Furthermore, Durkheim is credited with coining the phrase "altruistic criminal" to describe an individual who is offended by society's rules and seeks social change and an improved moral climate through his or her actions.

Anomie. Durkheim was also the first to consider that **anomie** or anomic stress was a cause of strain. Anomie, as seen by Durkheim, is a normlessness and apathy experienced by those unable to cope with the rapid social changes that occur around them (Bernard, Snipes, and Gerould, 2009). This perspective served as the basis for several subsequent explanations of crime and criminality. For the average American, it is common to live in some kind of community and to participate in socially acceptable behaviors such as going to school or being employed. Yet numerous individuals drop out of school at an early age, may not have a job, and may not even have a place to live. While many fall into this group as a result of unfortunate circumstances, some live apart, outside the norm, voluntarily. They do not want the responsibility of paying bills or owning property and would rather just be free to do whatever they want. In other words, they actually prefer being in an anomic state. However, while their lifestyles may be considered deviant, many of these people do not engage in criminal activities.

Robert Merton (1968) described anomic stress as the product of cultural values that counterpose a more or less common set of culturally defined goals that can be reached through socially accepted means. Based on this theory, criminal behavior is the result of an individual's inability to reach those goals through the approved means. The key to Merton's theory is adaptation to cultural norms through acceptable means. Merton (1968) supplied a typology of modes for adaptation: conformity, innovation, ritualism, retreatism, and rebellion. For each mode there is either an acceptance or denial of the cultural goals and institutional means of reaching those goals.

The conformist mode, which Merton believes leads to the most stable society, accepts both the cultural goals and the institutional means: a person should own a home and vehicle and get them by working. Criminal behavior is based on the innovation mode whereby the cultural goals are accepted, but the institutional means of reaching them are denied: I want a big house and a nice car but not a real job, so I sell drugs. The ritualist mode denies the cultural goals but accepts institutional means: I'll work to get what I want, but I don't need a big house or a nice car. The retreatist mode denies the cultural goals and the institutional means. Often these individuals retreat through the use of drugs or alcohol. Others may actually withdraw from society by becoming hermits or joining groups of like-minded people in isolated communities. The final mode is rebellion, in which people not only reject the cultural goals and institutional means but seek to change them, often through violence (see Table 7.1).

Anomie aids in explaining the existence of high-crime areas and the predominance of delinquent and criminal behavior among particular social and ethnic groups. Yet, while it manages to explain crime rates, it does not help explain particular behaviors. And while this theory led to advances in subsequent subcultural explanations of delinquency, it shares the weakness of its successors in not adequately explaining why many who suffer from anomie do not engage in criminal behavior.

Table 7.1   Merton's Typology of Modes for Adaptation

Mode	Goals	Means	Behavior
Conformity	+	+	Stable
Innovation	+	−	Criminal activities
Ritualism	−	+	Jaded compliance
Retreatism	−	−	Drugs, alcohol
Rebellion	+/−	+/−	Revolutionary activities

Source: Adapted from Robert K. Merton (1968), "Social Structure and Anomie," in *Social Theory and Social Structure* (New York: Free Press).
Notes: + indicates acceptance of the goals and/or means.
− indicates denial of goals and/or means.

Institutional anomie. Institutional anomie theory builds upon Merton's earlier work. Steven Messner and Richard Rosenfield (1994) argue that Americans are conditioned by our capitalistic society to accumulate material goods and wealth. We are socialized into devaluing other social institutions, such as family, church, and community, in our quest for financial success. When conflicts emerge between these other institutions and the workplace, they lose out. Ultimately economic norms and standards become dominant even within noneconomic areas.

According to Messner and Rosenfield (1994), the problem with this economic emphasis (other than the obvious neglect of other vital social institutions) is that it weakens informal social controls formerly exercised by families, churches, schools, and other institutions. When success is measured by financial status and social controls are weakened, crime becomes prevalent. This perspective offers an explanation of how, even in good economic times, criminal behavior can occur among those seeking to increase their wealth. It also can account for frustration-induced criminality on the part of those who are unable to do so. In addition, it is not limited to explaining lower-class behaviors but can also be applied to the middle and upper classes.

The weakness of this theory is that despite the emphasis on material success in the United States, citizens (of all classes) are rejecting lifestyles that are based solely on economic wealth. The American dream is being redefined by many as a comfortable life that may have fewer luxuries but enables them to enjoy their associations with other social institutions. In addition, even among the lower and middle classes, who are hard-pressed to make ends meet financially, anomie usually does not occur.

Relative deprivation theory. Another theory that builds on Merton's anomie is **relative deprivation** theory. In his discussion of anomie, Merton (1968) used the concept of relative deprivation to explain why many individuals remained law-abiding despite being in situations that led others to commit crimes. The premise is quite simple: You assess your situation based upon those who are around you. If you determine that others are better off than you are, you may become frustrated and anomic. If you decide that you are as well off or perhaps even better off than your peers, you will not.

Relative deprivation can be used to explain how individuals (even affluent people who believe that they are not as well off as other wealthy people) may experience anomie. It also is useful in explaining how the poor and ethnic minorities can believe that they are victims of income inequality and discrimination. J. Blau and P. Blau (1982) used relative deprivation to explain how the urban poor experience hostility and discontent because of their perceptions of social injustice. The closer their proximity to the affluent, the greater the likelihood that such feelings will develop among the urban poor. Therefore, urban restoration projects that bring the affluent back into inner-city areas are seen as both positive and negative in that they help rejuvenate cities and enhance the tax base for funding social programs, but they also emphasize class differences among urban dwellers.

The strength of relative deprivation is that it is useful for understanding individual behaviors as well as group behaviors. In addition to understanding the frustrations of ethnic minorities, it is useful in understanding the frustrations of lower-class, working-class, and lower-middle-class whites who believe that they are being unjustly penalized by governmental efforts to placate minorities. Therefore, the greatest strength of relative deprivation could also be said to be its greatest weakness in that it can actually be applied to all those who, for whatever reason, believe that they are not getting their due from society.

Integrated Strain Theories

Integrated strain theories include Delbert Elliot's integrated theory and Robert Agnew's **general strain theory**. These theories stress their integrated aspects but are solidly built upon the concepts of strain theory. For that reason, we are including them here rather than in Chapter 10.

Integrated theory. Elliott, David Huizinga, and Suzanne Agerton (1985) developed an integrated strain theory that draws heavily from social learning and control theories. In integrated theory, strain within family and school results in weakened bonds to conventional society and promotes stronger bonds with delinquent peers. Association with these delinquent peers increases the likelihood of delinquent behavior. This view differs from traditional social bonding theories in which socialization is seen as promoting conventional behaviors and reducing the risk of deviant behaviors. Instead, socialization is similar to Edwin Sutherland's **differential association theory** (see Chapter 8) in that deviant behaviors may be learned and reinforced within the bonding process.

This theory is similar to Weis's social development theory (discussed in Chapter 10). However, it goes further to explain how the bonds within the family and school are weakened by strain from various social factors. Living in disorganized communities, believing that legitimate opportunities for success are unavailable, and being involved in petty crimes lead to feelings of hopelessness. Strain occurs, which then causes deviant groups and activities to appear as acceptable substitutes. Experimentation with drugs while engaging in delinquent behaviors results in the development of a deviant lifestyle.

General strain theory. Agnew's (1985) general strain theory enhances traditional strain theory by using psychological concepts to explain how strain occurs within individuals. Whereas traditional strain theories focus on the effects of the social structure on lower-class youth in general, Agnew describes how internal stresses and strains can affect individuals regardless of social class. The negative affective states—anger, frustration, and hopelessness—are caused by failure to achieve goals, the removal of positive or desired stimuli, and the confrontation with negative stimuli.

Since the stressors that influence individuals' perceptions of themselves within the social order can occur to anyone, general strain theory is not limited to a racial or social category. Anyone affected by the strains described by Agnew may come to see him- or herself as isolated and rejected by society. Ultimately, Agnew sees social factors as being influential but concludes that personal temperament and the ability to positively cope with stress are more important.

Cultural Deviance Theories

The last category of social structure theories that we discuss is **cultural deviance theories**. These theories are based upon the general view that criminal behavior is an expression of conformity to lower-class cultural values and traditions. The argument is not that the lower class is less law-abiding than the middle class, but that it has fundamental differences in its cultural norms and standards that bring it into conflict with laws designed by the middle and upper classes.

Culture conflict. Thorsten Sellin's culture conflict theory is the oldest of the cultural deviance theories. This theory was an offshoot of Shaw and McKay's ecology of crime theory. Sellin's (1938) general view was that criminal behavior is an expression of conformity to lower-class cultural values and traditions. The two main assumptions of this theory are:

1. Criminal law is an expression of the rules of the dominant culture, therefore a clash may result between middle-class rules and splinter groups, such as ethnic and racial minorities who maintain their own set of conduct norms.
2. Obedience to the norms of their **lower-class culture** puts people in conflict with the norms of the dominant culture (Dantzker, 1998, p. 47).

This theory is best summarized through its strengths, which are that it identifies the aspect of lower-class life that produces street crime and adds the idea of culture conflict to Shaw and McKay's social disorganization theory. Its weaknesses are that it ignores middle-class crime completely and does not provide an adequate means of testing its theoretical premises.

Middle-class measuring rod. Anomie theory led the way to the development of extended theories, the first of which was the delinquent boys or middle-class measuring rod theory. This theory was introduced by Alfred K. Cohen in his 1955 text *Delinquent Boys: The Culture of the Gang.* The key points to Cohen's theory were that delinquency is due to status frustration, an inability to achieve success in a legitimate manner, and is a function of the social and economic limitations suffered by less fortunate individuals. Cohen also suggested that the lower-class youth commits crimes because he is unable to meet the standards of the middle class.

Cohen asserts that the lower-class child is constantly being measured by middle-class standards. The result is that the lower-class child, who accepts the middle-class standards but cannot reach them through socially approved means, turns to criminality to meet these goals. Cohen refers to these standards as the **middle-class measuring rod.**

Cohen identified three types of youth: the corner boy, the college boy, and the delinquent boy. Cohen pays the most attention to the delinquent boy, who adopts norms and principles directly opposite those of middle-class society and joins a gang in which activities are described as follows:

- Nonutilitarian: delinquents do things because they feel like doing them and because they do not believe they have ties to middle-class values and, therefore, there is no need to conform.
- Malicious: the delinquent enjoys defying social taboos.
- Negativistic: the norms of the gang are the opposite of those of adult society.
- Versatile: a delinquent can do anything as long as it is within the norms of the gang.
- Short-run hedonistic: the gang is interested in monetary pleasures.
- Autonomous: the only peer pressure is from within the gang (Cohen, 1955).

This theory offers little empirical support and assumes that lower-class youths really care what the middle class thinks or really want what the middle class wants. Furthermore, it should be noted that Cohen himself claimed that he was not trying to explain individual behavior but instead the development of the delinquent subculture.

Focal concerns. In line with Cohen's theory was a follow-up by Walter B. Miller, whose theory suggests that delinquency is a product of a united lower-class culture. **Focal concerns theory** claims that the lower class has a separate, identifiable culture distinct from middle-class values. The basis for Miller's theory is that slums are organized by a distinctive lower-class culture that emphasizes membership in one-sex peer groups. The one-sex peer groups, according to Miller (1958), are organized by a unique set of focal concerns that include trouble, smartness, toughness, fate, and autonomy. Ultimately, Miller suggested, the adherence to lower-class focal concerns is what produces delinquency (see Figure 7.4). The strength of this theory is that it more clearly identifies the aspects of lower-class culture that push people toward criminal behavior. Its weaknesses are that it does not provide empirical support for the existence of a lower-class culture, account for middle-class influence, or explain upper-class crime.

Differential opportunity. Another extension of anomie theory is **differential opportunity**, a theory introduced by Richard A. Cloward and Lloyd E. Ohlin in their 1960 text *Delinquency and Opportunity*. The aim of this theory is to explain how **delinquent subcultures** arise and persist in the lower-class areas of large urban cities. Their theory is based on the premise that the opportunities for lower-class youths to reach the American dream (education, wealth, status) are blocked, causing them to resort to illegitimate means. Furthermore, they contend that lower-class youths have the same wishes and needs as middle-class youths, so when legitimate means to success are not available, the lower-class youths resort to criminal means (see Figure 7.5). Cloward and Ohlin (1960) observed that as an alternative to reaching the American dream, youths gain satisfaction by adapting to one of three subcultures (gangs): the criminal gang, which is the training ground for adult criminal activity; the conflict gang, in which fighting and territorial protection are the norm; and the retreatist gang, which is content to search for kicks through alcohol, drugs, and sex.

Like any theory, differential opportunity theory has its flaws. Major criticisms of the theory include the following:

- Whether lower-class youths really want the same things their middle-class counterparts do is unknown.
- The theory is attractive to the middle class because it reinforces the values they themselves supposedly hold.

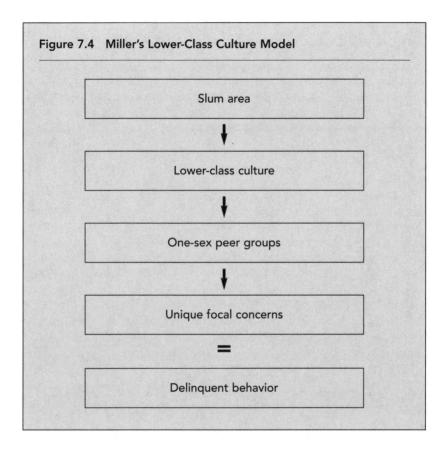

Figure 7.4 Miller's Lower-Class Culture Model

Slum area

↓

Lower-class culture

↓

One-sex peer groups

↓

Unique focal concerns

=

Delinquent behavior

- There is little support that lower-class youth become specialized in one of the three categories offered (Dantzker, 1998; Martin, Mutchnick, and Austin, 1990).

Despite its faults, differential opportunity theory actually seems to be more appropriate in its explanation of criminal behaviors among lower-class youths today than it was during the 1950s and 1960s.

Subculture of violence. Yet another distinction between lower-class culture and middle-class culture was proposed by Marvin E. Wolfgang and Franco Ferracuti (1967), who noted that lower-class males are quick to resort to physical aggression as a socially approved and expected response to insults and other interpersonal conflict. They opined that lower-class males often respond to physical force in situations where middle-class males tend to walk away. They argued that aggression as a response stems from the need of lower-class males to defend their honor and masculinity.

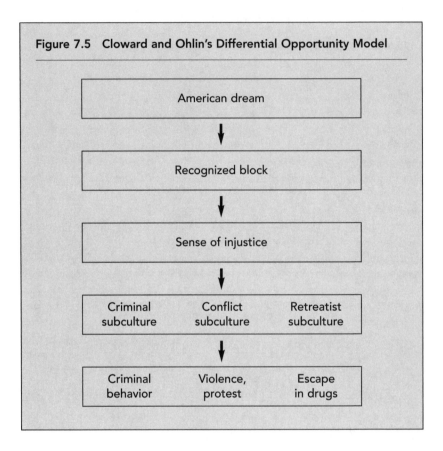

Figure 7.5   Cloward and Ohlin's Differential Opportunity Model

American dream

Recognized block

Sense of injustice

| Criminal subculture | Conflict subculture | Retreatist subculture |

| Criminal behavior | Violence, protest | Escape in drugs |

Critics of Wolfgang and Ferracuti stress that the higher incidence of violence among inner-city youth is a product of the social problems found within inner-city areas rather than the existence of a subculture of violence. They also criticize the concept of a subculture of violence as being racially biased in that it implies that young African American males are more violent.

It is our contention that Wolfgang and Ferracuti are correct and their critics are in error. Our view is that the willingness to resort to violence is a means of protecting one's image within one's social group and to maintain pride in self. The social conditions that others point out are exactly why young urban males have to do so: they are limited in other legitimate means of protecting themselves. While agreeing with the concept of a subculture of violence, we note that the lead author grew up in a working-class community within the rural South. The same limitations existed for young white males in that setting, with physical aggression as a primary means of protecting one's honor.

Code of the street. Elijah Anderson's (1999) ethnographic research in Philadelphia supports the existence of a subculture of violence among urban

Reality Check: Gangs

Gangs have been a problem within US society since the early days of the republic. The large cities of the Northeast had problems with young boys and teenagers who roamed the streets committing petty crimes. During the US Civil War, ethnic gangs composed of youth and adults developed as a defense against other groups and as a base of power for immigrants and first-generation Americans clustered within ethnic conclaves. Following that war, gangs were outlaws, such as the James-Younger gang that terrorized Missouri. Bitterness as to the war's outcome and the harsh treatment that ex-Confederates received were justifications for their atrocities.

Later, gangs were synonymous with organized crime. During Prohibition, groups led by individuals such as Al Capone competed for the lucrative markets in prostitution, bootlegging alcohol, running "speakeasies," gambling, drugs, and other vices desired by the public. In fact, Prohibition was repealed for the primary reason—protecting the welfare of the public— it was originally imposed.

While acknowledging the existence of organized crime, during the mid-1900s, the term "gangs" was used once again to refer to groups of young men who engaged in delinquent behaviors. Youth gangs were a focus of criminologists and led to the proliferation of theories covered within this chapter, although the title was also shared with motorcycle gangs who emerged after World War II.

During the 1960s, youth gangs grew along with the cities in which they were situated. The ethnic groups that had made up youth gangs (Italians, Hungarians, Poles, Irish, and Jewish immigrants) had successfully assimilated into American society. Youth gangs now consisted of African Americans, Hispanics, and other groups that were located within the impoverished areas of the inner cities. During the 1970s and 1980s, gang membership changed. In addition to the social support, camaraderie, and rebellion against authority found within youth gangs, other factors emerged to complicate the environment in which gangs existed.

The ready availability of modern firearms, along with huge sums of money from the sale of illicit drugs, transformed youth gangs in the United States. Instead of groups that most members outgrew as they matured, the lucrative drug market led to gangs in which older males remained involved and in which violence was not only accepted but encouraged. In fact, many inmates within our prison system are active members of national gangs that were originally local or, at best, regional affiliations of youth from similar ethnic groups. Today a gang's bitterest enemies may be members of the same ethnicity. This is further exacerbated by the increased involvement of young women in gangs and the organized crime associated with gang activities.

In light of the changes in American youth gangs, are the theories presented within this chapter still relevant? If so, which theories do you think best explain involvement in youth gangs?

youth in depressed areas. Anderson asserts that the perception that they are not respectable and have no legitimate power drives young African American males to attempt to gain respect by emphasizing their masculinity. These young men, like the settlers of the Wild West, feel that they cannot rely upon the police and the criminal justice system. Therefore, they rely upon themselves and their social group when there is a need to defend their honor. Anderson's work has resurrected subcultural research. Rather than running afoul of "political correctness" by designating urban youth as different, Anderson provides clear linkages between structural problems found within large cities and the need for respect.

To conclude, the social structure theories are relevant to current attempts to understand criminality. Still, one should be aware that these theories all focus on male youths who were drawn to gangs, which places serious limitations on the utility of these theories for other types of criminality.

Summary

The sociological theories are considered by many to be the "heart and soul" of criminological thought. This chapter addressed the social structure theories, that is, the theories that view criminality as a result of social structure. Three theoretical categories were identified: social disorganization, strain, and cultural deviance.

Social disorganization theories focus on the social environment as the cause of crime and criminality. The social disorganization theories discussed were concentric zone theory and social ecology theory. Concentric zone theory argues that the areas of the city in which people live influence how they are able to live. Social ecology theory abandoned Shaw and McKay's concentric zones but continued to examine the relationships that crime has with overcrowding, concentrated poverty, and social disorganization within urban areas.

Strain theories also examine the effects that the social structure has in producing crime. Strain theories differ from social disorganization theories in that they emphasize an individual's inability to reach higher goals or values because of his or her economic place in society. When goals for advancement are blocked or unattainable, strain occurs. The strain theories discussed include Durkheim's strain theory, anomie theory, institutional anomie theory, and relative deprivation. Durkheim's strain theory is based on the changes that occur within society and the pressures that are created for those who have difficulty in adjusting to those changes. Merton further developed the theory of anomie by identifying conformity, innovation, ritualism, retreatism, and rebellion as modes of adaptation. Institutional anomie theory argues that because Americans are conditioned by our capitalistic society to accumulate material goods and wealth, those who feel unable to do so are more likely to become deviant. Relative deprivation theory stresses how individuals or groups assess their social situation based upon those around them.

The last theoretical category was cultural deviance theory, which holds that there are distinct differences among the social classes. The lower classes come into conflict with societal norms and laws because of these cultural differences. The theories within this category are culture conflict, middle-class measuring rod, focal concerns, and differential opportunity. Sellin's culture conflict theory views crime as the product of a clash between middle-class rules and lower-class culture. The middle-class measuring rod theory holds that delinquency is due to status frustration of lower-class youths unable to meet the standards of the middle class. Focal concerns theory claims that the lower class has a separate, identifiable culture distinct from middle-class values. Last, differential opportunity theory is based on the premise that the opportunities for lower-class youths to reach the American dream are blocked, causing them to resort to illegitimate means.

Discussion Questions

1. How do the social structure theories apply to today's crime problems, especially among youths? Which one makes the most sense? Why?
2. Explain why social disorganization theory remains so popular today with social activists and governmental leaders.
3. Compare and contrast the strain theories.
4. Compare and contrast the cultural deviance theories.
5. What are the main shortcomings of the social structure theories? What are their strongest points?

8

Social Interaction
Theories

In the previous chapter, we discussed the first set of social-oriented theories, those dealing with social structure. Like social structure theories, social interaction theories fall under the umbrella of structural functionalism. Whereas the social structure theories tended to focus more on social conditions and are, therefore, more sociological, social interaction theories may be viewed as being more social-psychological in nature.

The social interaction theories present a relatively consistent theme in that social processes and interactions are seen as influencing criminality. Again, there is no consensus as to which theories (probably the majority of existing theories) should be discussed in this arena. Because of the number of theories and the somewhat differing perspectives found among them, we have chosen to divide them into two categories of interaction: social process and social reaction (see Figure 8.1).

Social Process Theories

Social process theories examine the social mechanisms by which criminal behaviors are said to develop. Traditionally, social process theories include social learning theories, **social control theories**, and labeling theory. Because labeling theory changes the focus from the individual offender to agents of social control, we have separated it from social process theories and included it, along with symbolic interactionist theories, under social reaction theories. Our discussion of social process theories will begin with social learning theories.

Figure 8.1 Social Interaction Theories

Social Process		Social Reaction	
Social Learning	Social Control	Symbolic Interactionist	Labeling
Differential association	Containment Control	Neutralization Commitment to conformity	Labeling Theory of deviant behavior
Differential anticipation			Differential
Differential reinforcement			social control
Imitation			Defiance theory

Social Learning Theories

The consistent theme of social process theories is that deviant socialization and intimacy with criminal peers breed criminality. Social learning theories see this socialization as occurring through a process by which offenders (usually youth) are taught that criminal or deviant behaviors are acceptable and perhaps even more desirable than legitimate behaviors. This chapter presents four social learning theories. Each emphasizes a different way that individuals learn to engage in criminal behavior. Our discussion begins with the oldest of the social learning theories, the theory of imitation.

Imitation theory. The first social learning theory that we discuss is Gabriel Tarde's theory of imitation. This is the oldest of the social learning theories and influenced subsequent learning theories in both sociology and psychology. Tarde (1912) noted:

- Individuals in close and intimate contact with one another imitate one another's behaviors.
- Imitation spreads from the top down.
- New acts and behaviors are superimposed on old ones and subsequently act to reinforce or to discourage previous customs (what Tarde referred to as the "law of insertion").

Tarde's theory is built upon by Albert Bandura's social learning theory, which claims that people learn to be aggressive and violent through life experiences. According to Bandura (1977), aggressive acts are often the result of modeling. He identified three principal sources or models: family members (e.g., if a parent is an alcoholic or abuser, chances are good the child will be); environmental experiences (e.g., getting "stoned" at a party with friends on cocaine); and the mass media (e.g., constant publicity of volatile events leading to violent actions).

Bandura's theory concludes by looking at the four factors he attributes to producing violent and aggressive behavior: an event that heightens arousal, aggressive skills, expected outcomes, and consistency of behavior with values.

Differential association. Edwin Sutherland's theory of differential association is based on the laws of learning and includes the concept of symbolic interactionism. The basic focus is on social relations—the frequency, duration, intensity, and meaningfulness of association—rather than on the individual's qualities or traits or on the external world of concrete and visible events. Sutherland's major premise was that people learn to commit crime through their exposure to antisocial definitions; in particular, individuals respond to the cultural standards of their associates, especially the intimate ones. In his textbook *Principles of Criminology,* which was first published in 1924, Edwin Sutherland (1939) offered the nine propositions that are the foundation of his theory:

1. Criminal behavior is learned.
2. Criminal behavior is learned in interaction with other persons in a process of communication.
3. The principal part of the learning of the criminal behavior occurs within intimate personal groups.
4. When criminal behavior is learned, the learning includes techniques of committing the crime, which are sometimes very complicated, sometimes very simple.
5. The specific directions of the motives and drives are learned from definitions of the legal codes as favorable or unfavorable. In some societies, an individual is surrounded by persons who invariably define the legal codes as rules to be observed, while in others he [or she] is surrounded by persons whose definitions are favorable to the violation of the legal codes.
6. *A person becomes delinquent because of an excess of definitions favorable to violation of law over definitions unfavorable to violation of law.* This is the principle of differential association *(emphasis added).*
7. Differential associations may vary in frequency, duration, priority, and intensity. This means that associations with criminal behavior and also associations with anticriminal behavior vary in those respects.
8. The process of learning criminal behavior by association with criminal and anti-criminal patterns involves all of the mechanisms that are involved in any other learning.
9. While criminal behavior is an expression of general needs and values, it is not explained by those general needs and values, since noncriminal

behavior is an expression of the same needs and values. Thieves generally steal in order to secure money, but likewise honest laborers work in order to secure money. The attempts by scholars to explain criminal behavior by general drives and values, such as the happiness principle, striving for social status, the money motive, or frustration, have been, and must continue to be, futile, since they explain lawful behavior as completely as they explain criminal behavior. They are similar to respiration, which is necessary for any behavior, but which does not differentiate criminal from noncriminal (Sutherland and Cressey, 1978, pp. 80–82).

Sutherland's theory has strengths and weaknesses. Its strengths include explaining the onset of criminality, the presence of crime in all elements of social structure, and why some people in high-crime areas refrain from criminality. An additional strength is that it can apply to both juveniles and adults.

On the other hand, the theory provides no answers to these questions: Where do antisocial definitions originate? How can we measure antisocial definitions or prove that someone has been exposed to an excess of them? The theory also fails to explain illogical acts of violence and destruction and offers no discussion as to how to adequately test the theory. Despite these concerns, differential association continues to be one of the more popular sociological theories. It may be seen as the foundation for later social learning theories.

Differential anticipation. The theory of **differential anticipation** is built on Sutherland's differential association theory. The main contributor of this theory was Donald Glaser, whose major premise was that people commit crimes whenever and wherever expectations of gain from the criminal act exceed the expected losses with respect to **social bonds** (Glaser, 1956). The strength of this theory is that it combines principles of social bonds, differential association, and classical thought. However, its weaknesses are that it has not been subjected to extensive empirical testing and it does not explain why expectations and crime rates vary.

Differential reinforcement. A third social learning theory is **differential reinforcement** theory. By adapting the views of B. F. Skinner and other psychologists on operant conditioning and integrating them with Sutherland's differential association concept, R. L. Burgess and R. L. Akers (1966) argued that criminal behavior and attitudes are more likely to be learned when they are reinforced or rewarded by friends and/or family. When the rewards for criminal behavior outweigh the rewards for alternative behaviors, differential reinforcement occurs and the criminal behavior is learned.

According to Burgess and Akers, people decide whether to commit crime after calculating whether the potential rewards will outweigh the potential risks. As Ronald Akers and Christine S. Sellers (2009, p. 92) noted, "Whether individuals will refrain from or commit a crime at any given time (and whether they will continue or desist from doing so in the future) depends on the past, present, and anticipated future rewards and punishments for their actions." Although much learning of criminal behavior occurs within the intimate personal groups emphasized by Sutherland, Burgess and Akers observed it can also result from the influence of school authorities, police, the mass media, and other nonprimary group sources. These sources all provide rewards and punishments that influence the learning of behavior (Akers and Sellers, 2009).

While Burgess and Akers stressed the social context of differential reinforcement, they also recognized that criminal behavior can provide its own rewards, such as excitement and increased wealth. Akers accepts the validity of Bandura's modeling (see Chapter 6) as a necessary factor in the initial acquisition of deviant behavior. But its continuation will depend greatly on the frequency and personal significance of **social reinforcement**, which comes from association with others.

The strengths of this theory are that it adds learning theory principles to differential association, and it links sociological and psychological principles. The weaknesses of this theory are that it fails to explain why those rewarded for conventional behavior commit crimes and why some delinquent youths do not become adult criminals despite having been rewarded for criminal behavior. In addition, some scholars consider it tautological, or circular, in that behavior is said to occur because it is reinforced, but it is reinforced because it occurs.

Kornhauser (1978) points out that there is no empirical support for this theory. Still, the theory remains a very popular one within both psychological and sociological criminology. We should also note that with its blend of psychological, sociological, and classical features, it would also qualify as an integrated theory of criminality.

Social Control Theories

The second group of theories in the social process typology is social control theories. These theories start with an assumption that human nature is the motivator for criminal behavior, and that if some type of outside control did not exist, individuals would naturally commit crimes. The first of the social control theorists, Albert Reiss, argued that the failure of personal controls (the inability to refrain from meeting personal needs in ways that conflict with society's norms and rules) leads to criminality (Reiss, 1951). However, he failed to consider the effect of family, environmental, and community controls on an individual's behavior. Despite the obvious flaws in his argument, Reiss's assumptions paved the way for two social control theories: containment and social bond.

Containment theory. Another of the social control theories is referred to as **containment theory**. The main theorist, Walter Reckless (1967), claimed that each person has inner and outer controls that push him or her toward conformity or pull him or her toward criminality. He further contended that society produces these pushes and pulls and that they can be counteracted by internal and external containments:

- Inner containment, or the individual's personality
- Outer containment, or the constraints that society and social groups use
- Internal pushes, or personal factors such as restlessness, discontent, and boredom
- External pressures, such as adverse living conditions
- External pulls, such as deviant associates

The strengths of containment theory are that it brings together psychological and sociological principles and can explain why some people are able to resist the strongest social pressures to commit crime. For example, despite situational influences that might predispose other youths toward criminality, the "good boys" studied by Reckless and his associates (1957) were able to resist temptation because of their positive self-image. This self-image was seen as the product of encouragement and support from significant adults.

The findings from containment theory studies have been criticized over the methodology used (Shoemaker, 2009). In particular, one might argue that the labeling and subsequent treatment of "good" and "bad" youths by adult authority figures may have more influence on their self-image and actions than do "inner containments."

Social bond. Finally, the last of the social control theories is T. Hirschi's **social bond** (or control) **theory**, whose main assumption is that it is the person's bond to society that prevents him or her from participating in criminal behavior. Should the bond weaken, the individual feels free to commit crime. Hirschi (1969) identified four elements of a bond to conventional society: attachment, commitment, involvement, and belief.

Attachment, which Hirschi claimed is the strongest bond, refers to how an individual attaches him- or herself to others. It takes into account the internalization of **social norms**, **conscience**, and superego. The bond of commitment involves how an individual invests his or her time and energy in certain activities. The individual also considers the costs of being involved in delinquent behavior. Perhaps the most pragmatic bond is involvement, in which an individual is just so busy participating in conventional activities that there is no time to engage in criminal acts. Last, the belief bond relates to an individual's acceptance of the moral validity of society's rules.

From a positive perspective, social bond theory explains the onset of criminality, applies to both middle- and lower-class crime, and explains its theoretical constructs in a manner that can be measured and empirically tested. From a negative perspective, it fails to explain the differences in crime rates, to show whether a weak bond can be strengthened, and to distinguish the importance of different elements of the social bond (which is more important, attachment or commitment, commitment or involvement?).

On the whole, social process theories have led to many discussions as to how criminal behavior is either learned or suppressed. Yet there are those who would argue that it is how one reacts or responds to society that leads to criminality. We shall examine those arguments in the next section.

Social Reaction Theories

The second typology of social interaction theories, social reaction, includes two categories: labeling and symbolic interactionist. Social reaction theorists have postulated that it is impossible to understand criminality merely through the study of criminals but insist that crime must be viewed in its entire social context. Therefore, social reaction theorists argue that criminal behavior can be understood only in the context of how others react to it. This includes official reactions in which individuals and events are legally defined as criminal. It has been argued that criminal behavior is defined solely by the reactions that others have to it, creating what can be referred to as a "reactive" definition of crime.

Social reaction theories can best be summarized as attempts to explain the initial occurrence of criminal behavior in light of societal reaction to individuals or groups who are different from the norm. Additional occurrences of criminal behavior after the societal reaction are seen as the result of socialization caused by the social reaction. This leads to the question "Is it the reaction of an individual, a group, or society as a whole that influences the behavior?" The following theories assist in responding to this question.

Symbolic Interactionist Theories

Symbolic interactionist theory focuses on how human behavior is influenced by how situations are perceived and interpreted. Individuals tend to alter their behavior based on how they think others perceive them. Therefore, behavior is a function of self. The roles that we think others have assigned to us determine our own self-image (Mead, 1934). We see ourselves in a mental looking glass that may or may not accurately depict how we are viewed by others. If these roles are positive, we adopt behaviors that we believe are compatible with them. Unfortunately, if these roles are believed to be negative, we are very likely to adopt negative behaviors.

Symbolic interactionism is an important theory in explaining all human behavior. It is particularly useful in explaining crime and criminality. The remaining theories all qualify as symbolic interactionist explanations. However, because of its importance in the development of criminology as a discipline, we have separated labeling theory and its direct descendants from the other symbolic interactionist theories. The first symbolic interactionist theory to be examined is **neutralization theory**.

Neutralization theory. Neutralization theory (sometimes called *drift theory*) was proposed by David Matza and Gresham Sykes. Their main assumption was that youths learn ways to neutralize society's moral constraints and will periodically drift in and out of criminal behavior. They contended that delinquency is essentially an unrecognized extension of "defenses to crimes" in a form of justifications (Matza, 1964). In other words, criminal behavior can be rationalized by the offender but not by the legal system or society. These rationalizations can precede or follow criminal behavior and are said to serve to protect the individual from self-blame and the blame of others after the act.

Matza and Sykes (1961) identified five ways that delinquents rationalize or neutralize their actions:

1. *Denial of responsibility*—implies that the deviant act resulted from forces beyond the individual's control.
2. *Denial of injury*—despite the fact that it was unlawful, the individual does not believe that the behavior really harmed anyone.
3. *Denial of victim*—again, despite the act's unlawfulness, the belief is that the victim deserved the action taken against him or her and that the action was actually a form of punishment.
4. *Condemnation of the condemners*—focuses attention from the deviant act to those who have condemned it.   ˎ
5. *Appeal to higher loyalties*—legal norms are replaced by a loyalty to other norms.

The strengths of neutralization theory include explanations of why many delinquents do not become adult criminals and why youthful law violators can participate in conventional behavior. However, the theory fails to show whether neutralization occurs before or after the criminal behavior, to explain why some youths drift and others do not, and to explain self-destructive acts such as alcohol and drug use.

Commitment to conform. To complement the theory of drift, there is Scot Briar and Irving Piliavin's **commitment to conformity theory**. This theory's main assumption is that short-term stimuli that influence behavior are controlled by the individual's commitment to conventional society (Briar and Piliavin, 1965). This commitment is believed to help the individual resist temptation. The positive aspects of this theory are that it helps explain both middle- and lower-class criminality and shows how control is maintained in the middle class, keeping members from committing crimes. The negative side of this theory is that it fails to explain variations in crime and crime rates and why some children develop commitments and others do not.

Labeling Theory

Edwin Lemert's labeling theory has been recognized as the leading social reaction theory. The main assumptions of this theory are:

1. Two types of deviance exist: primary, in which crimes are situationally induced, and secondary, which is the result of labels and sanctions resulting from primary deviance.
2. Individuals will enter into a career of law violations when they are labeled for their personalities, especially if the labeling is done by people important to the individual.
3. Labeling creates a stigma and affects self-image.
4. Labeled individuals view themselves as deviant and will increasingly commit criminal behavior (Lemert, 1951).

Furthermore, labeling theory emphasizes the process and does not see deviance as a state of being but as an outcome of social interaction. It also argues that one problem with labeling someone deviant is that standards and norms used to define transgressions are not universal in character. Ultimately, the assumptions of labeling theory provide two models (see Figure 8.2). In Model One, the individual who has committed a deviant act receives the label

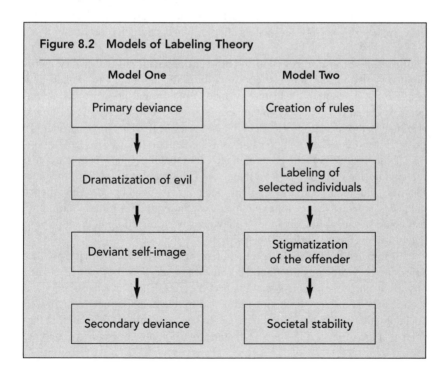

Figure 8.2 Models of Labeling Theory

Model One	Model Two
Primary deviance	Creation of rules
Dramatization of evil	Labeling of selected individuals
Deviant self-image	Stigmatization of the offender
Secondary deviance	Societal stability

of "deviant" and, accepting that label, continues to commit deviant acts. In Model Two, socially created rules automatically label a violator as "deviant," stigmatizing the individual and allowing society to maintain stability.

The strengths of labeling theory include explanations of the role that society has in creating deviance and why some juvenile delinquents do not become adult criminals. It also helps develop the concept of the career criminal. The weaknesses are that it does not explain the reason the crime was originally committed, and it places too much emphasis on society's role. The two theories that follow attempt to address the weaknesses of labeling theory by incorporating other social interaction theories into labeling theory.

Theory of deviant behavior. One effort to strengthen labeling theory involves using social control theory to explain how negative self-image can lead to criminal and/or deviant behavior. Individuals who lack desirable social traits may become isolated from others. This isolation leads to feelings of self-hate and low self-image. The product of this self-hate is that commitment to conventional values is lessened.

These social outcasts then associate with others like themselves, creating a deviant subculture that defies conventional values. Criminal acts are then committed as acts of defiance and/or acceptance of unlawful behaviors as appropriate responses to societal rejection (Kaplan and Fukurai, 1992; Kaplan and Johnson, 1991). The advantage of this theory over conventional labeling theory is that it explains how noncriminal deviance can actually lead to criminal behavior, rather than emphasizing society's responses after criminal activity has occurred.

Differential social control theory. **Differential social control** theory incorporates symbolic interactionist concepts into labeling theory to explain how youths' self-perceptions lead to deviance. Both formal and informal social controls are seen as causing young people to engage in reflective role-taking (Heimer and Matsueda, 1994). Parental labels are seen as having a particularly great impact upon the young person's self-perception (Matsueda, 1992).

If the youth's self-image is damaged by labeling, young people assume the deviant identity they believe they have been labeled with. With this new identity, the likelihood of criminal behavior is heightened. This theory enhances labeling theory by explaining how individuals who are "different" can come to accept the label they believe has been forced upon them prior to actual involvement in criminal behavior.

Before leaving the social reaction theories, we wish to note that these theories are of particular importance because they serve as the bridge between structural functionalist and social conflict theories. The previous sociological theories focus on how limitations imposed by the social structure or flawed social interactions might lead individuals to become criminal. The conflict theories that are discussed in the next chapter focus on how power and economic conflicts within society create criminality. The social reaction theories link these two perspectives by addressing how the actions of agents of social control might influence individuals or groups to engage in criminal behavior.

Defiance theory. The last of the social reaction theories that we will discuss is Lawrence W. Sherman's **defiance theory**. In an effort to evaluate the competing claims made by deterrence and labeling theorists, Sherman contrasted the competing and, in his view, limited perspectives they offered. To conduct his evaluation, Sherman attempted to construct a comprehensive theory that would account for sanctions that created defiance, deterrence, or irrelevance (Sherman, 2003). To accomplish this task, Sherman developed defiance theory. Defiance was defined as "the net increase in the prevalence, incidence, or seriousness of future offending against a sanctioning community caused by a proud shameless reaction to the administration of a criminal sanction" (Sherman, 2003, p. 459).

The key question addressed by Sherman was, does punishment control crime? He felt that deterrence was unattainable if offenders were indignant about a sanction they felt was unjust. Instead of teaching that crime was not worth the pain, offenders became angry and resentful toward society and criminal justice if they perceived that the sanction they received was too harsh or unwarranted. Sherman used Braithwaite's reintegrative shaming to explain how punishment can achieve diametrically opposite results. As discussed earlier, stigmatizing shaming creates resentment, whereas reintegrative shaming is seen as controlling crime.

Sherman builds on reintegrative shaming by incorporating concerns of fairness and emotional responses to shaming into a single theory. Defiance theory examines the concepts of legitimacy, social bonds, shame, and pride to describe how criminal sanctions can produce defiance rather than deterrence. He introduces specific or individual defiance as the reaction of one person to being punished. General defiance is how a group might react to the punishment of one or more of its members. The factors that determine whether a sanction produces defiance instead of deterrence are:

- The offender defines a criminal sanction as unfair.
- The offender is poorly bonded to or alienated from the sanctioning agent or the community the agent represents.
- The offender defines the sanction as stigmatizing and rejecting a person, not the lawbreaking act.
- The offender denies or refuses to acknowledge the shame the sanction has actually caused him or her to suffer.

Sanctions are defined as unfair under two conditions, either of which is sufficient:

Reality Check: Domestic Terrorism

Prior to 1978, the United States had experienced few activities that were terroristic. Since that time, Americans have been made aware of terrorism and its impacts. Five cases may be seen as the events that led to our unwelcome awareness. Three of them are acts of domestic terrorism by left-wing or right-wing extremists.

Ted Kaczynski: The Unabomber

Theodore John "Ted" Kaczynski was a mathematician who left his job as an assistant professor at the University of California, Berkeley, to move to a remote cabin in Montana. As development encroached on the wilderness around his cabin, Kaczynski began a mail bombing spree that spanned nearly twenty years, killing three people and injuring twenty-three others. His targets were universities, airlines, computer stores, scientists, and high-tech businesses. Kaczynski's motivation was to oppose what he perceived as the encroachment of science and technology on US society and to promote his views of "leftism." He was apprehended in 1996 after his brother read Kaczynski's manifesto, which had been published by the *New York Times* and *Washington Post*. He is currently serving a life sentence without parole in a federal prison.

Timothy McVeigh: The Oklahoma City Bomber

Timothy McVeigh was a former soldier who won a bronze star during the First Gulf War. After he left the army, he wandered around the country, becoming involved with people disenchanted with the federal government. His dislike became extreme hatred following the botched Bureau of Alcohol, Tobacco, Firearms and Explosives (ATF) and Federal Bureau of Investigation (FBI) sieges at Waco, Texas, and Ruby Ridge in northern Idaho, both of which resulted in the deaths of men, women, and children. Even though he was considered a loner, McVeigh conspired with Terry Nichols, Michael Fortier, and Lori Fortier in detonating a truck bomb in front of the Alfred P. Murrah Building in Oklahoma City on April 19, 1995. The attack killed 168 people (including 19 small children and babies) and injured 450. After being captured, McVeigh showed no remorse for his actions. He was executed by lethal injection on June 11, 2001.

Eric Rudolph: The Olympic Park Bomber

Eric Robert Rudolph was responsible for a series of bombings across the southern United States from 1996 to 1998. His attacks killed 2 people and injured at least 150 others.

continues

Reality Check, *continued*

Rudolph is best known for the Centennial Olympic Park bombing in Atlanta during the 1996 Summer Olympics. The blast killed 1 spectator and wounded 111 others. Rudolph later bombed an abortion clinic in Sandy Springs, Georgia; a lesbian bar in Atlanta, injuring 5; and an abortion clinic in Birmingham, Alabama, killing a Birmingham police officer and critically injuring a nurse. After being identified, Rudolph evaded capture for ten years by hiding out in the mountains near Murphy, North Carolina (it is speculated that he received assistance, but no one was ever identified). In 2005, as part of a plea bargain, Rudolph pled guilty to numerous federal and state homicide charges and accepted four consecutive life sentences in exchange for avoiding a trial and a potential death sentence. Rudolph's motivation for the bombings was allegedly to draw attention to the evils of abortion and homosexuality, and many have claimed that Rudolph's actions were Christian terrorism. However, it is interesting that one of his brothers is gay, and Rudolph at one point made the comment, "I really prefer Nietzsche to the Bible" (Morrison, 2005).

All three of these men are designated "lone wolf terrorists" who either acted on their own (Kaczynski and Rudolph) or were aided by one or two others but carried out the attack on their own (McVeigh). According to Bartol and Bartol (2011), lone wolf terrorists are the most challenging type of terrorist. They operate individually, do not belong to an organized group, act without direct influence of a leader or hierarchy, and claim to be acting on behalf of an interest group. They also carefully plan their attacks, appear to be emotionally disturbed, and demonstrate poor interpersonal and social skills (p. 337).

Identify another "lone wolf" domestic terrorist, describe his/her actions, and discuss what his/her motivations might have been. Which of the theories discussed within this chapter best explains the actions of this terrorist?

1. The sanctioning agent behaves with disrespect for the offender or for the group to whom the offender belongs, regardless of how fair the sanction is on substantive grounds.
2. The sanction is substantively arbitrary, discriminatory, excessive, undeserved, or otherwise objectively unjust (Sherman, 2003, p. 328).

Defiance theory is quite interesting in its ability to explain how offenders can reject unjust sanctions or unfair treatment by agents of social control. However, it does not explain why offenders who have been treated fairly and who have received a just sanction become defiant.

Summary

Social interaction theories present a relatively consistent theme in their claim that culture and intimacy with criminal peers breed criminality. Because of the number of theories and the somewhat differing perspectives found among them, we chose to divide them into two levels of interaction: social process and social reaction. The social process theories were further subdivided into social learning and social control theories. The consistent theme of social learning theory is that intimacy with criminal peers breeds criminality; we examined several social learning theories.

The first social learning theory examined was Tarde's theory of imitation. Tarde's theory suggests that individuals in close and intimate contact with one another imitate one another's behaviors. This theory was further developed through Bandura's social learning theory, which claims that people learn to be aggressive and violent through life experiences.

The next social learning theory to be discussed was differential association theory, which is based on the laws of learning. The basic focus is on social relations rather than on the individual's qualities or traits or the external world of concrete and visible events. Differential association theory led to the development of several learning theories that sought to better explain how the process of association influences criminality. Differential anticipation was the first such theory discussed. The main premise of this theory is that people commit crimes whenever and wherever expectations of gain from the criminal act exceed the expected losses with respect to social bonds. Yet another social learning theory is Akers's differential reinforcement. The major assumption of this theory is that criminal behavior depends on the person's experiences with rewards for conventional behaviors and punishments for deviant ones.

The second group of social process theories was the social control theories. These theories start with an assumption that human nature is the motivator for criminal behavior. It is believed that if some type of control did not exist, individuals would naturally commit crimes. Two social control theories evolved from Reiss's assumptions of social control. Reckless's containment theory argues that each person has inner and outer controls that push him or her toward conformity or pull him or her toward criminality. Society produces these pushes and pulls, which can be counteracted by internal and external containments. The second control theory was Hirschi's social bond theory. Its main assumption is that it is the person's bond to society that prevents him or her from participating in criminal behavior.

The second overall category of social interaction theories discussed was referred to as social reaction theories, which can best be summarized as attempts to explain the initial occurrence of criminal behavior in light of societal reactions to individuals or groups who are different from the norm. Additional occurrences of criminal behavior are seen as the result of socialization caused by the social reaction.

Symbolic interactionist theories focus on how human behavior is influenced by how situations are perceived and interpreted. Neutralization theory proposes that youths learn ways to neutralize society's moral constraints and will periodically drift in and out of criminal behavior. Criminal behavior can be rationalized by the offender. These rationalizations can precede or follow criminal behavior and are said to serve to protect the individual from self-blame and blame of others after the act. Complementing neutralization theory is commitment to conform theory. This theory's main assumption is that short-term stimuli that influence behavior are controlled by the individual's commitment to conventional society. This commitment is believed to help resist temptations to engage in criminal behavior.

The final grouping of social reaction theories is Lemert's labeling theory and its derivatives, the theory of deviant behavior and differential social control. These labeling theories assume that two types of deviance exist, primary and secondary. Primary deviance is the offender's first involvement with criminal behavior resulting from situational factors. Secondary deviance is the offender's subsequent involvement in criminal activities after having been sanctioned or labeled for primary deviance. Individuals are thought to enter into a career of law violations when they are labeled as deviant, especially if done so by "significant others." The labeling theories were seen by the authors as having particular importance because they serve as the bridge between structural functionalist theories and social control theories.

Discussion Questions

1. What is the underlying theme of the social process theories? How would you apply these theories to current criminality?
2. What is the underlying theme of the social reaction theories? How would you apply these theories to current criminality?
3. What is the underlying theme of the social control theories? How would you apply these theories to current criminality?
4. Compare and contrast the three sets of social interaction theories. Which set appears to be the most useful in explaining today's criminal behavior?

9

Social Conflict Theories

In the preceding coverage of sociological theories, there has been an assumption that the social structure is functional and that despite the ills that lead to crime and criminality, there is a consensus among the majority of citizens within society in regard to how the overall system is administered. The focus of both social structure and social interaction theories is to determine why individuals or groups deviate from societal norms. As we noted in Chapter 8, the social reaction theories, most notably labeling theory, see society as functional but change the emphasis to explain how agents of social control can lead to criminality.

Social Conflict and Structural Functionalism

Social conflict theories expand this analysis of social institutions. However, they do not start from a view of structural functionalism but from continuous competition and conflict within a society that is politically, economically, and socially divided. Unlike previously discussed positivist theories that take into account biological, psychological, and individual sociological factors as the basis for explaining criminal behavior, **conflict theory** focuses on society as the major influence on criminal behavior. The position of conflict theorists is that imposition of law and justice is determined by those who are in power (i.e., those in control of government and/or business). The conflict perspectives have as their foundation power struggles between those who are in power and those who are not. Non-Marxist theories focus on interest group competition and power relationships. Marxist theorists focus on the effects of capitalism and social class. Contemporary theorists examine social conflicts from a variety of perspectives that may or may not include class struggle.

The Social Conflict Perspective

Conflict theories attempt to identify society's power relations and draw attention to their role in promoting criminal behavior. Although conflict is viewed as an essential social process upon which society depends (Durkheim, 1984), group interests and their influence on legislation that arises from these conflicts are linked to criminal behavior. The conflict model espouses three themes:

1. *The relativity of criminal definitions*—conflict theory says that every act defined as immoral, deviant, or criminal must be viewed as tentative, at best, and that it is always subject to redefinition (depending on the group with the most power).
2. *Control of institutions*—conflict theorists debate that there are three basic means to maintaining and enhancing society's interests: to force compromise, and the dominance of social institutions, such as law, church, schools, and government.
3. *Law as an instrument of power*—conflict theory views the law as an extremely potent weapon of social conflict; whoever has control over the laws retains power (Dantzker, 1998, p. 59).

According to conflict theory, the power of those with control over the laws to protect themselves and their interests leads those not in power toward criminal behavior. In this chapter, three categories of conflict theories are offered: traditional conflict (pluralist or group explanations), Marxist (including critical, radical, structural, and instrumental), and contemporary (left realism, feminism, and peacemaking). While myriad other theories qualify as social conflict theories, we limit our discussion to these better-known subjects (see Figure 9.1). Our examination begins with the non-Marxist conflict theories.

Non-Marxist Conflict Theories

Non-Marxist conflict theories can be traced to the writings of George Vold and Rolf Dahrendorf during the 1950s. Their arguments that competition and conflict, rather than consensus and stability, governed the social order challenged the basic premise of structural functionalism. In their works, and in the works of criminologists who succeeded these pioneers, the focus of research moved from individual offenders who were somehow "out of step" with society to society and its institutions. The result of this approach is seen not only in the non-Marxist theories but in the application of all conflict theories (both Marxist and non-Marxist) that followed.

Figure 9.1   Social Conflict Theories

Non-Marxist	Marxist	Contemporary
Group conflict	Instrumental	Feminist
Status	Structural	Postmodernist
Class conflict	Critical	Peacemaking
Criminalization	Radical	Elitist
Social reality	Left realist	Power control
	Integrated	
	structural Marxist	

Group conflict theory. George Vold (1958) incorporated the premises of political pluralism and Thorsten Sellin's (1938) culture conflict into his theory of group conflict. Vold's **group conflict theory** postulates that conflict between groups should be viewed as one of the principal and essential social processes upon which the continuance of society depends. Like Emile Durkheim (1984), Vold saw social conflict as normal and beneficial. **Interest group competition** serves to hold all groups in check to keep any one from becoming too powerful. Both the making of laws and the breaking of laws were seen as products of this competition. Unlike Marxist theorists, Vold saw capitalism as but one of many political interests that led to interest group competition.

Status theory. Max Weber (1953, pp. 121–124), like Vold, believed that the Marxist theories and a capitalist economy were only part of the many issues involved within social conflict. However, Weber did emphasize social class within his perspective. In **status theory**, power and prestige are seen to be key issues within the conflict that exists in society. According to Weber, "criminality exists in all societies and is the result of the political struggle among different groups attempting to promote or enhance their life chances" (Bartollas and Schmalleger, 2010).

Class conflict theory. Dahrendorf (1959) expanded Weber's perspective on power and authority. Like Weber, he rejected the Marxist emphasis on property ownership as the sole determinant of political and social power. However, he did view **class conflict** as integral to social conflict. Class was seen as determining the allocation of power and authority within society, and struggles between the classes were seen as being regulated by legal sanctions, to the advantage of the upper classes.

Criminalization theory. Austin Turk (1966, 1977) incorporated Dahrendorf's views into his own extension of Weber's perspective on power and authority. The conflicts that Turk described were seen as covering a wide range of social and cultural issues. Those holding power were viewed as using their abilities to make, interpret, and enforce legal standards to maintain control. Those out of power were seen as resisting those legal standards that they perceived to be contrary to their own interests.

Turk's (1966, 1977) **criminalization theory** centers on (1) the conditions under which cultural and social differences between authorities and subjects will probably result in conflict, (2) the conditions under which criminalization will probably occur in the course of conflict, and (3) the conditions under which the degree of deprivation associated with becoming a criminal will probably be greater or lesser.

Social reality theory. Another theory that advocates power and authority relationships as the basis of social conflict was presented by Richard Quinney. Quinney's (1970) **social reality theory** argues that conflict is intertwined with power and that differential distribution of power produces conflict, which is rooted in the competition for power. Quinney offered six postulates for explaining conflict as social reality: (1) the *definition of crime*—authorized government agents define criminal conduct; (2) the *formulation of criminal definition*—criminal definitions are interpreted by those who have the power to shape public policy; (3) the *application of criminal definition*—those in power enforce their definitions of criminal behaviors; (4) the *development of behavioral patterns in relation to criminal behaviors*—behavioral patterns within society are structured by how criminal behaviors are defined and enforced; (5) the *construction of criminal conceptions*—the conceptions of crime are constructed and diffused within the different segments of society through various means of communication; (6) the *social reality of crime*—crime is the product of the previous propositions, meaning that those in power attempt to use criminal definitions to impose their will on the rest of society (adapted from Quinney, 1970, pp. 15–23).

These conflict theories not only influenced non-Marxist criminological research but also served to expedite the development of Marxist perspectives on crime and criminality, which are presented in the following section.

Marxist Theories

The economic and social philosophies of Karl Marx are the foundation of several conflict theories. Marx's view was that class biases result from class division in a capitalist society made up of two classes—elites (bourgeoisie) and subordinates (proletariat)—and inevitably lead to conflict. His solution was a classless society that would be created by overthrowing capitalistic society and adopting a socialistic system (Marx, Engels, and Malia, 1998).

The explanation of critical and radical theories of criminality begins with **Marxist theory**. Marxist theory includes the following:

1. A struggle exists between the proletariat (working class) and the bourgeoisie (owners and controllers of production).
2. The political and economic philosophies of the dominant class influence all aspects of life.
3. Society's structure(s) are unstable and can be changed through slow and evolving violence. (Dantzker, 1998, p. 59)

The Marxist view of law and behavior is that individuals are not naturally inclined to be either criminal or noncriminal, but the inclination toward criminal behavior is a result of social laws designed to maintain control of the powerless by the powerful. Willem Bonger (1969), the individual credited with first applying Marxist theory to the study of criminology, noted:

1. The abnormal element of crime is of social and biological origin.
2. The response to crime is punishment—the application of penalties considered more severe than spontaneous moral condemnation.
3. No act is naturally immoral or criminal.
4. Crimes are antisocial acts harmful to those who have the power at their command to control society.
5. In every society divided into a ruling class and an inferior class, penal law serves the will of the former.
6. Crime is a function of poverty.

The views of Marx and Bonger are the starting point for the various Marxist perspectives currently found within criminology. Bruce Arrigo (1999) identifies several theories derived from Marxist perspectives (instrumental Marxists, structural Marxists, anarchists, structural interpellationists, left realists, socialist feminists, postmodernists, critical race theorists, and peacemaking criminologists are but a few) within modern criminology. Our overview discusses the following: instrumental Marxism, structural Marxism, critical theory, and radical theory.

Instrumental theory. Adherents of **instrumental Marxism** see capitalism as the root of social conflict within society. Property ownership and perpetuation of social injustices by the owners of production against the poor and the powerless are the basis for crime and criminality. The owners of production control the economy. They also determine how laws are enacted, how crimes are constructed, and how deviance is defined. These powerful elites are seen by instrumental Marxists as the true criminals because they use their power to impose poverty and powerlessness on the poor in order to maintain their own power. Poverty is seen as the cause of crime. Ordinary criminals are viewed as victims who have reacted to the social injustices perpetrated against them (Arrigo, 1999; Bohm, 1982).

Structural theory. **Structural Marxism** shares the view of instrumental Marxism that capitalist society produces social inequities that lead to crime. Like instrumental Marxists, structural Marxists see the rich as abusing the criminal justice system to impose their will on the poor. They also see poverty and hopelessness as the root causes of criminality. They believe, however, that other autonomous forces within society also influence crime and criminal behavior. While capitalism is evil, all capitalists need not be. Nor are all criminals revolutionaries railing at social injustice (Arrigo, 1999; Bohm, 1982). However, they do agree with the instrumental Marxists in their belief that class struggle is the basis of social conflict.

Critical theory. Based to a large degree on structural Marxism, the emphasis of **critical theory** is that the social order is dominated by class interests and that crime is the product of social inequality (Quinney, 1974). Critical criminologists study the impact of capitalism on government and society. They call for governmental actions to redistribute the wealth, regulate business, and protect the poor from elites (Bohm and Vogel, 2011). While the basis of their critique may be seen as Marxist (although one might argue that liberal criminology now shares many of these criticisms), they do not necessarily call for the total restructuring of society, but instead call for increased governmental intervention on behalf of the poor and the powerless. Their proposed solutions would be appropriately labeled as socialistic.

Radical theory. Radical criminologists also study the effects of capitalism. Their views are more in line with those of instrumental Marxists. Big business is seen as acting in its own behalf. Government is seen as being corrupted by economic interests. Capitalistic society is seen as promoting greed and self-interest, which lead directly to poverty and crime (Quinney, 1980). Unlike critical theory, **radical theory** sees society as needing a total overhaul in which capitalism is replaced by a communist society. Only through the creation of such a society can the twin evils of poverty and crime be eliminated.

Left realism. Criticisms of Marxist theory have flourished. Generally these critiques focus on the lack of quantitative support for Marxist interpretation and its ideological interpretation of social events. Karl Klockars (1980) has provided one of the stronger criticisms of Marxist theory, listing several elements in which it is found lacking. His argument is that Marxists set themselves up as being morally superior and then examine issues through their own ideologically biased prism in order to justify their views. By doing so, they fail to consider their own theoretical weaknesses or the existence of criminality in socialistic societies.

In an effort to address the issues raised by Klockars as well as common assertions of methodological weaknesses, a new generation of Marxists has emerged. These neo-Marxists are more pragmatic and tend to provide empirical rather than subjective support for their arguments. Proponents of **neo-Marxist theories** are recognized as left realists.

Left realism has its roots in the works of Ian Taylor, Paul Walton, and Jock Young. The approach used by Taylor, Walton, and Young (1973) acknowledges that criminals may be found at all levels of the society. Instead of railing about the injustices of capitalistic society, left realists demonstrate how social inequities produce criminal activities at all levels. While acknowledging that socialism would be a preferred solution to easing the burdens of crime and poverty, left realists advocate providing solutions within the existing capitalistic social order. Because of these views, left realists are often criticized by other Marxists as having sold out to pressure from mainstream criminology (Bohm and Vogel, 2011).

Contemporary Criminology

Contemporary criminology covers a variety of modern conflict theories that may or may not include Marxist interpretations. Of the theories that we discuss, all but elitist theory have been categorized as being critical or even radical perspectives (Arrigo, 1999; Bohm and Vogel, 2011). Left realism could also be categorized as a contemporary theory. The contemporary theories presented here include feminism, postmodernism, peacemaking, and elitist theory. Contemporary theories may also be called *neocritical theories.*

Feminist theory. **Feminist theory** covers a spectrum of arguments related to the effects of gender and the inequitable treatment of women within society. While these perspectives vary considerably in their orientation, they share a feminist emphasis not generally found in the criminology literature. As a whole, feminist theories hold that society has traditionally been dominated by males who have sought to subjugate women. Despite considerable advances within contemporary society, women are still seen as being constricted by the chauvinism and paternalism of society's male-oriented power bases (Daly and Chesney-Lind, 1988). The purpose of feminist theory is to provide a female perspective on social inequality and crime.

Liberal feminists argue for more equitable treatment of women within social institutions and recognition of the feminist perspective in dealing with social issues such as the administration of justice. Governmental intervention is seen as necessary to create opportunities for female empowerment and equality. Education of both males and females is viewed as an important mechanism for achieving these results.

Marxist feminists call for the elimination of capitalism as the means of achieving equity for women, the poor, and ethnic minorities (Bohm and Vogel,

2011). Radical feminists see "male aggression and control of female sexuality as the basis for patriarchy and female subjugation" (Hagan, 2011, p. 165). Socialist feminists see capitalistic society as reinforcing male dominance in both the workforce and the home. Rather than seeking to rectify inequitable treatment through education and governmental intervention, socialist feminists stress the need to promote socialism as the cure for the injustices of capitalism (Messerschmidt, 1986).

N. Jane McCandless argues that despite differences within the feminist perspectives, four common principles should be considered in addressing the social inequality of women:

1. *Education*—the necessity of producing and disseminating information so that women can make informed choices.
2. *Egalitarianism*—the need for women to be treated as equals within society.
3. *Empowerment*—enacting changes in the fundamental structure of society that will provide women with the ability to meet their own needs and solve their own problems by taking control of their lives.
4. *Inclusion*—providing women access to career opportunities and equity in pay and earnings potential (McCandless and Conner, 1999).

Postmodernism. A response to the pressures of contemporary society, **postmodernism** argues that the modern emphasis on scientific rationality has reduced the importance of humanistic thinking, causing a multitude of social ills. Proponents of postmodernism desire a return to a simpler, more caring social order that stresses cooperation rather than competition. Branches of postmodernism include poststructuralism, which calls for a simplification of the complex social processes found within modern society; semiotics, which calls for reducing the myriad signs, symbolism, and complex wordings that have complicated social interactions; and deconstruction, which calls for the realignment of the social hierarchy into a simpler, more understandable, and therefore less stressful social order based on social harmony and cooperation (Bohm and Vogel, 2011; Hagan, 2011). Thus far, postmodernism has received only limited support within criminology.

Peacemaking. The reader may have noticed that the work of Richard Quinney has been cited several times. The reason is quite simple. Quinney has been actively involved in the development of several social conflict perspectives. He has, at different stages of his career, advocated social reality theory (Quinney, 1970), critical theory (Quinney, 1974), and radical theory (Quinney, 1980). More recently, he has been instrumental in developing peacemaking criminology theory (Quinney, 1991). While one might wonder at his changes in ideological orientation, he has remained consistent in his zeal for social justice and equity, which are important components of peacemaking criminology.

Peacemaking theory includes a variety of issues within its overall philosophy. These issues are built around the concepts of dispute resolution, restorative justice, and nonviolence. John Fuller (1998) presents the primary tenets of peacemaking criminology within his Peacemaking Paradigm Pyramid (see Figure 9.2). The foundation of peacemaking is nonviolence. Peacemakers stress that the criminal justice system should not condone violence in the application of justice. Coercion, excessive force, and the imposition of the death penalty are seen as contradictory to the goals of justice.

According to Fuller (1998), the following components build on the nonviolence foundation:

- *Social justice*—social injustices such as sexism, racism, and ageism must be dealt with to provide equity and harmony within society.
- *Inclusion*—attempts must be made to involve both the victim and the offender in the dispute resolution process rather than just imposing governmental edicts upon them. Deterrence and punishment goals should be subverted to the mutual needs of victims and offenders.
- *Correct means*—the process by which justice is attained must be addressed, and the legal safeguards of due process must be accorded to offenders.

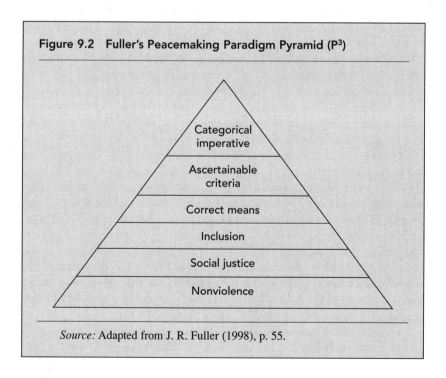

Figure 9.2   Fuller's Peacemaking Paradigm Pyramid (P³)

Categorical imperative

Ascertainable criteria

Correct means

Inclusion

Social justice

Nonviolence

Source: Adapted from J. R. Fuller (1998), p. 55.

- *Ascertainable criteria*—the justice process must be conducted in a manner that all participants understand and have confidence in.
- *Categorical imperative*—the decisions and outcomes of the justice process must be based on moral precepts (reasoning) that are universally applicable to all situations and all persons (Fuller, 1998, pp. 54–57).

These principles are not all-inclusive, but they serve as a model of how the peacemaking perspective is applied. The current strategies for administering justice are believed to actually promote crime and social conflict. By using the peacemaking approach throughout the justice system, peacemakers hope to rectify the shortcomings of a system that is seen as perpetuating its own failure.

Elitist theory. The last neocritical theory that we present is our own **elitist theory**. Our view is that all of the social conflict explanations have merit in their critiques of society and the administration of justice. In particular, theories that consider class and wealth but focus on power struggles between competing interest groups as universal rather than as uniquely the product of capitalism have special appeal. However, the previous theories have looked on the use of power and group conflict as means by which the powerful maintain control over the powerless. Instead, we see power brokers on all points on the political spectrum (conservative, liberal, socialist, communist) conspiring with one another to maintain control over the poor, the working class, and the middle class.

The elitist perspective holds that every society is ruled by an elite oligarchy. These elites may preside over totalitarian governments or they may permit their citizens to enjoy considerable freedom in allegedly democratic societies. Regardless of the nature of the government, the elites conspire to maintain their political control. However, we argue that the behavior of elites may actually benefit the lower classes.

Using precepts espoused by G. William Domhoff (1998), Thomas R. Dye and L. Harman Zeigler (1999), C. Wright Mills (2000), and Thorstein Veblen, (1998), we view power relations as defined through a conflict in which the middle class is exploited by advocates of both the **haves** and **have-nots**. Class struggle is seen as normal and continuous whether the society is capitalist, socialist, or communist. In order to maintain control, the powerful make concessions to the "dangerous classes." However, the concessions are at the expense of the middle class, not the upper class. Through a process known as symbolic reassurance (described in detail in Chapter 14), elites co-opt those who would oppose them. In addition, threats to power are diminished by pitting the lower class and the middle class against each other.

Political and economic elites, despite the considerable differences they present to the public, are in general consensus. Whether they espouse the conservative policies of the traditional capitalistic bourgeois or the liberal policies of the new "bohemian bourgeois" (Brooks, 2001), their actions are based on their own upper-class self-interests. Ironically, they maintain their power by promoting conflict within society. By appealing to class, race, and gender divisions, they are able to impose their collective will on the populace. Only when there is such considerable discontent within society that their position of authority is threatened will they respond to pressures from the middle class. However, the response is measured only to the extent necessary to defuse the perceived threats.

Posturing on issues such as "making the rich pay their fair share" and "tax cuts benefit only the affluent," and alleging that "certain programs would hurt women, minorities, and the poor" enable liberal elites in government to generate support for their programs. Posturing by conservative elites on issues such as "eliminating welfare" and "eliminating affirmative action," and arguing that "big government is causing economic harm to the working and middle classes" help conservative elites find support for their programs. These are actually only tokens provided to ensure that their control is continued. For the most part, there are few differences in how elites actually govern. An example of elitism in action is the operation of the social security system as a pyramid scheme that would be unlawful in the private sector. Likewise, the theft of social security funds to create an alleged budget surplus was a result of agreement between Democrats and Republicans in Washington, DC.

Elitist theory holds that seeking to dramatically overhaul the current system of government (through either revolution or the ballot) would only replace one group of elites with another. Therefore, the key to reducing conflict and crime within society lies in educating the middle class about how they are being used to provide the resources to placate the lower class. These efforts would not result in a change in the political structure but would obtain more concessions on behalf of the middle class, whose conformity is the source of stability for the continuance of society.

Integrated Conflict Theories

Integrated conflict theories are premised on the conflictive nature of society. John Hagan's power control theory and Mark Colvin and John Pauly's integrated structural Marxist theory are innovative mergers of different conflict perspectives.

Power control theory. As the reader will have noted, many of the integrated sociological theories focus on the influence of families on youthful deviance. Hagan (2003) continues this focus with an innovative description of relations within the family setting to explain why female delinquency is less frequent than male delinquency. In power control theory, females are seen as less likely

Reality Check: Ponzi Schemes

Charles Ponzi

Charles Ponzi was an Italian immigrant who had big dreams. As a clerk in a Montreal bank, he was caught forging checks and served three years in prison. When he was released in 1917, Ponzi blundered upon a scheme in which he was able to cash postal reply coupons for five times their value. He shared his secret with friends, who were delighted with the return on their money. Soon he was making $250,000 a day. In less than eight months he collected $10 million.

Despite fears that he was using monies from new investors to pay older investors, Ponzi soon collected another $5 million. When he was arrested by federal agents for running a pyramid scheme, Ponzi had bilked 40,000 investors out of a total of $15 million. He was sentenced to five years in a federal prison and an additional seven years in a Massachusetts prison. In 1934 he was deported back to Italy. From that time onward, illegal schemes that defraud investors have been known as "Ponzi schemes."

Bernie Madoff

Bernard Lawrence "Bernie" Madoff was a stockbroker and investment banker in New York. In 1960 he formed a Wall Street firm, Bernard L. Madoff Investment Securities, LLC. He served as its chairman until his arrest on December 11, 2008. Although Madoff's wealth-management business ultimately grew into a multibillion-dollar operation, none of the major derivatives firms traded with him because they didn't think his numbers were real. Federal investigators began looking into Madoff's operation in 2007 when complaints began arising about his questionable business practices. In 2008, he was finally arrested on federal felony charges of securities fraud, wire fraud, mail fraud, money laundering, making false statements, perjury, theft from an employee benefit plan, and making false filings with the US Securities and Exchange Commission.

Madoff claimed that he did not begin his scheme until 1990, but federal investigators believe that he may have begun as early as 1970. While the amount of money that he defrauded from his investors is not known for certain, it is estimated that he collected more than $36 billion in recent years, of which he paid out about half to investors to make it appear that he was running a legitimate business. In 2009, Madoff pled guilty to eleven federal charges. He received a maximum sentence of 150 years in prison.

continues

> **Reality Check,** *continued*
>
> The federal complaint that motivated Madoff to plead guilty stated that over twenty years, Madoff had defrauded his clients of almost $65 billion. Investors included such diverse groups as celebrities, educational institutions, and charitable organizations. It is believed that Madoff's operation was the largest Ponzi scheme in history. So far only $1.5 billion has been recovered.
>
> *How would a non-Marxist conflict theorist view the fraudulent activities that led to Madoff's arrest? How would a Marxist theorist describe them?*

to engage in risk-taking because of the socialization that occurs within the home. Male dominance within the home is thought to impose submissive behaviors on young women. Since young men are given more "freedom to deviate" within this chauvinistic environment, they are more likely to engage in deviance.

Hagan argues that larger gender differences in delinquent activities will be seen in patriarchal families. Conversely, egalitarian families will have smaller gender differences in delinquency. Female-headed households produce higher levels of female delinquency than other types of households. Using this knowledge, Hagan postulates that as female equality within the workplace creates a more equitable home environment, female delinquency will increase. Conversely, it will also eventually have the positive effect of lowering levels of female victimization in domestic situations.

Integrated structural Marxist theory. Colvin and Pauly (1983) also explore domestic relations in their integrated structural Marxist theory, wherein the coercive workplace environment of capitalism contributes to coercive family environments. Negative relations in the workplace are said to create strain and alienation in the domestic setting. Frustrations that the parents bring home from their jobs are displaced onto family members. In particular, parents are likely to excessively exercise the controls that they have over their children as compensation for their powerlessness at work and in a capitalistic society.

This repressive home environment causes strain in the family. Consequently, the normal bonds of family are drastically weakened. Coercive school situations further aggravate the frustrations that young people feel. They may, in expressing their frustration and hopelessness, act out in a violent manner and/or engage in deviant behaviors as a means of seeking positive rewards that are otherwise unattainable. This theory is thought to be a significant contribution to the Marxist literature in that it clearly demonstrates how capitalism can promote delinquency.

Summary

Conflict theories attempt to identify society's power relations and draw attention to their role in promoting criminal behavior. Basically, conflict theory views crime as the ability of those groups in power to protect themselves and their interests, thus leading those who are not in power toward criminal behavior. Three categories of conflict theories were examined: non-Marxist, Marxist, and contemporary.

Non-Marxist conflict theories stress that social conflict is prevalent within society. Interest group competition and power and authority relationships create power struggles within society. Class and economic issues are only a part of the myriad political causes contested within these struggles. Vold's group conflict theory postulates that conflict between groups should be viewed as one of the principal and essential social processes upon which the continuance of society depends. Weber's status theory presents power and prestige as key issues within social conflict. Dahrendorf saw class conflict as integral to social conflict. Quinney's social reality theory advocates that conflict is intertwined with power and that differential distribution of power produces conflict, which is rooted in the competition for power. Turk's criminalization theory examines the conditions under which cultural and social differences between authorities and subjects will probably result in conflict.

The two main individuals credited with the development of Marxist criminology are Marx and Bonger. Marx was the social philosopher who developed the economic concepts upon which Marxism is based. Bonger was the social scientist who first applied Marxist concepts to criminology. There are many Marxist views. Those discussed within this chapter include instrumental Marxism, which sees capitalism as the root of social conflict and crime; structural Marxism, which also views capitalism as evil but considers other social influences; critical theory, which is comparable to structural Marxism; and radical theory, which is comparable to instrumental Marxism. Left realism is a more pragmatic approach that uses empirical techniques in the study of social conflict.

Contemporary theories may also be called neocritical theories. The contemporary theories discussed are feminist, postmodernism, peacemaking, and elitist theory. Feminist theories include liberal, Marxist, socialist, and radical. However, they share a common concern for education, egalitarianism, empowerment, and inclusion of women. Postmodernism seeks to return to a kinder, gentler society by reducing the complexities of modern life. Peacemaking offers the precepts of nonviolence, social justice, inclusion, correct means, ascertainable criteria, and categorical imperative to create a fair and equitable justice system. Elitist theory sees society's elites as forcing concessions from the middle class to placate the lower class.

Integrated conflict theories are innovative mergers of differing conflict perspectives. Hagan's power control theory explores the family dynamics that influence delinquency. Patriarchal families are seen as having greater gender differences in regard to delinquency. Egalitarian families are more likely to have smaller gender differences in delinquency. Colvin and Pauly's integrated structural Marxist theory argues that the coercive workplace environment of capitalism contributes to coercive family environments.

Discussion Questions

1. Conflict theory says that the definition of any behavior as immoral, deviant, or criminal must be viewed as tentative, at best, and that it is always subject to redefinition. Do you agree? Who should make this redefinition?

2. Conflict theorists debate that there are three basic means to maintaining and enhancing society's interests: force, compromise, and the dominance of social institutions such as law, church, schools, and government. Which means do you believe is the best for the United States? Are there other means?

3. Law is viewed as an instrument of power, that is, as an extremely potent weapon of social conflict in that whoever has control over the laws retains power. If this is true, how will any other class but the elite ever have power? Isn't there power in numbers regardless of social status?

4. On what should contemporary criminologists focus their energy? Does female criminality really differ so much from that of males such that it requires a separate set of theories?

10

Integrated and Holistic Theories

As noted in Chapter 3, criminology does not draw its theoretical basis from any one discipline. In the previous chapters, you were exposed to a variety of legal, psychological, biological, and sociological explanations of crime, ranging from individual offender orientations to societal interpretations. Just as no one medicine cures all illnesses, no one theory explains all crime. Therefore, criminologists approach the study of crime and criminality from a number of perspectives.

While an individual criminologist may prefer a particular discipline's perspective (e.g., biological or psychological), another may use a very different technique (e.g., sociological or legal) in his or her studies. Indeed, there is often a great deal of disagreement among criminologists who share similar views of the fundamental causes of crime (variation is readily apparent among critical criminologists). It is for these reasons that better criminology programs tend to hire faculty from divergent disciplines or those whose training was interdisciplinary.

Integrated Theories

An interdisciplinary approach to the study of criminology produces explanations that use two or more of the "standard criminological theories" within their theoretical perspectives. These are known as integrated theories. This chapter examines the better-known integrated theories: integrated classical theories, integrated biological theories, integrated psychological theories, and integrated sociological theories. The integrated theories to be discussed are shown in Figure 10.1.

Integrated Biological Theories

Integrated biological theories stress the importance of physiological factors on an individual's behaviors. Yet, they seek to explain how these natural fea-

Figure 10.1 Integrated Theories

Integrated Biological Theories	Integrated Psychological Theories	Integrated Sociological Theories
Bioconditioning	Delinquency development	Integrated learning
Human nature	Age-graded	Integrated control
Developmental theory	Self-derogation	Integrated strain

tures are influenced by psychological and/or sociological factors. A number of integrated biological explanations were discussed as biosocial theories in Chapter 5. In this section, we limit our discussion to Hans Eysenck's bioconditioning theory and James Q. Wilson and Richard Herrnstein's **human nature theory**.

Bioconditioning theory. **Bioconditioning theory** (Eysenck and Gudjonsson, 1989) merges biology, behavioral psychology, and classical criminology. The premise of bioconditioning theory is that guilt and conscience are conditioned responses to pleasure and pain. How well behavior is conditioned is due to biological influences. Extroverts are seen as being more outgoing and needing more external stimulation than are introverts. As a result of these stimulation needs, extroverts are less likely to accept pleasure/pain conditioning. Therefore, they are more likely to engage in behaviors that are delinquent or criminal. This theory was discussed briefly in Chapter 5.

Although biological factors are said to contribute to crime and delinquency, social factors are seen as providing the conditioning that leads to crime. Eysenck argues that permissive child-rearing practices result in underdeveloped consciences. To remedy this problem, he contends that behavioral psychology should be applied to modify deviant behaviors (Eysenck and Gudjonsson, 1989).

Human nature theory. James Q. Wilson and Richard J. Herrnstein (1985) proposed another integrated biological theory, human nature theory. They contend that genetic makeup, intelligence, and body type have considerable impact on human behavior. Individuals' personalities are influenced by these physical features that shape how they see themselves as well as how others see them. Like Eysenck, Wilson and Herrnstein stress the importance of biological and psychological factors in the behavioral choices that humans make. They differ from Eysenck in their recommendations for influencing those choices.

According to Wilson and Herrnstein (1985), human decisionmaking is a product of the interactions of biological, psychological, and sociological influences. To overcome predispositions that may lead to crime choices, they call for programs to aid families and schools in teaching children moral standards. Personal responsibility is an integral component of these moral teachings. These precrime interventions are seen as preferable to imposing harsh punishments after criminal behaviors have occurred.

Developmental theory. Terrie E. Moffitt and her associates have developed a theoretical explanation as to why most antisocial children do not become adult criminals. This theory is a blend of biological, psychological, and sociological theories. As such, this theory is considered to be biosocial, in that it blends biological factors with environmental influences. This perspective may also be seen as *life course criminology* in that it explains how personality changes as adolescents mature bring about behavioral changes.

Moffitt's perspective clearly demonstrates that personality and behavior changes are products of nature and nurture. To explain why most youthful offenders do not become adult offenders, Moffitt (1993) developed a two-path explication. Those people who persist in misbehavior throughout life are referred to as *life course persisters*. These offenders are influenced by neuropsychological deficits (such as early brain damage or chemical imbalances) that, combined with poverty and family dysfunction, cause them to fail in school and become involved in delinquency in early life. As time passes, their opportunities for legitimate success become increasingly limited (Moffitt, 1993; Schmalleger, 2012). A greater number of adolescents are *adolescence-limited offenders*. These young people may be involved in significant offending during their mid-teens due to structural disadvantages. The more influential of these structural disadvantages is status anxiety of teenagers as they transition from adolescence to adulthood. Biological maturity at an early age (and children's subsequent desire for sexual and emotional relationships as well as personal autonomy) conflicts with social restrictions to create a "maturity gap" (Moffitt, 1993). This creates conflicts in which adolescence-limited offenders engage in delinquent activities.

Caspi and colleagues (2002) further determined that maltreatment of children can lead to changes in genetic makeup that influence antisocial behavior. Therefore, the social condition of maltreatment can cause psychological and biological changes that may lead to them becoming life course persisters. Their findings are supported by recent studies indicating that teen behaviors such as fast driving, drug use, and risky sex may be due to a neurological gap in the developing brain (Zimmer, 2011). This research supports the thesis that the human brain is designed to help adolescents face the risks that come with a new stage in life but can create an affinity for taking risks that explains the actions and later movement from delinquency found in adolescence-limited offenders.

Integrated Psychological Theories

Integrated psychological theories explain how social factors can influence individual self-perception. These may also be called psychosocial theories or social psychological theories. Some of the theories that were discussed in Chapter 7 could just as readily have been located here; conversely, these theories could also have been discussed within Chapter 7. We selected them for inclusion here because they are good examples of the integration of psychological and sociological approaches, not exclusive examples of such. The theories included here are David Farrington's delinquency development theory, Robert Sampson and John Laub's age-graded theory, and Howard Kaplan's self-derogation theory.

Delinquency development theory. Farrington (1988) used his analyses of longitudinal studies of delinquent boys to theorize that delinquent behavior patterns emerge early in life and that these behaviors become more developed as the child matures. According to Farrington's **delinquency development theory**, there is continuity in criminal behavior that reaches from early childhood into the adult years. Social and economic conditions are seen as influencing children and their parents, and the actions of parents and older siblings in response to these conditions serve as models for the children. Children raised in poverty who have role models who are criminal are likely to adopt criminogenic tendencies.

The development of a deviant personality is the likely product of poor child rearing, economic deprivation, and resentment of social responses to prior deviance. After the deviant personality has emerged, it is reinforced by continued criminal activities. Life experiences influence future behavior choices. Some individuals will abandon deviant behaviors in adulthood. However, the personality is often so well established that behavior change is not possible. The cycle of criminality continues as the children of these deviant-personality adults are subjected to the same bonding and social learning influences that shaped their parents' personalities.

Age-graded theory. Sampson and Laub (1993) used a delinquent maturation approach similar to Farrington's. Social structure factors (e.g., poverty) and social control processes (e.g., family and peer deviance) interact with individual factors (e.g., temperament, learning difficulties) to create delinquent behaviors. Outcomes from social responses to delinquent behaviors then interact with the prior influences to reduce or reinforce future behaviors. Unlike Farrington's delinquency development theory, Sampson and Laub's **age-graded theory** does not see the deviant personality as necessarily being developed at an early age. Therefore, positive life events as the delinquent matures may well lead to a cessation in delinquent activity. The building of social capital (i.e., obtaining work, school success, and marriage) enables the previously delinquent person to reject future criminal behaviors.

Self-derogation theory. Howard B. Kaplan (1975) proposed the **self-derogation theory** of delinquency, which emphasizes **self-esteem** as integral to the occurrence of delinquent behavior. According to Kaplan, each person has a "self-esteem motive" that causes him or her to try to maximize positive perceptions of self and minimize negative perceptions of self. In a process that uses strain, social control, labeling, social learning, and cognitive concepts, youths are seen as turning to deviant groups and activities if they are unable to construct positive self-perceptions within conventional groups or activities.

If young people are unsuccessful in school, in their family, or in peer activities, they are less likely to accept social controls imposed by those groups. Conventional behaviors are seen as contributing to self-derogation. Delinquent alternatives are seen as means of enhancing self-esteem and countering self-derogation. The importance of peer groups is stressed within this perspective. Subsequent involvement in conventional or deviant activities is influenced by the individual's self-perceptions. If conventional opportunities emerge (such as participating in extracurricular activities) that enhance self-perceptions, the youth may return to conventional behaviors. If conventional opportunities are not available or do not enhance perceptions, deviant activities and associations will continue.

Integrated Sociological Theories

Perhaps the best-known integrated theory is Robert Burgess and Ronald Akers's (1966) differential reinforcement theory. Because we have discussed it in Chapter 8, we will not do so again, but we use it as an example of how criminologists may disagree on the nature of a theory and where it should be classified. For the most part, the theories discussed in this section combine two or more sociological explanations of crime and criminality. **Integrated sociological theories** include **integrated learning theories** and **integrated control theories**. Integrated strain theories and integrated conflict theories were discussed in Chapter 7.

Integrated learning theories. Integrated learning theories emphasize social learning theory as the foundation for their explanations of criminal behavior. The theories reviewed here are Marvin Krohn's network analysis and Terence Thornberry's interactional theory.

Network analysis theory. Marvin D. Krohn (1986) merged aspects of social learning theory with social bonding theory in his network analysis approach.

The nature and extent of social learning and social bonding are said to be based upon social and personal networks. These networks include friends, family, peers, teachers, and other people and institutions with whom the young person interacts. How these networks influence the youth is said to depend on multiplexity and density. *Multiplexity* refers to the number of activities that specific individuals have in common with one another in their daily activities; *density* refers to the total number of contacts that an individual might have with others in the community.

According to Krohn, the learning that occurs and the bonding that takes place within a community may be either conventional or deviant. If contacts with deviant individuals are frequent due to multiplexity (several common activities) and significant due to a lack of density (few interactions with others), then deviant behaviors are reinforced. Conversely, if conventional contacts dominate, conventional behaviors are reinforced.

Interactional theory. In interactional theory, Terrence P. Thornberry (1987) incorporates social learning theory, social bonding, cognitive theory, and social structure theories of criminal behavior to explain delinquency. As in the maturation theories discussed earlier, Thornberry sees delinquency activities as changing over time. As youths enter adolescence, their bonds to their parents and social institutions are said to weaken. Peer groups become more important to them. If these young people reside in socially disorganized environments, they are at high risk to have weak social bonds and peers who engage in deviance. Adolescents who are from more stable environments may engage in deviancy (they are, after all, adolescents), but their actions are better controlled by stronger social bonds and associations with peers who engage in more conventional behaviors.

Thornberry sees delinquent behaviors as influenced by age. As young people enter their late teens, the influence of peers gives way to perceptions of their roles in society (i.e., work activities, involvement in social institutions, and domestic relationships). As commitment to these conventional influences increases, deviant activities decrease. Therefore, Thornberry argues that involvement in delinquency is a dynamic social process that changes over time.

Integrated control theories. Integrated control theories use the social control perspective as the foundation of their integrated approaches. The social control emphasis may be easily observed in Charles Tittle's control balance theory, Joseph Weis's social development theory, and John Braithwaite's reintegrative shaming.

Control balance theory. **Control balance theory** merges concepts from social control, social learning, rational choice, and anomie. Charles R. Tittle (1995, p. 142) proposes that "the amount of control to which people are subject relative to the amount of control that they exercise affects the general probability that they will commit specific types of deviance." In other words, you do not always have control over your behavior, but are subject to the control of others. Even in those situations in which you do have control over your behavior, it is not certain that you will exercise that control. Whether or not you choose to exercise behavioral control is dependent upon four factors: predisposition, provocation, opportunity, and constraint.

Predisposition is defined by Tittle as deviant motivations. For any number of reasons, a potential offender may be inclined to engage in criminal behavior. Provocation refers to the positive or negative stimulation that will be derived from the behavior. Opportunity is the actual chance to commit an act of deviance. And constraint is the actual or perceived likelihood of being subject to restraints imposed by others.

According to Tittle, the probability of deviance is higher when the control ratio (likelihood of control to actual ability to control) is not in balance. When the control ratio is balanced, the probability of deviance is lower. The rationale for these actions is that people who have control surpluses (a great deal of actual control over their actions, with little restraint from others) are likely to engage in exploitative or decadent behaviors. People with control deficits (little actual control over their behaviors) are likely to engage in predatory, defiant, or submissive behaviors. People who have a balance of control are not as likely to engage in deviance. This view of deviance as responding to control opportunities is useful in explaining not only juvenile delinquency but adult behaviors as well.

Social development theory. Another integrated control theory has been presented by Weis and his associates at the Seattle Social Development Project (Weis and Hawkins, 1981; Weis and Sederstrom, 1981). **Social development theory** is based on social control theory augmented by social learning and structural modeling. According to social development theory, young children are socialized through family interactions. The opportunities for interactions, the degree of involvement in interactions, the skills to participate in interactions, and the reinforcement of participation are all thought to affect the family bonds that develop. In strong, supportive families, children develop prosocial bonds that will aid them in resisting antisocial behaviors as they mature. If the family bonds are lacking or the family's commitment to conventional behaviors is weak, the child will be more susceptible to developing antisocial behaviors.

Even in supportive, law-abiding families, as the child matures, interactions with peers and other adults outside the family may result in the development of antisocial bonds that facilitate antisocial behaviors. Young people's position within the social structure, their interaction skills, the strength of their family interactions, and their perceptions of the rewards of engaging in deviance all factor into whether they will participate in antisocial behaviors. They also influence whether they will develop antisocial values from having done so.

The strength of family commitments provides a foundation for the development of commitments to school and other social institutions but does not guarantee that interactions with deviant others or social influences will not overcome these commitments by providing rewards for antisocial behaviors. Subsequent attachments to deviant peers and antisocial activities may then result in the adoption of antisocial beliefs and values.

Despite the impact of antisocial influences and deviant peers, Weis and his associates see strong bonds to family and school as integral in young people's ability to resist delinquent behaviors.

Reintegrative shaming theory. Braithwaite (1989) integrates the theories of control, labeling, social learning, and strain in his **reintegrative shaming theory**. Shaming, as seen by Braithwaite (1989, p. 100), includes "all social processes of expressing disapproval which have the intention or effect of invoking remorse in the person being shamed and/or condemnation by others who become aware of the shaming." Shaming is divided into two categories: stigmatization and **reintegration**. Stigmatization occurs when the labeling of the offender causes that person to feel deviant; reintegration occurs when, despite the shaming, the condemners ensure that they maintain bonds with the offender. Stigmatization is seen as causing additional criminality stemming from the acquired sense of deviance. Reintegration is seen as allowing the offender to acknowledge his or her wrongful behavior and then gain reentry into the conforming group.

According to Braithwaite, offenders who have stronger social bonds are more likely to reject deviance and return to conformity. The cohesiveness of the social structure and opportunities for legitimate behaviors affect the strengths of the social bonds. In turn, the strengths of the bonds affect the nature and extent of the shaming as well as how the offender responds to it.

Holistic Incorporation Theories

The benefit of criminology taking an interdisciplinary science approach rather than adhering to a single discipline is that it enables scholars to view a specific type of crime or criminal offender from several perspectives (Jeffery, 1977a, 1977b, 1990). Rather than a one-dimensional picture, multiple disciplinary approaches allow criminologists to see the entire panorama. Unfortunately, such an approach can be so general in nature that it is difficult to test and even more difficult to apply (Hagan, 2011). Because of these difficulties, most contemporary theories of crime and criminality emphasize a single disciplinary approach to a specific crime or criminal type. However, one should not become so fixed on one perspective that the benefits of other methods are overlooked.

Despite the problems inherent in using an integrated theoretical perspective, a number of efforts have combined multifactor perspectives regarding crime and criminality into more holistic (general) explanations. Four of the better-known efforts at **holistic incorporation** of criminological theories are C. Ray Jeffery's bioenvironmental theory, Ronald Akers's conceptual absorption, Frank Pearson and Nerl Weiner's conceptual integration, and Bryan Vilas's general paradigm. The theories discussed in this chapter are shown in Figure 10.2.

Jeffery's Bioenvironmental Theory. Jeffery's (1977, 1977a, 1977b, 1990) **bioenvironmental theory** argues that human behavior is the product of complex and constantly changing interactions between the physical environment and the social environment. Nature creates a predisposition for certain behaviors. Nurture creates opportunities for the behaviors to occur and also provides reinforcement for subsequent occurrences.

According to Jeffery, the physical environment includes biochemical activities within the brain, the effects of air and water pollution, ingestion of chemical substances, physiological defects that impact the brain and central nervous system, and damage from physical trauma. The social environment includes all social interactions at all levels (individual to societal) that might influence an individual's perceptions of him- or herself and others. Because of the enormity of investigating all social and physical interactions, Jeffery has focused his efforts on exploring how biological deficiencies can cause maladaptive behaviors.

Akers's Conceptual Absorption Theory. Akers and Sellers (2009) argue that we already have theory integration in criminology because of conceptual absorption. In his **conceptual absorption theory**, Akers posits that the concepts used to explain the behaviors of criminal offenders are compatible and in some cases the same as concepts used by other theories. Akers compares social learning theory and other sociological theories to demonstrate that they explain the same behavioral processes. Therefore, integration is

---

Figure 10.2　Holistic Theories

Holistic Incorporation Theories	General Theories
Bioenvironmental theory	Self-control theory
Conceptual absorption theory	Integrative delinquency theory
Conceptual integration theory	Identity theory
General paradigm theory	

said to have already occurred to a considerable degree. The difference is one of terminology.

In short, Akers and Sellers (2009) argue that all criminal behavior can be said to be based on social learning because every other theory uses social learning components. However, Akers is the first to acknowledge that such a broad interpretation provides little insight into criminal behavior other than noting that learning is involved in all the social theories.

Pearson and Weiner's Conceptual Integration. Yet another holistic interpretation is provided by Pearson and Weiner (1985). Like the previous two explanations, **conceptual integration theory** does not provide an integrated theory as much as a framework that demonstrates how other theories complement one another. The basis for the theoretical framework is that eight concepts can be identified in all criminological theories. Concepts that determine behavior are:

1. Utility
2. Behavior skill
3. Signs of opportunities to commit crimes
4. Behavioral resources
5. Rules of expedience
6. Rules of morality

Consequences of the behavior are interpreted by:

7. Utility receptions
8. Information acquisition

Like Akers's theory, the Pearson and Weiner framework is predominantly an effort to incorporate all other theories into a social learning explanation. While it has received some support, most notably from Akers and Sellers (2009), it has limited application as a theoretical model.

Vila's General Paradigm. The fourth holistic approach is Vila's **general paradigm theory** for understanding criminal behavior. According to Vila (1994), a theory must include ecological, integrative, developmental, and both macro- and micro-level explanations if it is to explain all types of criminal behavior. Theories that include only one component or explain only one type of crime are seen as only partial theories. General theories, in Vila's view, must incorporate biological, sociocultural, and developmental factors into complex and constantly changing ecological interactions.

A primary assumption in Vila's paradigm is that all crimes are the product of human desire to acquire "resources." The type of resource desired (material, hedonistic, or political) and ecological factors determine the type of crimes committed (or not committed). How these interactions occur is demonstrated within a complex "mathematical chaos model" that incorporates all factors rather than using a traditional linear model of analysis. Like the previous explanations, Vila's paradigm has great appeal in its general explanation. However, it shares the same weakness as the others in that the broadness of the approach limits its applicability. The complex methodology required for assessing this paradigm is also an impediment to its application.

General Theories of Crime and Criminality

Single-factor approaches to crime causation do not adequately explain the myriad criminal offenders and criminal behaviors studied within criminology. However, **multifactor approaches** (such as the integrated theories presented in Chapter 7 and holistic incorporation efforts presented thus far in this chapter) attempt to apply a particular theoretical framework to a specific crime or crime type. Other explanations (as seen in the Akers model, the Pearson and Weiner model, and Jeffery's bioenvironmental approach) are so broad as to require single-factor assessments in order to be applied to criminal behavior. What is needed is a theoretical explanation that can be applied to a number of crimes and offenders without being so broad as to be useless in its practical application. The following section reviews two attempts at theoretical integration that accomplish this goal with varying degrees of success. These theories are Michael Gottfredson and Travis Hirschi's self-control theory and Donald Shoemaker's integrative delinquency theory.

Self-control theory. Gottfredson and Hirschi's (1990) **self-control theory** merges concepts of control theory with rational choice, routine activities, and biological and psychological explanations. Integral to their explanation is that crime and criminal behavior are different concepts. People who engage in criminal acts are seen as having low self-control. They engage in many conventional behaviors, but due to low self-control, they are predisposed to committing crimes if opportunities arise. This explanation explains all types of crimes and criminal behaviors.

According to Gottfredson and Hirschi, the causes of crime are impulsive personality, low self-control, weakened social bonds, and criminal opportunities. An impulsive personality is developed by certain biological and psychological factors. Low self-control is a product of impulsive personality combined with social factors such as deviant parents and poor supervision. Weakened social bonds are the product of low self-control and the subsequent development of alternative attachments, involvements, commitments, and beliefs. If criminal opportunities should come about, the combination of low self-control and weakened social bonds will very likely result in crime.

While self-control theory has been criticized as too general as well as tautological, it is perhaps the clearest and most understandable theory to date that incorporates biological, psychological, and sociological influences (Akers and Sellers, 2009).

Integrative delinquency theory. Gottfredson and Hirschi explain how low self-control can influence criminality; in his theory of integrative delinquency, Shoemaker (2009) emphasizes self-esteem as integral to understanding juvenile delinquency. According to Shoemaker, a juvenile's self-esteem is determined by interactions with conforming adults, and these interactions may result in a positive or negative **self-concept**. The linkage of self-concept to criminal behavior may be direct but is more often an indirect influence that interacts with other influences. Influences on behavior are said to be structural (relating to social conditions), individual (biological and psychological), and social psychological (social controls, self-esteem, and peer associations).

In this model, individual and structural conditions indirectly influence delinquency, first through social controls and later through self-esteem and peer associations. Weakened social bonds created by structural and/or individual situations lead to lowered self-concept and increased association with deviants. As attachments to deviant associates are strengthened, conventional attachments are weakened. The combination of weakened social bonds, lowered self-concept, and negative peer influences directly and powerfully influence delinquency (Shoemaker, 2009).

Like self-control theory, **integrative delinquency theory** provides a rational explanation of how biological, psychological, and sociological factors can be incorporated into a general explanation of criminality. Unfortunately, it may also be seen by critics of multifactor approaches as too general and as having restricted applicability.

A Synopsis of Integrated and Holistic Theories

Integrated theories must emphasize both the physical and social environments. Otherwise, they offer little more than do single-factor explanations. Integrated crime explanations cannot just provide a broad framework, however; they must be adaptable to explain specific behaviors. Some of the theories discussed in the previous chapters accomplish this task, but most do not. The complexities of holistic incorporation theories limit their application in explaining specific criminal behaviors.

The two general theories that we have just discussed are more readily adapted to explaining specific criminal behaviors, though Shoemaker's integrative delinquency theory is limited in that its focus is to explain how delinquent behavior develops. Of the theories that we have discussed, it is our opinion that Gottfredson and Hirschi's self-control theory best explains crime and criminality. Nevertheless, we believe a need for improvement remains.

Identity Theory

The final holistic theory that we discuss is our own **identity theory**, which might also be called enviro-classical conflict, in that it draws from a variety of approaches that might ordinarily be seen as incompatible. It is our view that rather than being incompatible, these seemingly contradictory perspectives actually complement one another in creating a general theory of crime and criminality. Our premise is quite simple: criminal behavior is the product of nature and nurture. The determination of whether behavior will be criminal depends on how the individual and society interrelate. These interrelationships are influenced by complex and constantly changing biological, psychological, and social factors.

The biological factors that influence human behavior include physiological (physical attractiveness, physical size, and gender), genetic (gender, ethnicity, and intelligence), and environmental (effects of pollution and diet). These influences interact with psychological factors, including problem-solving abilities, emotional stability, personality, and belief systems. These combined influences interact with sociological factors, such as social structure, economic systems, culture, family, religion, class, ethnicity, gender, and sexual orientation. These complex interrelationships are constant and frequently conflictive. Compared to this complex approach, single-factor theories, though useful to describe group activities, can be seen as inadequate to explain the actions of individual offenders.

In order to understand crime and criminality at the individual level, the combined effects of the previously discussed factors must be considered. However, this does not mean that criminologists must evaluate a lengthy checklist of environmental factors for each criminal offender. Instead, it means that we must locate an indicator of those influences that will then enable us to assess criminality. Previous considerations of self-concept and self-esteem have proven valuable in explaining the development of criminal and deviant behaviors. It is our belief that these concepts should be expanded into a theory of human behavior based on personal identity.

Human beings have an innate need to feel worthy. It is important that people significant to us feel that we are worthwhile, but it is even more important that we feel self-worth. Every action that we take in dealing with others and in dealing with ourselves is a product of our desire for positive self-worth. All human behavior, no matter how compassionate or selfless, is driven by the desire to feel good about ourselves. Thorstein Veblen (1998) saw greed as motivation not only for seemingly selfish acts but for altruistic acts as well. The basis of this view is that we will do whatever is necessary to have positive feelings.

As human beings we have many desires. Food, shelter, and material comforts are fundamental concerns. But ego needs ultimately determine behavior. It is our argument that ego gratification is necessary for mental and emotional well-being. Without this gratification, we cannot maintain a positive self-image, and without a positive self-image, we have no identity. Therefore, in order to develop and maintain our personal identity, we do what we think is necessary to enhance our self-worth.

If our ecological makeup has disposed us to being gregarious and outgoing, our self-identity is influenced by what others think of us. If we have suffered rejection, frustration, and loneliness, we may come to rely solely upon our own self-image. Social bonds and controls are important but only if they contribute to a positive identity. If such social influences should happen to lead to identity conflict, we will do what is necessary to remove negative stimuli so as to reestablish our positive identity. The means by which we remove negative stimuli may be to conform to social pressures or it may be to reject the sources of those pressures. These actions may range from internal responses (cognitive acceptance or denial) to efforts on a societal level (attempting to change the social and economic order). Whether these individual responses are criminal or lawful may be due more to the opinions of others than to the personal ideology of the respondent. The choice of lawful or criminal behavior is determined by whether compliance or deviance best serves our identity needs.

While ecological concerns have substantial impact, broad social factors are also influential. As indicated earlier, we choose our actions based on what aids us in maintaining our identity. If we have been socialized into the view that work status is important, we shall seek to enhance our work status. If we are unable to do so, maintaining our positive identity requires that we reject such status labels. This rejection may not be deviant and may seek to lawfully alter the system or circumstances that created the threat to our identity.

Identity theory is compatible with all other explanations of criminal behavior. Classical theory stresses the need for individual responsibility; so does identity theory. But whether that responsibility is socially acceptable is not as important as whether it promotes a positive identity. Fortunately, because of early socialization efforts, most of us comply with classical mandates not out of fear of punishment but because it makes us feel good about ourselves.

We support the punishment of others because that also makes us feel good about ourselves. We may support positive theories for similar identity support. Likewise, we may advocate Marxist ideologies because our perceived involvement in the struggle for equality enables us to maintain (or further develop) our positive identity.

Identity theory can explain both legal and illegal behaviors committed by all classes of people and all categories of crime. For example, racism can be explained as the product of socialization that leads to hostility and contempt for other races. This hostility may result in any number of behaviors, but ultimately those behaviors will be selected based on what is deemed most bene-

Reality Check: The Problem of Toxic Agers

One issue that often emerges in separating victims from offenders is that of age. Usually, when we discuss the elderly and crime we are referring to their vulnerability to becoming victims. However, people do not necessarily become nicer as they grow older. In fact, some people actually become more evil. This is so frequent that gerontologists actually have a title for them, "toxic agers." According to Gloria Davenport (1999, p. 8), "Toxic agers are older adults, usually in their 70's and 80's who consistently act out defensive, negative behavior that is based upon ego-distorted perceptions, values, beliefs, messages and experiences."

The development of toxic behavior in elder adults is seen as a product of life events going all the way back to the individual's youth. Or as an elderly woman described a particularly offensive octogenarian, "I've known 'Emmalee' her entire life; she has always been a self-serving bitch. Now that she's old, people cater to her and she has gotten even worse." The individual in question had been involved in political intrigues within a small town for more than fifty years. During that time, she had consistently misused her authority as a school administrator and member of the city council to reward her friends and punish her enemies. She later gained control of the local historical society and a city park. It is estimated that as much as $300,000 that had been raised within that park had been misappropriated by her and her associates over many years.

When questions arose about her activities from a new park board member, Emmalee organized supporters to protest the involvement of "outsiders" in daring to question her behaviors. These activities included physical threats and vandalism, in addition to threatened legal actions, organized disruptions of board meetings, and false accusations about park board members and their families. The small-town politicians chose to ignore what was occurring. Interestingly, when the local district attorney was asked for assistance, she refused, stating, "You've got to be crazy. No one in this county is going to convict a bunch of 80 year olds."

This story is an extreme example of how toxic agers not only may affect their families and caregivers but can also actually impact the well-being of an entire community. Do you know of any toxic agers in your community? If so, what integrated theory do you think would best describe them?

ficial to the individual's personal identity. Whether that selection be cool indifference, nonviolent protest, or violent action is determined by personal identity. What seems to be an irrational act to some may be a deliberate (and personally rewarding) act of martyrdom to others. All actions, even on the part of those thought to be deranged or mentally incompetent, are rational—to them—efforts to enhance their personal identity.

Assessment of Holistic Theories

Like the computers we have come to rely upon, human beings are affected by hardware issues (nature) and software issues (nurture) that determine the ability to process information and provide adequate responses. To ignore biological or physiological influences on human behavior is akin to ignoring hardware aspects of our computers; to ignore psychological and sociological influences is the same as trying to use a computer without having software installed. Like the computer, we must understand what issues are relevant when a particular problem emerges. The question then arises, is it important that we debate a plethora of competing and/or complementary theories, or that we understand the variables that are found to influence criminal behavior?

The holistic approaches discussed earlier in this chapter tend to use multifactor orientations while emphasizing specific approaches (i.e., biology with Jeffery or social learning with Akers). According to Bernard, Snipes, and Gerould (2009), theories that emphasize individual-level data should be classified as **individual difference theories**. Theories that emphasize aggregate-level data should be classified as **structure/process theories**. Most of the single and multifactor approaches that we discussed can be located within these categories.

For the most part, aggregate-level and individual-level data should not be combined (this leads to a dilemma referred to in methods texts as the "ecological fallacy"). Following this logic, the primary concern of criminological research is not to adhere to artificial theoretical delineations, but to use the correct level of analysis in evaluating the individual or societal variables that influence criminality. In our opinion, it is in those common areas, where cautious explanation of how individual factors and societal factors are interrelated, that multifactor (holistic/general) criminological theories are not only proper but necessary.

Summary

Criminology is an interdisciplinary science. This interdisciplinary nature has been both a blessing and a hindrance in understanding crime and criminality. Integrated theories attempt to address the shortcomings of individual theories by merging two or more theoretical explanations into a more complete explanation.

Integrated biological theories stress the importance of biological factors in human behavior. The biological theories include bioconditioning theory and human nature theory. Integrated psychological theories explain how social factors can influence self-perception. Integrated psychological theories include delinquency development theory, age-graded theory, and self-derogation theory.

Integrated sociological explanations include integrated learning, integrated control, integrated strain, and integrated conflict theories. Integrated learning theories include network analysis and interactional theory. Integrated control theories are control balance theory, social development theory, and reintegrative shaming theory.

Despite the problems inherent in using an integrated theoretical perspective, there have been a number of efforts to combine different perspectives regarding crime and criminality into more holistic explanations. Four of the better-known efforts at holistic incorporation of criminological theories are Jeffery's bioenvironmental theory, Akers's conceptual absorption theory, Pearson and Weiner's conceptual integration theory, and Vila's general paradigm.

Jeffery argues that human behavior is the product of complex and constantly changing interactions between the physical environment and the social environment. Akers argues that we already have theory integration in criminology because of conceptual absorption. He posits that the concepts used to explain the behaviors of criminal offenders are compatible and in some cases the same as concepts used by other theories. Pearson and Weiner provide a framework demonstrating how other theories complement one another. The basis for their theoretical framework is that eight common concepts can be identified in all criminological theories. Vila's paradigm for understanding criminal behavior assumes that all crimes are the product of human desire to acquire resources. The type of resource desired (material, hedonistic, or political) and ecological factors determine the type of crimes committed (or not committed).

Each of the four holistic theories has great appeal in its general explanation. However, they all share the same weakness in that the broadness of the approach limits applicability. Two theories thought to better represent holistic theoretical integration were categorized as general theories.

Gottfredson and Hirschi merge concepts of control theory with rational choice, routine activities, and biological and psychological explanations within their general theory of crime. People who engage in criminal acts are seen as having low self-control. Although they may engage in many conventional behaviors, due to low self-control, they are predisposed to committing crimes if opportunities arise.

In his theory of integrative delinquency, Shoemaker (2009) emphasizes self-esteem as integral to understanding juvenile delinquency. In this model, individual and structural conditions indirectly influence delinquency, first through social controls and later through self-esteem and peer associations.

Our identity theory provides a general explanation that can be applied to all crimes and criminal typologies. Criminal behavior is seen as the product of nature amid nurture. The determination of whether behavior will be criminal depends on how the individual and society interrelate. These interrelationships are influenced by complex and constantly changing influences of biological factors, psychological factors, and social factors. Personal identity was identified as the best indicator of how those influences may create crime and criminality.

Last, integrated and holistic theories were assessed on the basis of their strengths and weaknesses. It was concluded that a holistic approach is both proper and necessary in explaining crime and criminality.

Discussion Questions

1. Debate the pros and cons of integrated approaches in explaining crime and criminality.
2. Select the integrated theory that you think best explains crime and criminality. Justify your selection.
3. Using at least one biological, one psychological, and two sociological concepts from the explanations offered, create your own integrated theory of crime causation.

11

Victimization Theories

Discussions in previous chapters focused on the causes of crime and on criminal offenders. This chapter discusses the victims of crime and the causes of victimization. The study of crime victims and issues related to victimization is known as **victimology**.

Victimology is seen by some scholars as a separate discipline (Wallace, 1998). Others see victimology as an important subfield within criminology (Doerner and Lab, 2012). Regardless of one's viewpoint as to victimology's disciplinary status, the study of crime and its consequences would not be complete without examining the issues leading to victimization, the subsequent effects of crime on victims, and society's responses to victims' needs.

Concern for victims is not a new phenomenon. Offenders in early tribal societies were held accountable to victims for the harm they had caused them. Social customs such as the blood feud placed responsibility on the victim's family to exact **vengeance**. Offenders could often avoid retribution by paying restitution to the victim or the victim's family in compensation for the harm caused (Territo, Halstead, and Bromley, 2004). This arrangement prevented future violence, reinforced societal prohibitions against specific crimes, and also aided victims.

As tribal societies evolved into nation-states, the need of the state to collect revenues took precedence over concern for victims. Compensation paid to victims gave way to fines paid to the government for the harm crime caused to society. Victims gradually became witnesses in the governmental efforts to promote justice, and criminal offenders became the focus of these enforcement efforts (Doerner and Lab, 2012). This emphasis on offenders would continue as modern nations developed, and it remains the focal concern of criminal justice administration to this day.

Only since the 1960s have victims become a subject of study for social scientists. Furthermore, justice system concerns for the welfare of victims did not gain impetus until the mid-1970s, when victim-assistance programs and crime-compensation efforts began to emerge. In recent years, victimology has become an important area of study within sociology, criminology, and criminal justice programs. More important, perhaps, criminal justice practitioners have become more aware and responsive to the needs of crime victims.

Early Victimization Theories

Chapters 4 through 10 presented numerous theories of crime causation. This chapter discusses several different theories of victimization. Whereas the earlier theories of crime focused on the motivations and actions of criminal offenders, these theories concentrate on the behaviors of victims. The victimization theories discussed in this chapter are shown in Figure 11.1.

Personal Factors Theory

Hans von Hentig's research was instrumental in drawing the attention of other social scientists to the victim's role in the commission of crime. After much research on criminal offenders, von Hentig began focusing on the events that caused certain types of individuals to become victims. He was among the first to claim that the victim could be a contributing factor to his or her successive victimization (von Hentig, 1941); this is known as **victim precipitation**. Von Hentig's later research developed the premise that victims could actually be provocateurs of the crimes committed against them (von Hentig, 1948).

Figure 11.1   Victimization Theories

Early Theories	Contemporary Theories
Personal factors theory	General victimology theory
Situational factors theory	Critical victimology theory
Functional responsibility theory	Compatible victimology
Crime event theory	Lifestyle theories
Victim precipitation theory	Equivalent group hypothesis
	Proximity hypothesis
	Deviant place hypothesis
	Routine activities theory

In examining victims' roles in their own victimization, von Hentig developed a typology of potential victims. These characteristics were based on physical, social, and psychological disadvantages that made victims less able to resist criminals' efforts (Doerner and Lab, 2012). While von Hentig did not blame victims for their misfortunes, he was the first to argue that studying victims' personal factors might provide understanding of their susceptibility to criminal victimization. Figure 11.2 shows the **victim typology** developed within his **personal factors theory**.

Situational Factors Theory

Benjamin Mendelsohn is credited by some as the father of victimology. As a practicing attorney, Mendelsohn investigated the situational factors that led to a criminal event. His research resulted in the belief that a relationship often existed between offenders and victims that set up the victimization episode (Wallace, 1998). Like von Hentig, he believed that victims could be categorized within a victim precipitation typology. However, Mendelsohn focused on factors within the social relationship rather than on features of the victims.

While Mendelsohn did not argue that victims warranted the crime that occurred against them, he did believe that they should be assigned some of the blame for having placed themselves at risk. The typology Mendelsohn

---

Figure 11.2 Von Hentig's Victim Typology

1. *The Young.* Children.
2. *The Female.* Women.
3. *The Old.* The elderly.
4. *The Mentally Defective.* The feebleminded, mentally ill.
5. *Immigrants.* Newly arrived and naive about the culture.
6. *Minorities.* Disadvantaged due to racial bias.
7. *Dull Normals.* The slow or ignorant.
8. *The Depressed.* The dejected and emotionally drained.
9. *The Acquisitive.* Greedy people seeking to gain.
10. *The Wanton.* Promiscuous individuals.
11. *The Lonesome/Heartbroken.* Suffering from emotional loss.
12. *The Tormentor.* The abuser who provokes violence.
13. *The Blocked, Exempted, or Fighting.* Those whose actions have placed them in losing situations.
14. *The Activating Sufferer.* Victim as perpetrator.

Source: von Hentig, 1948, pp. 404–438.

developed in his **situational factors theory** is displayed in Figure 11.3. One can see that Mendelsohn was more than willing to hold victims partially, if not fully, accountable for having become victims. This perspective developed the concept of victim precipitation beyond that initially discussed by von Hentig.

Functional Responsibility Theory

Stephen Schafer examined the earlier works of both von Hentig and Mendelsohn before developing his own classification of victims. Rather than categorizing victims based on risk factors, as had been done by von Hentig and Mendelsohn, Schafer (1968) used responsibility as his rationale for categorization. He believed that examining the relationship between criminals and victims would enable the criminal justice system to better deal with the problem of crime.

The key to Schafer's **functional responsibility theory** is that everyone within society has a responsibility to conduct him- or herself appropriately. Crime is a social phenomenon that is in most cases the product of inappropriate behavior on the part of both victims and offenders. Therefore, in order to deal with the problem of crime, victim responsibility must be acknowledged. Schafer's victim precipitation typology is shown in Figure 11.4.

Figure 11.3   Mendelsohn's Victim Precipitation Typology

1. *The completely innocent victim.* Individuals who did nothing to precipitate the act against them.
2. *The victim with minor guilt.* Persons whose ignorance or inadvertent actions placed them in jeopardy.
3. *The victim who is as guilty as the offender.* Those whose voluntary actions helped create the situation.
4. *The victim more guilty than the offender.* People who provoke others to commit a crime against them.
5. *The most guilty victim.* Perpetrators who initiate a crime against another and end up being killed or harmed by their would-be victim.
6. *The imaginary victim.* Individuals who are delusional and believe that they have been victimized or who deliberately fabricate a crime to cover up their own responsibility for their misfortune.

Source: Adapted from Wallace, 1998, p. 6.

Figure 11.4 Schafer's Victim Precipitation Typology

1. *Unrelated victims*	No criminal responsibility; victim is unfortunate target.
2. *Provocative victims*	Victim shares responsibility due to provocative actions.
3. *Precipitative victims*	Some degree of victim responsibility due to careless or inappropriate actions.
4. *Biologically weak victims*	No victim responsibility due to physical conditions that led to being targeted.
5. *Socially weak victims*	Immigrants, minorities, and others who are seen as easy targets.
6. *Self-victimizing*	Total victim responsibility due to individual's own criminal activity.
7. *Political victims*	No victim responsibility due to abuses by those in power.

Source: Doerner and Lab, 2012.

Crime Event Theory

In 1964, yet another typology of crime victims was offered by Thorston Sellin and Marvin Wolfgang. Instead of concentrating on the relationship between victims and offenders, they focused on crime situations in a manner similar to that of Mendelsohn's earlier work. However, they emphasized the actual crime event more than Mendelsohn did. As a result of their research, Sellin and Wolfgang (1964) offered five categories of victimization in their **crime event theory**:

- *Primary victimization.* **Primary vicitimization** refers to personalized or individualized victimization in which the victims were selected for victimization based on personal attributes. This would be exemplified by an attack on an individual because of knowledge about that person or because that individual fit the offender's victim profile.
- *Secondary victimization.* **Secondary victimization** occurs when the victim is an impersonal but available target of the offender. The victim in this situation may merely be in the wrong place at the wrong time.
- *Tertiary victimization.* **Tertiary victimization** occurs when the public or society as a whole is considered to be the victim of criminal activity— for example, when public officials engage in unlawful or corrupt behavior that is detrimental to the welfare of their constituents.

- *Mutual victimization.* This victimization occurs when one offender is victimized by an associate or accomplice. For example, a falling-out among gang members might result in a shooting incident.
- *No victimization.* This occurs when willing participants engage in allegedly **victimless crimes**, such as gambling or prostitution.

Victim Precipitation Theory

Most of the early victimization theories classify victims in order to better understand the offender-victim relationship or the situational factors leading to victimization. The theories themselves received very little empirical support. However, **victim precipitation theory**, or the idea that the victims' actions could possibly influence or actually cause their victimization, received a great deal of attention from scholars and criminal justice practitioners.

One study that does provide support for the idea that victims' actions could lead to their victimization was conducted by Marvin Wolfgang. In a study of homicide victims in Philadelphia, Wolfgang (1958) found that the victims often had prior interpersonal relationships with the offender, that the act of homicide was the product of a disagreement that escalated to violence, and that alcohol consumption often exacerbated the situation. This led Wolfgang to conclude that many homicides result from victim precipitation. Individuals who engaged in behavior that was provocative or instrumental in causing their victimization are said to have engaged in **active precipitation**. When victims unwittingly contribute to their victimization through actions (or inaction) that make them more vulnerable, **passive precipitation** occurs.

Another study that provided further support for the concept of victim precipitation was conducted by Menachim Amir (1971), who analyzed rape data from Philadelphia police records. Amir concluded that 19 percent of all forcible rapes were victim-precipitated. When this controversial study was publicized, the negative reactions not only to Amir's conclusion but also to the concept of victim precipitation were immediate and strong.

The study of victimology was actually disrupted because of disagreements about victim precipitation among scholars, criminal justice practitioners, the media, and the public. Proponents argued that the victim's involvement in crime must be understood in order to prevent future victimization. Critics argued that victim precipitation was nothing more than blaming the victim for what the offender had done. Ultimately, a compromise was reached (Doerner and Lab, 2012) as victimologists established a middle ground that recognized that in some situations victims had some responsibility, but that in many other situations victim behavior had little or no bearing on their victimization.

Contemporary Victimization Theories

As the study of victimology has developed, several other theories have emerged to either supplement or complement the earlier hypotheses. This section presents three theoretical perspectives that allow for broad differentiation on the part of victimologists. We then discuss two theories that revisit the issue of victim behavior in preventing or precipitating victimization.

General Victimology Theory

In an effort to promote stability within the discipline, Mendelsohn (1976, p. 59) called for **general victimology theory** to "investigate the causes of victimization in search of effective remedies." To emphasize the concern for victims, Mendelsohn offered five new definitions of victims:

- *Victim of a criminal*—covers all acts initiated by other individuals or groups of individuals.
- *Victim of one's self*—involves acts of self-abuse or injury such as suicide.
- *Victim of the social environment*—refers to incidents such as discrimination based on race or class, as well as governmental abuses of power.
- *Victim of technology*—alludes to people who fall prey to technological advances and their impacts.
- *Victims of the natural environment*—those affected by natural disasters such as floods, earthquakes, and tornadoes (Doerner and Lab, 2012).

While the reader may object that such a typology of victims makes everyone a potential victim, it does manage to allow victimologists to pursue different perspectives within victimology without splintering the field of study.

Critical Victimology Theory

The general victimology described previously allows for many diverse views on what victimhood is and what causes it. Earlier we saw that many critical criminologists define crime based on social conflict and the actions of those in power against those deemed powerless. R. I. Mawby and S. Walklate (1994) exemplify the perspective of critical victimologists who seek to examine the wider social context of power and control within society that results in different definitions of and responses to victimization. **Critical victimology theory** tends to focus more on social conditions that are thought to influence the incidence of crime and victimization than does contemporary victimology. Indeed, to a critical victimologist, the offender-victim relationship as defined by a contemporary victimologist or criminologist may be the reverse of that which he or she sees.

Compatible Victimology Theory

A theory that perhaps best describes the multidisciplinary nature of victimology and the divergent views that are held within this emerging discipline (or criminological subfield) was offered by Andrew Karmen. Like Mendelsohn's general theory, **compatible victimology theory** provides for divergent perspectives in the study of victimization. Karmen (2010) noted three compatible areas of concentration for victimologists:

1. Victimologists study the reasons (if any) why and how the victim entered a dangerous situation. This approach does not attempt to fix the blame on the victim; rather it examines the dynamics that resulted in the victim's being in a dangerous situation.
2. Victimology evaluates how police, prosecutors, courts, and related agencies interact with the victim, and how the victim is treated at each stage in the criminal justice system.
3. Victimologists evaluate the effectiveness of efforts to reimburse victims for their losses and meet the victims' personal and emotional needs.

Lifestyle Theory

Lifestyle theory holds that people may increase or decrease their potential to become victims of crime based on their lifestyle. Some individuals have lifestyles that are very high-risk, whereas others tend to live more sedate or conventional existences, which are much lower in risk. The premise is actually quite simple: the more you place yourself in harm's way, the more likely you are to be harmed. Therefore, proponents of lifestyle theory seek to educate potential victims about their propensity for victimization. The three distinct hypotheses that may be found among lifestyle advocates are **equivalent group hypothesis**, **proximity hypothesis**, and deviant place hypothesis.

Equivalent group hypothesis. Individuals who become victims of crime often exhibit the same lifestyle characteristics as their offenders. People who engage in criminal activities are frequently victimized by their associates. Indeed, for law enforcement officials, it may sometimes be difficult to determine who is the offender and who is the victim when investigating an act of violence. It is within this equivalent group that we frequently see repeat **victimization** or victim recidivism (Doerner and Lab, 2012), in which victims tend be victimized on a continual basis.

Proximity hypothesis. Proximity hypothesis is similar to equivalent group hypothesis in that it considers the influence of the victim's lifestyle on his or

Reality Check: Human Trafficking

Recently a human trafficking ring was discovered within a few miles of the Georgia Gwinnett College campus. We were shocked to learn that women from South America and Mexico had been tricked into coming to the Atlanta area in the belief that they would be able to obtain legitimate jobs. Instead, they were forced into prostitution in area brothels. One victim indicated that she had been forced to "service" as many as fifty men in one day. Human trafficking in which women and children are sold as sex slaves is something that one imagines happening in third world nations, not in the United States. Unfortunately, the United States is the second leading destination for women and children trafficked for sexual exploitation, behind Germany (Bartol and Bartol, 2011).

Victims of sexual trafficking come from Asia, South America, Africa, and Europe. They may be manipulated by someone who they think is a friend; they may be misled by advertising promoting jobs in the United States; they may be abducted from bars, hotels, or even from their homes; and they may be sold by impoverished parents. They live lives (often shortened to a few years) in which violence, intimidation, and rape are common experiences. Death from forced drug addiction, exposure to sexually transmitted diseases, physical injuries, and even murder are all too frequent.

It is estimated that 800,000 to 900,000 victims are trafficked each year, with 7,500 to 18,500 being brought into the United States (Office of the Undersecretary for Democracy and Global Affairs, 2007). Human and sex trafficking is a worldwide industry. The United Nations has attributed this growth to global smuggling rings, established transnational routes, weak legislation, lax border control, corrupt officials, and the power of organized crime networks (Office of the Undersecretary for Democracy and Global Affairs, 2007).

Discuss the different forms of human trafficking that exist. What do you think can be done to combat these atrocities?

her vulnerability to crime, but it emphasizes where victims live rather than their individual characteristics. Often there is no victim precipitation other than the misfortune of being in close proximity to would-be offenders. For example, urban dwellers may have no choice but to reside and conduct their daily activities near those who are predisposed to victimize them (Meadows, 2010). The more people are compressed within an area, the greater the potential for victims and offenders to come into contact.

Deviant place hypothesis. Deviant place hypothesis takes the concept of proximity further by focusing on those areas in which social disorganization and crime tend to flourish. The supposition is that proximity to offenders is increased among those who live in areas in which crime flourishes. Despite precautions taken by potential victims, they are still at high risk of victimization (Stark, 1987). Many areas within US society are more dangerous than others, and people who are forced to live within these areas will most certainly experience higher incidences of victimization.

Routine Activities Theory

The routine activities theory was discussed in Chapters 4 and 10. The basic premise of the theory is that there are always individuals who are motivated to commit crimes. If these motivated offenders either consciously or unconsciously note suitable targets (either for property or personal offenses), and capable guardians (police, vigilant homeowners, etc.) are absent, they commit crimes (Cohen and Felson, 1979). When motivated offenders and suitable targets come into contact in the same place and time in the absence of any deterrent, crime will occur. The routine activities approach goes beyond the lifestyle theories in that it encourages potential victims to reduce their potential for victimization by reducing their attractiveness as victims and by using various crime-prevention strategies.

Summary

The study of crime victims and issues related to victimization is known as victimology. Victimology is seen by some scholars as a separate discipline in itself. Others see it as an important subfield within criminology. Victimology has its origins in early societies, where concerns for the victim outweighed concerns for exacting societal punishment on the offender. It has only been within the last thirty years that concerns for the welfare of the victim have reemerged.

As scholars, politicians, criminal justice practitioners, and the public as a whole have become more knowledgeable about victimization, strategies for determining the nature and extent of victimization have changed dramatically. Similarly, theories of victimology have developed from simple typologies that classified victim characteristics to diverse explanations of victimization. As the study of victimology developed, it was both helped and hindered by the concept of victim precipitation. While victim precipitation was seen by many scholars as an important means of understanding both victim-offender relationships and situational factors, critics believed that it unfairly blamed victims for the offenses committed against them.

More recent theories of victimology allow for scholars from diverse perspectives such as critical criminology and routine activities theory to pursue their particular interests in understanding and, it is hoped, remedying the problem of criminal victimization. Victim precipitation is no longer believed to be as divisive a topic within victimology. Indeed, situational and personal factors originally discussed in the early victim precipitation discussions are dealt with within contemporary lifestyle theories.

Discussion Questions

1. Discuss how early societies dealt with the problems of victims. How has this changed over time? What do you think could be done to make our current criminal justice system more victim-friendly?
2. Describe how victimology came to be a field of study. Do you believe that victimology should be seen as a subfield of criminology or as a separate discipline? Justify your answer.
3. Which theory of victimology best explains victimization? Justify your selection.
4. Discuss how the concept of victim precipitation has been both a useful tool and an impediment to the study of victimology. What is your personal view of victim precipitation?

12

Dealing with Lawbreakers

Since the beginning of time, society's wrongdoers have been punished in some form or fashion. For many centuries, punishment was primarily physically oriented—from whippings, brandings, and mutilations to hangings and beheadings. However, as society matured, the emphasis of punishment changed from the physical to more humane approaches: incarceration, community service, fines, and so on. Unfortunately, today's results may not be as beneficial as society would like. Therefore, we continue to be faced with the problem of how to deal with lawbreakers. This chapter discusses the rationales for imposing sanctions on lawbreakers and the means by which these sanctions are applied.

The Rationales for Imposing Sanctions

The imposition of criminal sanctions has historically been tied to a particular society's views of human nature. In ancient societies, lawbreakers were considered to be inherently evil and deserving of the direst of punishments for their alleged sins against society, God, or the gods. The Enlightenment, which took place from the late 1600s through the 1700s, brought about new perspectives on human nature that ultimately led to the precepts of the classical school of criminological thought. In Western societies, draconian measures such as torture and mutilation were replaced by efforts to match the punishment with the seriousness of the crime in order to benefit both the offender and society. Later, the positive school of criminological thought called for treatment based on the needs of the offender in order to address factors that caused the offender to engage in unlawful behaviors. As these philosophies have developed, the responses to criminal behavior have changed (Albanese, 2004).

The earliest historical accounts of response to crime date from the ancient civilizations of biblical Israel, the Greeks, and the Romans (Johnson and Wolfe, 1996). It is within these societies that we find the foundation for punishment; all three cultures established strict laws and delivered swift, harsh punishment. The form of punishments varied depending on the type of crime. For example, someone who intentionally killed another might suffer the punishment of banishment or execution. Similar punishments were given for crimes of a sexual nature and theft.

Delivering punishment (e.g., mutilation, banishment, flogging, torture, and execution) was the main method of serving justice in many early societies, including America, until the transition from harsh and often arbitrary punishment to the provision of strong constitutional rights, rehabilitation, and more appropriately applied punishments prevailed. This transition included the development of more acceptable jails and prisons, separation of juveniles from adults, more lenient sentencing and punishments, and enforcement of constitutional guarantees.

The Classical Response to Crime

The main focus of the classical response to crime was that crime could be controlled by punishing identified offenders. Instead of imposing harsh punishments that often had no relationship to the severity of the offense, punishment was to be applied fairly and equitably based on the severity of the offense committed. This punishment should be carried out in a way that would make potential offenders fearful of the consequences of committing crime. The foundation for this approach is found in the tenets of the classical school of criminology (see Chapters 3 and 4), which stressed that individuals

- were bound to society only by their own consent, and the society was responsible to them, creating the "social contract";
- chose to act as they did, using their "free will";
- sought pleasure and avoided pain;
- should be punished and the punishment used as a means of deterring criminal behavior; and
- committing identical crimes should receive identical punishments (Bernard, Snipes, and Gerould, 2009).

Ultimately, the classical response is to punish individuals for their criminal behaviors with the belief that the punishment serves also as a means of deterrence. This has led to the acknowledgment of two types of deterrence: general and specific (see Chapter 3). Punishment as a general deterrent refers to the belief that based on the type of punishment issued, others will be deterred from committing the same act. Punishment as a specific deterrent is meant to deter the individuals from committing additional criminal acts by teaching them that the crime was not worth the pain it caused. In order for deterrence to work, the imposition of punishment must be equitable, swift, severe, and certain. In this context, equity means that all similar crimes should be punished in a similar manner (allowing for legal considerations such as mitigating and aggravating circumstances; see Chapter 4). **Swiftness** means that the time between the commission of the crime and the imposition of punishment should be reasonably short so that both the offender and the public will be able to note the connection between the two. **Severity** means that the punishment should exceed the benefits of the crime so that it discourages future criminality, but not so much that it is unreasonable or unduly harsh. Finally, **certainty** means that the likelihood of being caught, adjudicated, and punished is perceived as high enough to discourage both the offender and similar-minded individuals.

Under the classical model, prison became the primary form of punishment used in the United States. Since 1990, the number of individuals incarcerated has continued to rise (see Table 12.1). As of June 30, 1998, more than 1.8 million people were incarcerated in jails or prisons (*Sourcebook of Criminal Justice Statistics,* 1999). However, the high rates of **recidivism** in this country suggest that punishment does not have the specific deterring effect desired. This may be seen as the failure of the criminal justice system to accomplish the goals of equity, swiftness, and certainty (see Table 12.1).

Differences in sentencing have led to charges that the poor and ethnic minorities receive harsher penalties and lengthy waits or delays before the implementation of sanctions contradict swiftness. Estimates that only one-half to one-third of serious crimes committed in the United States are reported to the police (Schmalleger, 2012) preclude certainty. This leaves us to emphasize severity as the means of dealing with criminal behavior. Unfortunately, while we have seen declines in the overall crime rates during recent years, the general deterrent effect of punishment is considered to be minimal (Albanese, 2004). Advocates of the positive school of criminology argue that strategies that deal with the root causes of crime and criminal behavior are more appropriate and effective than punishment models.

The Positive Response to Crime

During the 1930s, there was a major shift from the classical school to the positive school of criminology. Here the emphasis was placed on treatment based on offender needs as opposed to punishment based on the crime. The positive school's (see Chapter 3) tenets include the following:

• Denial of the concepts of the social contract and free will.
• Suggestions that there are multiple causes of criminal behavior, including biological and environmental factors.
• Belief that actions toward the criminal should be to correct the behavior, not punish it (Bernard, Snipes, and Gerould, 2009).

The efforts of the positive response have led to three means of dealing with criminal behavior: rehabilitation, reintegration, incapacitation, and **prevention**.

Rehabilitation

The main concept of the positive approach to criminal behavior is that of rehabilitation. The underlying basis of rehabilitation is that criminal behavior results from sociological, psychological, or physical imperfections. These imperfections require correction through treatment or training. This concept of "fixing the offender's problems" is the mainstay of rehabilitation. Today, rehabilitation includes medical treatment, individual counseling, group therapy, education, job training, and reintegration (Barlow, 2000).

Physiological problems such as chemical imbalances are treated with medication, surgery, or other medical solutions. Individual counseling is a psychological strategy that strives to deal with the mental and emotional ailments thought to have precipitated the criminal behavior. Group therapy is a social-psychological technique of teaching offenders how to deal with the circumstances that may have led to their illegal actions. Educational programs and job training seek to provide offenders with the educational or vocational credentials necessary to obtain adequate employment when they reenter society. In many cases, such as the rehabilitation of drug offenders, several strategies (e.g., medication, individual therapy, group counseling, and job training) may be used.

The success of rehabilitation has been questioned since its beginning. Conservatives have challenged rehabilitation as being unsuccessful and as coddling criminals instead of punishing them. Liberals have criticized treatment efforts for "experimenting" on criminals, and for often being more punitive than therapeutic. Much is still left to be learned about whom to target and which rehabilitative efforts to practice in dealing with those who commit crime.

Reintegration

This is a newer strategy advocated by positivists. It calls for offenders to either remain within the community or be placed within the community prior to their release from correctional custody. The object is to retain or restore offenders' ties to the community (family, social network, job, etc.) so that they have an established support network to help them remain crime-free (Barlow, 2000). We talk more about this technique later in the chapter.

Dealing with Lawbreakers   201

Table 12.1 Adults on Probation, in Jail or Prison, and on Parole in the United States, 1980–2009

	Total Correctional Population[a]	Probation	Jail	Prison	Parole
1980	1,840,400	1,118,097	182,288	319,598	220,438
1981	2,006,600	1,225,934	195,085	360,029	225,539
1982	2,192,600	1,357,264	207,853	402,914	224,604
1983	2,475,100	1,582,947	221,815	423,898	246,440
1984	2,689,200	1,740,948	233,018	448,264	266,992
1985	3,011,500	1,968,712	254,986	487,593	300,203
1986	3,239,400	2,114,621	272,735	526,436	325,638
1987	3,459,600	2,247,158	294,092	562,814	355,505
1988	3,714,100	2,356,483	341,893	607,766	407,977
1989	4,055,600	2,522,125	393,303	683,367	456,803
1990	4,350,300	2,670,234	405,320	743,382	531,407
1991	4,535,600	2,728,472	424,129	792,535	590,442
1992	4,762,600	2,811,611	441,781	850,566	658,601
1993	4,944,000	2,903,061	455,500	909,381	676,100
1994	5,141,300	2,981,022	479,800	990,147	690,371
1995	5,342,900	3,077,861	507,044	1,078,542	679,421
1996	5,490,700	3,164,996	518,492	1,127,528	679,733
1997	5,734,900	3,296,513	567,079	1,176,564	694,787
1998	6,134,200	3,670,441	592,462	1,224,469	696,385
1999	6,340,800	3,779,922	605,943	1,287,172	714,457
2000	6,445,100	3,826,209	621,149	1,316,333	723,898
2001	6,581,700	3,931,731	631,240	1,330,007	732,333
2002	6,758,800	4,024,067	665,475	1,367,547	750,934
2003	6,924,500	4,120,012	691,301	1,390,279	769,925
2004	6,995,000	4,143,792	713,990	1,421,345	771,852
2005	7,045,100	4,166,757	740,770	1,448,344	780,616
2006	7,176,000	4,215,361	759,717	1,492,973	799,875
2007	7,267,500	4,234,471	773,341	1,517,867	821,177
2008	7,274,600	4,244,046	777,852	1,522,834	824,834
2009	7,225,800	4,203,967	760,400	1,524,513	819,308

Source: Adapted from Sourcebook of Criminal Justice Statistics Online, table 6.1.2009, http://www.albany.edu/sourcebook/pdf/t612009.pdf.

Note: a. Due to rounding, the column numbers may not match the correctional population totals.

Incapacitation

In the classical sense, incapacitation generally refers to incarceration: locking someone away for a specific period of time based on the seriousness of the crime committed. The logic is that past behavior is the best predictor of future behavior and that, while incarcerated, offenders will not be preying on society (a belief that may no longer be true because of technological advancements in communication). The positive approach to incapacitation is oriented toward enabling the offender to return to society by delivering needed treatment. Under this approach, to incapacitate is to make unable to perform or act. Mandatory drug testing, required medications, chemical castration of sex offenders, and interlocking devices for convicted drunk drivers are but a few examples of the positive approach to incapacitation.

Prevention

The final aspect of the positive response to crime is prevention. Whereas the classical approach uses the threat of punishment to prevent crime, the positive approach uses education. These efforts may be applied to society as a whole or specifically to offenders. Teaching predelinquent adolescents (youths who have not been charged with crimes but appear to be headed for trouble) the difference between acceptable and unacceptable behavior and emphasizing what may happen if criminal behavior is chosen are such strategies. Warning about the detrimental effects of drug use is another. Working to address social ills thought to create criminogenic environments is yet another aspect of prevention.

Applying Criminal Sanctions

Whether one prefers the classical approach or the positive approach to crime, the first consideration in administering justice is deciding what is criminal. This section discusses the making of laws, arrest of alleged offenders, adjudication, and correctional techniques.

Making Law

Perhaps one of the most difficult and controversial aspects of dealing with criminal behavior is determining what is criminal. The enactment of criminal laws has long been an area of debate. While there is common agreement among the diverse members of our society that acts such as rape, robbery, murder, arson, burglary, larceny, and automobile theft should be criminal, there is great disagreement about how to apply the law to offenses. In addition, numerous behaviors, such as sexual relations between consenting adults and the use of alcoholic beverages, tobacco products, and recreational drugs, cause great debate within society (Hancock and Sharp, 2004).

An important component in discussions of criminal law is the concept of **overcriminalization**. When one considers the great number of laws and ordinances that exist and all the activities they affect, the question arises, what behavior will be next? Some argue that one reason there is so much "crime" is that there are so many laws that, in effect, our society is overcriminalized. People who in their other behaviors are law abiding therefore become violators. This can lead to disrespect for the justice system as a whole. A solution to this dilemma is decriminalization. Basically, **decriminalization** refers to redefining certain criminal behaviors and making them lesser offenses or lawful (Schmalleger, 2012). For example, making the possession of a marijuana cigarette a civil infraction rather than a criminal offense would lessen the sanction against it. An example of legalizing behaviors would be lifting existing sanctions against consensual sexual acts between adults.

Regardless of how many laws there are or what level of punishment they exact, the reality is that criminal law requires a criminal sanction. Therefore, the issue becomes the type of sanction. Four types of criminal sanctions are commonly used in the United States: **fines**, **incarceration**, **probation**, and **capital punishment**. Corporal punishment was once common but has not been used in the United States since the 1950s (Albanese, 2004). In fact, corporal punishment of adult offenders is banned in most states as cruel and unusual. Interestingly, it is still permitted as a "reasonable means of discipline" for children. The types of sanctions applied will be discussed in the section on sentencing.

Arrest and Prosecution

As we suggested in our discussion of deterrence, a major weakness of the criminal justice system is that so few offenders are actually apprehended (Hancock and Sharp, 2004). Our purpose in this section is not to detail the process by which an individual is apprehended and later judged guilty of a crime (for a detailed overview of this process, we direct the reader to the many excellent introductory texts on criminal justice that are currently available). We do wish, however, to make several important points about this process. The first is that in order for an individual to be arrested, authorities must have a legal reason for doing so, that is, there must be probable cause that a crime has occurred and that the arrestee is responsible.

Following an arrest, a series of legal procedures must be observed. Failure to follow proper procedures may result in the case being dismissed as a result of violation of the individual's right to due process of law. If a person's constitutional protections are not observed during the police investigation, after the time of arrest, or during the prosecution, an argument can be made that his or her rights to due process have been violated. Violation of due process can be grounds for the trial judge to suppress improperly obtained evidence or even to dismiss the charges, or it might serve as a basis of appeal to a higher court if the individual is found guilty by the trial court (Territo, Halstead, and Bromley, 2004).

Under the US system of justice, the accused is considered to be innocent until proven guilty. This means that a jury (or a judge, if a bench trial has been accepted by the defendant) must listen to the evidence and determine beyond a **reasonable doubt** that the defendant is guilty of the crime of which he or she has been accused. It is the burden of the prosecution to prove guilt to the jury or the judge.

In addition to the previous safeguards, an accused person may offer any of several defenses to refute the charge or excuse his or her actions. The first defense is to present an **alibi**. Quite simply, an alibi is verification from others that the accused could not have committed the crime because he or she was elsewhere or was physically incapable of committing the crime and can prove it. **Duress** is another defense. In this situation, factors out of his or her control caused the accused to violate the law to avoid a greater harm (such as breaking into a remote mountain cabin to escape a blizzard). **Coercion** is also a defense. In this scenario, the offense was committed because of threats or force applied by another person capable of causing the accused or the accused's loved ones harm. Yet another legal defense is **self-defense**. Here the accused argues that his or her actions were necessary for self-protection or to protect others from physical harm. **Youth** is still another defense when the age of the offender precludes him or her from being held accountable for the actions, requires more lenient treatment, or requires transfer to the juvenile justice system. Still another legal defense is **entrapment**, which occurs when the police or their agents actually entice someone into committing a criminal act that he or she would not have contemplated doing on his or her own initiative.

The last legal defense that we shall discuss is **insanity**. In this situation, the accused claims to have been insane at the time of the crime or claims to be incapable of assisting in preparation of his or her legal defense. Under the US system of justice, an accused individual must be able to understand the charges against him or her and to aid in his or her own defense. The determination of insanity varies among the fifty states and the federal government. In many states, the so-called McNaughton Rule—"was the defendant capable of knowing right from wrong"—is the standard. This is the standard under which it is most difficult to prove insanity as a defense. McNaughton is sometimes augmented by the irresistible impulse test, which stresses that although the accused knew it was wrong, he or she could not keep from acting. This defense is particularly useful for crimes of passion.

In the District of Columbia and New Hampshire, the Durham Rule—"the action was the product of a diseased mind"—is used. This is the easiest standard by which to prove insanity. It was the standard under which John Hinckley was found not guilty by reason of insanity of the 1981 shooting of President Ronald Reagan and James Brady. Acceptance of the diseased-mind defense was based on Hinckley's history of irrational actions, including his excessive infatuation with actress Jodie Foster. Currently, a majority of the states and the federal courts are using the substantial capacity test, which is modeled on the American Bar Association's Model Penal Code. The substantial capacity rule defines a defendant who is "lacking the substantial capacity to appreciate the wrongfulness of the action that was taken" as legally insane. This is also known as the Brawner Rule after the case in which it was first applied by a federal court (Gaines and Miller, 2009; Schmalleger, 2012).

The controversial nature of the insanity defense has led several states to amend their statutes to provide for a "guilty but mentally ill" finding so that emotionally disturbed individuals, such as John Hinckley, can be held more accountable for their actions. Anyone contemplating an insanity defense should be aware that, if convicted, defendants often are confined longer in mental institutions than they would be in prison. Despite the outcry following Hinckley's trial in 1982, at this writing he is still confined in Saint Elizabeth's Hospital in Washington, DC.

Adjudication

Once a determination of guilt has been made either by a trial or a plea bargain, the next step in the process is sentencing. **Adjudication**, as the term is used in relation to the criminal justice system, actually refers to determining a punishment. Historically, we have sentenced or punished individuals for their criminal behavior for any or all of the following reasons: retribution, atonement, incapacitation, deterrence, and rehabilitation. **Retribution** occurs when the punishment given supposedly satisfies the victim's and society's need for revenge. **Atonement** is the idea that an offender must "pay his or her debt to society" so that, having atoned for the crime, he or she can then reenter society with a clean slate. Incapacitation is the removal of the offender from society or the imposition of restrictions that negate his or her ability to commit a specific type of crime. Deterrence, as noted earlier, can be either general or specific and is meant to keep the individual and others from repeating the behavior. Rehabilitation is meant to treat the behavior in an attempt to prevent it from recurring.

The United States relies more on imprisoning individuals for criminal behavior than any other democratic nation in the world. Sentencing may meet one of three forms: mandatory, determinate, and indeterminate. **Mandatory sentencing** exists in several states and refers to the automatic imprisonment for a specified period of time of an offender convicted of a certain crime. **Determinate sentencing** is the assessment of a specific number of years in prison (e.g., ten years). In theory, the offender is to serve the exact amount of time for which he or she is sentenced. **Indeterminate sentencing** refers to a sentence within a range of years (e.g., five to ten years). The type of sentencing imposed is based on state statutes. For example, Minnesota uses determinate sentencing, while the state of Texas is an indeterminate sentencing state. The actual release date is determined by a parole board that reviews the inmate's behavior during incarceration. It should be noted that despite the method used, the amount of time actually spent in prison usually ends up being considerably less than the actual imposed sentence because of credit awarded for "good time," that is, for compliance with prison rules while incarcerated (Territo, Halstead, and Bromley, 2004).

One of the most recent developments in sentencing is habitual offender laws, most often referred to as "Three Strikes." Habitual offender laws require that an individual who is convicted of a third felony offense, regardless of what it is, receive a mandatory sentence, which can be as severe as life imprisonment. These laws seek to remove from society hard-core offenders who are said to be dedicated to a life of crime. However, the application of these laws in some cases to lesser felons with a history of property crime has caused some criminologists to question their appropriateness (e.g., Skolnick, 2000). It has been argued that these laws, along with mandatory sentencing and the "war on drugs," have led to the excessive reliance on imprisonment in the United States (Currie, 2000).

The ultimate punishment in the United States is capital punishment. The most debated of sanctions, the death penalty has a long history of use, misuse, and abuse. One of the major issues accompanying imposition of the death penalty is concern as to its constitutionality. The Eighth Amendment to the US Constitution guarantees the right to be free from cruel and unusual punishment. Opponents of the death penalty cite this clause in their opposition. However, it is the arbitrariness and capriciousness of the death penalty's use that have motivated the appellate courts to intervene. Such an intervention led to a moratorium on the death penalty in the United States from 1967 through 1976. Two landmark US Supreme Court cases impacted both the beginning and ending of the moratorium.

In 1972, in the case of *Furman v. Georgia,* the US Supreme Court ruled that the Georgia death penalty statute was unconstitutional on grounds of capriciousness and arbitrariness. This affected the death penalty statutes in thirty-four other states. However, in the 1976 case of *Gregg v. Georgia,* the US Supreme Court ruled that the newly written Georgia statute on capital punishment was acceptable. This ruling, which created a two-trial system (one to determine guilt and a second to determine the sentence), opened the door once again for states to execute prisoners. Utah was the first to break the moratorium with the execution of Gary Gilmore in 1977. As of April 1, 1999, more than 3,200 individuals were sitting on death row awaiting execution (*Sourcebook,* 1999). However, in the year 2000, a movement to once again place a moratorium on the use of the death penalty gained support when Illinois governor George H. Ryan did so.

Sentencing Options

The sentence imposed by the trial court judge may be severely limited by mandatory sentences or restricted by sentencing guidelines that proscribe the range of sanctions from which he or she may choose. However, judges often have great latitude in the decisions that they make. The judge's decision is primarily based on the severity of the offense and the offender's past history of crime. In most cases, judges are aided in their decisionmaking by a presentence investigation report compiled by a probation officer. The choices available to judges in routine cases include fines, incarceration, and community corrections. In recent years, judges have also used alternative sanctions such as **restitution, community service,** and **restorative justice**.

Although primarily used as punishment for ordinance violations, traffic offenses, and minor misdemeanors, fines may also accompany felony punishments. Fines basically consist of a monetary value set by the judge that the offender must pay to the court. Usually this money is used to pay court-related costs. In the case of serious misdemeanors (e.g., driving under the influence) and felonies, the fine may be in the thousands of dollars. In a few sensational cases of white-collar crime (such as the Michael Milken insider trading case in the mid-1980s), the fine may be in the millions (Territo, Halsted, and Bromley, 2004).

Incarceration is a popular means of dealing with criminal behavior. Incarceration or institutional corrections sentences may be served in a variety of settings, including jails, prisons (maximum, medium, and minimum security), rehabilitation centers, boot camps, and work camps. Assignment to a specific type is based on the sentence of the judge and the correctional system's classification scheme.

Community corrections programs allow offenders to remain within the community under correctional supervision. The leading type of community correction is probation. Probation is a means of keeping a person under supervision without incarceration. Although often used for first-time offenders, it is not unheard of that repeat offenders receive probation. Probation usually requires the offender to follow certain restrictions imposed by the court. Such impositions may include attending a drug or alcohol program, being employed, going to school, staying away from certain types of people, and curfews. The person on probation must report to a probation officer, who determines whether the individual is abiding by the rules of his or her probation. At the end of 1997, more than 3.2 million individuals were on probation in the United States (*Sourcebook,* 1999).

Other forms of community correction are residence in a halfway house, house arrest, electronic monitoring, intensive probation, and shock probation. These techniques place more restrictions and requirements upon probationers

Reality Check: The Imposters

In an earlier reality check, we discussed conmen who defrauded investors out of millions of dollars. In this chapter, we will discuss another category of con artist, the imposter. Below are three of the most successful imposters who have operated in the United States.

Ferdinand Demara: The Great Impostor

Ferdinand Waldo Demara was a famous imposter who reached his zenith during World War II. His antics earned him the title "the Great Impostor." Demara began his career as an imposter when he joined the US Army in 1941. He "borrowed" the name of an army buddy and went AWOL (absent without leave). He later joined the US Navy. He faked a suicide, and after stints as a monk in two different monasteries, Demara borrowed another name and moved to another identity in which he became a religiously oriented psychologist. After being apprehended by the navy and army, Demara served time in prison. After being released from prison, he posed in a number of roles: a civil engineer, a sheriff's deputy, an assistant prison warden, a doctor of applied psychology, a hospital orderly, a lawyer, a child-care expert, a Benedictine monk, a Trappist monk, an editor, a cancer researcher, and a teacher.

Demara's most famous exploit was masquerading as surgeon Joseph Cyr aboard HMCS *Cayuga*, a Canadian Navy destroyer, during the Korean War. When a number of combat casualties were transferred to his ship, Demara used knowledge that he had obtained from reading a book on surgery to save the lives of sixteen men. The public acclaim that he received resulted in his exposure as a fake. The Canadian Navy chose not to press charges, and Demara returned to the United States.

Demara's notoriety inspired a book in 1960 and a movie, *The Great Imposter*, in which he was portrayed by Tony Curtis. He was a Baptist minister when he died in 1982 at the age of sixty.

Frank Abagnale: Catch Me If You Can

Frank William Abagnale Jr. was a professional imposter in the 1960s. His first con was committed at the age of twelve when he began writing checks on his own overdrawn account by printing out his own copies of checks. He also obtained many thousands of dollars by printing his account number on blank bank deposit slips. Over a five-year period that began when he was just sixteen, Abagnale used eight different identities through which he passed bad checks totaling more than $2.5 million in twenty-six countries.

continues

Reality Check, *continued*

For years, Abagnale masqueraded as Pan Am pilot Frank Williams to get free rides around the world on scheduled airline flights. Later, he impersonated a pediatrician for eleven months in a Georgia hospital under the name Frank Conners. He also forged a Harvard University law diploma, passed the bar exam of Louisiana, and got a job at the office of the State Attorney General of Louisiana.

After he was caught at age twenty-one, Abagnale served less than five years in prison before starting to work for the federal government. He is now a lecturer at the FBI Academy and operates Abagnale and Associates, a financial fraud consultancy company. The movie *Catch Me If You Can* is based upon his exploits.

Christopher Rocancourt: The French Rockefeller

Christophe Thierry Rocancourt (aka Christopher Rocancourt) is an imposter and con artist who frequently scammed affluent people by masquerading as a French member of the Rockefeller family. As a young man, Rocancourt made his way to Paris, where he sold a property that he did not own for the equivalent of $1.4 million. After arriving in the United States, Rocancourt used more than a dozen aliases, including that of a movie producer, a boxing champion, and a venture capitalist. He later moved to Canada to avoid prosecution for his many scams. Rocancourt wrote an autobiography in which he ridiculed his victims. In March 2002, he was extradited to New York. He pled guilty to three of eleven charges, including theft, grand larceny, smuggling, bribery, and perjury. Rocancourt has estimated making at least $40 million from his various scams.

What do you think motivates these people to become imposters? How do you think they are able to successfully fool so many people?

than does normal probation. Shock probation refers to when youthful offenders are sentenced to a boot camp or a short term in jail or prison to make them aware of the consequences of their actions should they fail to meet their probation requirements. House arrest, electronic monitoring, and intensive probation are used for higher-risk offenders. Halfway houses and **parole** are means of allowing inmates, who have served prison time, to be phased back into society. With the exception of parole and halfway houses, the type of sanction imposed is usually based on the judge's decision. Parole decisions are generally left up to a parole board or set by mandatory regulations.

Alternative Sanctions

Since the 1980s, we have seen a return to sentencing designed to ease the burden that the victim has experienced because of the offender's actions. Chapter 13 discusses the issue of victims' rights. Restitution for the harm incurred is one of many victims' issues. Restitution is also seen as a means of benefiting the offender. Compensating the victim for his or her loss is a means of atonement on behalf of the offender. It is also viewed as rehabilitative in that it forces the offender to see the humanity of the victim and to realize the impact of his or her actions (Doerner and Lab, 2012). This is a particularly useful strategy for lesser offenders and youthful offenders.

Restorative justice is another strategy that is used for many lesser offenses. This is a peacemaking approach that uses mediation in lieu of judicial sanctions to seek to restore both victim and offender to their precrime status (Fuller, 1998). In these scenarios, disputants agree to accept the resolutions offered by a trained mediator instead of seeking a criminal prosecution. This method is appropriate in disputes in which there is confusion as to who initiated the situation that led to conflict. Often a simple apology may satisfy the aggrieved party. Restorative justice is especially useful for dealing with disputes within a community.

Last, judges (or prosecutors) may use creative sanctions that do not involve fines or incarceration. Mandatory community service is a common sentence for lesser offenders. This compulsory service on public projects may involve menial tasks (e.g., picking up trash, washing police cars) or actually using job skills (carpentry, mechanical abilities) to benefit the community. **Diversion programs** that require the offender to receive counseling, attend school, obtain job training, acquire employment, or spend weekends observing emergency room arrivals are also common. Less common sentences may involve the public wearing of placards that declare the offender's culpability or the mandatory placing of an offender's photograph in local newspapers (a return to ancient shaming rituals) or having the offender agree to leave the community in exchange for the charges being dismissed. During the 1980s, Utah judges banished several offenders to California when California authorities refused to extradite several wanted felons back to Utah.

We still have much to learn about how to effectively deal with criminal behavior. Whether it is a fine, probation, incarceration, treatment, or death, no one means has proven to be the answer. Obviously, review and research the best ways to deal with criminal offenders will continue to be necessary.

Summary

The imposition of criminal sanctions has historically been tied to a particular society's view of human nature. The US legal system is based on the precepts of the classical school of criminological thought. The main focus of the classical response to crime is that crime can be controlled by punishing identified offenders. However, during the sentencing and corrections phases, precepts of the positive school of criminology are often used. The main concept of the positive approach to criminal behavior is rehabilitation.

While there is agreement among the diverse members of society that certain acts should be criminal, there is great disagreement about how to apply the laws to these offenses. In addition, there are numerous other behaviors for which there is no consensus as to criminality. Some argue that there are too many laws, which actually causes law-abiding citizens to become violators. Regardless of how many laws there are or at what level of punishment they exist, the reality is that criminal law requires a criminal sanction. Four types of criminal sanctions are commonly used in the United States: fines, incarceration, probation, and capital punishment. An accused may present several defenses to excuse his or her actions. These include presenting an alibi and arguing duress, coercion, self-defense, youth, or insanity.

Historically, we have sentenced or punished individuals for their criminal behavior for any or all of the following reasons: retribution, atonement, incapacitation, deterrence, and rehabilitation. The United States relies more on imprisoning individuals for criminal behavior than any other democratic nation in the world. The ultimate sentence possible in the United States is capital punishment. The major issues that have accompanied the use of the death penalty are questions as to its constitutionality and its application.

Judges often have great latitude in sentencing criminals. The judge's decision is primarily based on the severity of the offense and the offender's criminal history. The choices available to judges in routine cases include fines, incarceration, and community corrections. In recent years, judges have also used alternative sanctions, such as restitution, community service, and restorative justice.

Discussion Questions

1. It has been said that we try to use classical methods to determine guilt and positive methods to punish offenders. Explain how this occurs.
2. Advocates of decriminalization argue that excessive laws create contempt for the criminal justice system that may actually result in more crime. Explain how you think this might occur or why you think it doesn't occur.
3. Discuss the pros and cons of decriminalizing the sale and use of marijuana.
4. Discuss the pros and cons of capital punishment.
5. Discuss the pros and cons of the insanity defense.

13

Dealing with Victims

Chapter 12 focused on the criminal justice system's response to criminal offenders. This chapter discusses the impact of crime on victims. The study of crime victims and issues related to victimization were also discussed in Chapter 11.

The Extent of Crime Victimization

As shown in Chapter 2, there are several means of determining the incidence of crime. Uniform Crime Reports (UCR) provide information on crimes reported to law enforcement agencies within a given year. These reports are augmented by the National Incident-Based Reporting System (NIBRS), which gathers more specific crime data such as incidence of family violence. Hate crime statistics are also gathered by the Federal Bureau of Investigation. In addition, the Bureau of Justice Statistics conducts the National Crime Victimization Survey (NCVS), which surveys households to try to obtain information beyond that reported to police agencies. Despite these efforts, there is still a great deal of uncertainty among scholars as to the true extent of crime and the actual number of crime victims in the United States at any given time. Fortunately, we can track crime trends by reviewing the changes within the various methods of data gathering (UCR, NIBRS, or NCVS). The good news at the time of this writing is that crime rates for both property offenses and violent crimes continue to decline.

According to the Uniform Crime Reports (Federal Bureau of Investigation, 2010a), 10,639,369 crimes were reported in 2009. Of these incidents, 12.4 percent were violent crimes and 87.6 percent were property crimes (see Table 13.1). The National Crime Victimization Survey (Bureau of Justice Statistics, 2010) yielded a much higher finding of 19.9 million crimes reported by victims in

2009. Of these, 21.6 percent were reported to be violent crimes and 72.4 percent were said to be property offenses. While these numbers in themselves may appear to be impersonal presentations, they represent individuals who have been harmed financially, physically, and/or emotionally as crime victims.

Victim characteristics in 2009 remained similar to those in previous years:

> Males, blacks, and persons age 24 or younger continued to be victimized at higher or somewhat higher rates than females, whites, and persons age 25 or older. Males were victims of violent crime at rates slightly higher than females, indicating a continuing convergence of male and female victimization.
>
> Differences between male and female rates of simple assault were not statistically significant in 2009. Males experienced higher rates of robbery and aggravated assault than females. Females were more likely than males to be victims of rape or sexual assault.
>
> African Americans were more likely than whites to be victims of overall violent crime, robbery, and aggravated assault, and somewhat more likely than whites to be victims of rape or sexual assault. African Americans also experienced higher rates than persons of other races (American Indian, Alaska Native, Asian, Native Hawaiian, and other Pacific Islander) of overall violence, robbery, aggravated assault, and simple assault. Persons of two or more races were victims of overall violent crime at higher rates than whites and persons of other races, and somewhat higher rates than African Americans. Hispanics and non-Hispanics were equally likely to experience overall violent crime, rape or sexual assault, aggravated assault, and simple assault.
>
> Hispanics were victims of robbery at rates higher than those of non-Hispanics. Generally, persons age 25 or older experienced violent victimization at lower rates than younger persons. Persons ages 12 to 15 experienced simple assault at rates higher than persons age 20 or older, and slightly higher rates than persons ages 16 to 19. (Adapted from Truman and Rand, 2010, p. 4)

It is obvious from these data that despite the decline in criminal occurrences, millions of Americans are victimized each year.

Table 13.1   UCR Crime Incidents in 2009

Total crimes	10,639,369
Violent crimes	1,318,398
Murder/manslaughter	15,241
Forcible rape	88,097
Robbery	408,217
Aggravated assault	806,843
Property crimes	9,320,971
Burglary	2,199,125
Larceny/theft	6,327,230
Motor vehicle theft	794,616

Source: Federal Bureau of Investigation, 2010a, table 1.

The Consequences of Victimization

In 2007, for crimes both reported and not reported, the total economic loss to victims was $2 billion for violent crime and $16 billion for property crime (Bureau of Justice Statistics, 2010). Of this amount, only about 35 percent was recovered by law enforcement officials. These costs reflect only the value of property taken and not the costs of medical treatment for victims of violent crimes. Nor do they reflect the costs of property and/or injuries in incidents not reported to the police. It is not unreasonable to assume that the financial consequences of crime victimization in the United States could be several times higher.

Individual Costs of Victimization

Individual victims of crime suffer many costs. The financial losses due to theft, arson, burglary, robbery, fraud, and other economic crimes can lead to financial difficulties for victims and their families. Medical costs for those who have been victims of violent crimes could run into thousands and even hundreds of thousands of dollars. In addition, families in which a wage earner has been incapacitated or lost to homicide may well face severe economic hardship.

The financial aspects of victimization may be minor in relation to the pain and suffering experienced by victims and their families. The emotional turmoil of losing a loved one to homicide or the trauma of being a victim of sexual assault or other violent crime can cause long-lasting grief and anguish. The physical harm from violent assaults may result in permanent pain, illness, or disability. Even the less painful experience of having one's privacy violated by a burglar can cause victims to become fearful of being victimized again. These fears may actually result in an individual's inability to cope with the pressures of work or school, family life, and social activities. Depending on the nature of the crime, victims may lose confidence in society's ability to protect them from harm and may withdraw (Karmen, 2010).

Societal Costs of Victimization

In addition to the cost to individual victims, the cost of crime for society as a whole is great. The economic costs to victims are often passed on to others. Retail establishments pass on the costs of employee theft, shoplifting, and robbery to their customers in price hikes. Insurance companies do the same with rate hikes. In a like manner, governmental intervention in compensating victims, investigating criminal incidents, adjudicating accused offenders, and dealing with convicted offenders is funded by taxpayer dollars that must be taken either from other governmental projects or from increased tax revenues.

The social costs of criminal victimization are also high. The fear of victimization may affect citizens who have not actually been crime victims but who are nonetheless fearful due to knowledge of real or alleged criminal incidents. Such fear can lead to a curtailment in social activities, limitations on travel, withdrawal from community involvement, restrictions in job potential and earnings, as well as a loss of confidence in the criminal justice system or even in the society in which they live. If such fears become widespread among a community, government officials will find it extremely difficult to maintain order and stability. Ultimately, the loss of citizen involvement and support will lead to further social disorganization with increases in crime and victimization (Karmen, 2010).

Types of Victimization

Chapter 11 included a substantial discussion of victim precipitation. Studies of victim precipitation generally focus on violent crimes in which there is, if only briefly, an interaction between victim and offender. However, the majority of crimes are not violent but are property crimes. In these incidents, the victim precipitation may have been flowers left on a front porch or simply being away from home. Different strategies are required to avoid being victimized by property and violent crimes. Preventing property victimization is often straightforward. You wish to protect your home from burglary and arson, your car from burglary and theft, and your other valuables from theft. Most of these protections are provided by using crime-prevention strategies, such as locks, security devices, lighting, and other target-hardening techniques. We limit our discussion here to the complex issue of victimization by violence.

Victimization by Strangers

Criminologists used to stress that you were more likely to be a victim of violence by a friend or family member than by a stranger. While this adage continues to have some merit, many of today's violent crimes are committed by strangers. Robbery, home invasion, carjacking, serial killing, road rage, sexual assault, aggravated assault, and hate crime are but a few examples of how one might be violently victimized by strangers. Safety precautions such as not walking alone on campus at night and not provoking other drivers are not only wise but necessary actions.

According to Robert Meadows (2010, p. 90), 52 percent of victims of nonfatal violence did not know their assailant, 45 percent of murder victims were related to or knew their killers, and 15 percent of murder victims were murdered by strangers. In 40 percent of murder cases, the correlation between victim and offender was unknown. Seven of ten robberies were committed by strangers, as were three out of ten reported rapes. The implications of these data are clear: in today's complex and diverse society, one must be cautious of strangers and in one's dealings with them. Caution moderated with politeness and a nonconfrontational demeanor are good strategies to avoid victimization.

Victimization in the Workplace

Violence within the workplace has gained the attention of criminologists, victimologists, criminal justice practitioners, the media, and the public in general because of highly publicized incidents at post offices, office complexes, governmental buildings, shopping centers, and schools. Much workplace violence is committed by strangers against taxicab drivers, police officers, hotel clerks, gas station workers, convenience store clerks, security guards, stock handlers, store managers, and bartenders (to name the occupations with higher rates of victimization). However, many incidents are the actions of disgruntled employees who take out their frustrations on coworkers, supervisors, and customers (Doerner and Lab, 2012).

Because of the increasing incidence of workplace violence, many organizations within the public and private sectors seek to reduce the potential for such incidents with proactive human resource programs designed to lessen tensions among employees. However, the pressures of modern society too frequently overwhelm these efforts.

Victimization by Family

The victimization of family members by other family members is a "dirty little secret" that most families wish to suppress. For example, a son learned that his father had ignored his elderly mother's request for help to deal with verbal and physical abuse on the part of his sister, who was living with the mother. It was later discovered that the sister had stolen money, as well as forged and cashed checks sent to her mother. The father's response was, "I just couldn't believe that she would do such a thing." That response is not uncommon; in many cases, victims and witnesses are actually ostracized and even threatened by family members to keep them from reporting their victimization to the police.

Of 421,493 victims of violent crime reported to the National Incident-Based Reporting System in 1998, 27 percent were related to the offender (Federal Bureau of Investigation, 1999, p. 280). The impacts of family violence are more frequently associated with the areas of spouse abuse, child abuse, and elder abuse. Table 13.2 displays the family relationships of victims to offenders as shown in the 1998 NIBRS report. Violence by family members outside the immediate family is not included in Table 13.2, but several hundred incidents by in-laws were also reported to the NIBRS in 1998.

Spouse abuse. Traditionally, **spouse abuse** meant an intentional assault resulting in injury to a married female by her spouse. Women living in common-

Table 13.2   **Friend and Family Violence by Victim's Relationship
to Offender**

Type of Crime	Total	Spouse	Ex-Spouse		
Crimes of violence	1,731,170	133,890	95,030		
Rape	105,760	6,790	NA		
Robbery	137,240	1,990	7,670		
Aggravated assault	289.440	17,140	8,920		
Simple assault	1,198,730	107,970	78,440		
Type of Crime	Parent	Own Child	Other Relatives	Well-Known	
Crimes of violence	29,870	59,120	190,710	1,222,550	
Rape	NA	NA	5,220	93,750	
Robbery	4,860	NA	28,350	94,380	
Aggravated assault	3,230	11,550	38,940	209,670	
Simple assault	21,780	47,570	118,210	824,750	

Source: Bureau of Justice Statistics, 2011, table 33.
Note: NA = not available because unable to estimate.

law marriages (that is, partners who have never exchanged vows but live together as husband and wife under the old English common law, which considers a couple married after a specified period of cohabitation) were often not considered spouses unless state statutes specifically included these relationships. Likewise, individuals who were cohabitating did not qualify as spouses. Most certainly, individuals living in same-sex relationships were not covered by spouse abuse statutes. As societal practices have changed, so has the interpretation of spouse abuse. Many states have now changed the term in their statutes to **domestic violence** to cover individuals living together within a "familial environment."

As the status of women within society has changed from subservience to equality, the tolerance of spousal violence has declined. Unfortunately, women's increased status and the changing relationship between men and women actually cause many batterers to intensify their efforts to assert their authority through violence (Karmen, 2010). Factors that influence the incidence of spousal abuse are many, and the factor that has more impact in a given situation varies with each relationship. Some factors leading to spouse abuse are social stress, power struggles or assertion of power by the batterer, marital dependency (which prevents women from leaving abusive relationships), and the influence of alcohol (Wallace, 2006). The common-law tradition that permitted a husband to "discipline" his wife was also ingrained within many domestic relationships.

Child abuse. Just as wives were historically viewed as the chattel of their husbands, children were often seen as the property of parents who were free to use and punish them as they saw fit. In today's society, children's advocates argue that corporal punishment such as spanking is not to be tolerated and cite nations such as Denmark where spanking is prohibited by law. We will not take a stance in this debate except to point out that while parents in the United States have the right to use corporal punishment, there is a clear distinction between a spanking and a beating. Unfortunately for hundreds of thousands of children, their parents or guardians are not aware of this distinction. The continued use of corporal punishment does not mean that society has turned a blind eye to **child abuse**. Injuries to children that once brought clucks of disapproval now result in law enforcement or family service agencies investigating the incident.

As with spouse abuse, the family dynamics that lead to child abuse are complex, and there are no simple remedies. The problem is exacerbated in that physical abuse is only one type of child abuse (Doerner and Lab, 2012). Many children are mistreated and/or neglected by their parents and suffer from malnutrition and disease due to inadequate food, shelter, and clothing. Still others suffer from emotional neglect by absentee or inattentive parents. Educational neglect occurs when parents fail to ensure that their children's educational needs are met. While less frequent in occurrence, the too common incidence of sexual abuse of children is a major concern of child advocates because of the severity of both physical and emotional harm the child suffers as a result. Last, the most common form of mistreatment is emotional abuse. Parents who would be horrified to be accused of any of the previous forms of mistreatment may not think twice when they berate, verbally abuse, or emotionally torment their children.

Elder abuse. A problem that has only recently gained the attention of victimologists is **elder abuse**. The elderly experience victimization at lower levels than do other age groups, but the impact of the victimization is often more devastating. As the number of senior citizens within our society continues to increase, the number of offenses against them is also expected to increase. One by-product of longevity is that as senior citizens become less able to care for themselves, they must depend more on family members or paid residential care. This dependence can lead to elder abuse by caregivers.

The types of abuse experienced by the elderly include physical, psychological, material, active, and passive abuse (Doerner and Lab, 2012). Physical abuse ranges from slapping to sexual molestation. Psychological abuse includes verbal abuse, threats, and intimidation. Material abuse consists of theft of money or property. Active abuse is the intentional neglect or failure to meet a caretaking obligation. Passive abuse occurs when caretakers unintentionally, through incompetence or lack of concern, fail to meet the needs of their charges.

Victimization of Special Populations

In addition to the problems already discussed, some attention to special populations is warranted. These **special populations** include women, young people, gays and lesbians, and the disabled.

Women. Women deserve classification within a special population because of the large number of sexual assaults committed against them each year by both strangers and acquaintances. According to a 1992 study by the National Victim's Center, one in eight women will be raped at some time in her life (Wallace, 2006). Often the rapist is not a stranger but an acquaintance, coworker, fellow student, friend, or even a family member.

Rape is a traumatic event that can leave lasting harm both physically and emotionally, but it is not the only type of victimization women must fear. Sexual harassment is a common experience for women of all ages and walks of life. Sexual harassment consists of demands for sexual favors, subjection to overtly sexual conversations and imagery, sex-based denigration and ridicule, a superior permitting a hostile work or school environment, and merchants or professionals charging more for products or services sold to women.

Young people. Young people are a special population because immaturity, dependence issues, and minority status make them vulnerable to abuse. As indicated earlier, young people have the highest incidence of victimization of any age group. In addition to abuse within the home, victimization of young people outside the home is a major concern for child advocates, parents, and law enforcement officials. The many changes that children experience during the teenage years and their desire to gain independence from adult domination make them particularly susceptible to victimization by adults as well as by other youths (Hunter and Barker, 2011).

The elderly. The fear of abuse within a residential setting is not the only one faced by the elderly. As they move into late adulthood, people become increasingly aware of their vulnerability to crime. Loss of physical prowess, health concerns, the constraints of reduced income, and feelings of powerlessness cause the elderly to fear victimization (Hunter and Barker, 2011). While statistics show these victimization rates to be relatively low, some offenders selectively prey upon the elderly. Con artists in particular often target older citizens for their scams.

Gays and lesbians. Whether gay and lesbian people constitute a special population is a matter of debate. Despite stereotyping on the part of straights, gays, and lesbians, sexual orientation is often not as obvious a characteristic as race or gender. However, because of the highly publicized incidents of violence against gay and lesbian people, this community warrants attention. As exemplified in the Matthew Shepard murder, which received national attention in 1998–1999, people are often targeted for victimization due to their sexual orientation.

The disabled. Individuals who suffer from physical or mental disabilities also deserve special consideration by criminologists and victimologists. Despite the equal protections guaranteed by the Americans with Disabilities Act of 1990, many disabled people are disenfranchised within US society (Hunter and Barker, 2011). Physical incapacitation, such as blindness or deafness, and limited mobility make these individuals susceptible to victimization both inside and outside the home. Likewise, people suffering from mental illness and mental retardation are also susceptible to victimization.

Hate Crimes

Individuals who make up special populations are often singled out for victimization because of their increased vulnerability. For example, according to his killers, Matthew Shepard was selected not because of hatred for gays, but because they thought he would be an easy target for robbery. Whether one accepts this argument or that of gay advocates, that Shepard was selected and viciously murdered because of his sexual orientation, is moot. Gay people are frequently victimized by those who have disdain for their lifestyle. Such acts, which are based not on situational factors but on animosity toward individuals who are "different," are classified as hate crimes.

In addition to sexual orientation, hate crimes often target members of ethnic or racial minorities (such as the dragging death of African American James Byrd Jr. by three white racists in Jasper, Texas). Disabled persons are also sometimes victimized by assailants who consider them unworthy, as in the case of the mentally retarded young woman who was brutally gang-raped by teenage boys in a New Jersey suburb. Members of religious minorities are also occasionally targeted, as was exemplified by the 1999 shooting of several young children at a Jewish child-care center in California.

Concern about the apparent increases in hate crimes have led to the gathering and publication of hate-crime statistics by the Federal Bureau of Investigation. Most states have created hate-crime laws that impose more severe penalties if the victim was selected on the basis of race, disability, sexual orientation, or religion. These often model the federal hate-crime law discussed in Chapter 2.

Responding to Victimization

Victims, concerned citizens, government officials, criminal justice practitioners, and scholars respond to victimization in a number of ways. Some of these responses are specific to victims, others target offenders, and still others emphasize community or societal solutions.

Crime Prevention

Programs designed to reduce the vulnerability of citizens to victimization are frequently implemented by law enforcement agencies, governmental agencies, civic organizations, and community action groups. The various types of crime-prevention programs that are available range from individual efforts to programs at every level of society. They may be educational or **victim awareness** programs and self-defense training at the local levels, special assistance programs at the local and state levels, or the enactment of prohibitive legislation at the state and federal levels.

Victim Assistance Programs

Victim assistance programs may be run by governmental agencies such as a district attorney's office, by private organizations that contract with the state or local government to provide services, or by volunteer organizations. The nature and extent of assistance vary, but victims can often find counseling and support from individuals who have had similar experiences. They may receive free medical or mental health services, or they may find someone who will assist them in understanding and enduring the strain of the criminal justice process.

Victim Compensation

Most states and the federal government have programs in which victims of crime who have filed police reports and indicated a willingness to cooperate in having their cases prosecuted are eligible for financial support from governmental agencies. Florida was one of the first states to implement a **victim compensation** program on a statewide basis when it created the Florida Crime Compensation Commission in the 1970s. Depending on the circumstances, victims may receive support in paying medical bills and/or living expenses incurred due to injuries resulting from a crime. Regrettably, at the time of this writing, most compensation programs of which the authors are aware tend to be underfunded, so financial assistance to victims is often limited.

Reality Check: Stalking

During the past twenty years the federal government, all fifty states, Washington, DC, and the US Territories have enacted laws making stalking a criminal act. Stalking is defined as a course of conduct directed at a specific person that would cause a reasonable person to feel fear. The more common stalking behaviors are making unwanted phone calls; sending unsolicited or unwanted letters or e-mails; following or spying on the victim; showing up at places without a legitimate reason; waiting at places for the victim; leaving unwanted items, presents, or flowers; posting information; and other actions that seek to force a relationship. In 2006, an estimated 14 in every 1,000 persons age eighteen or older were victims of stalking. About half (46 percent) of stalking victims experienced at least one unwanted contact per week, and 11 percent of victims said they had been stalked for five years or more. The risk of stalking victimization was highest for individuals who were divorced or separated—34 per 1,000 individuals. Women were at greater risk than men for stalking victimization; however, women and men were equally likely to experience harassment. Male (37 percent) and female (41 percent) stalking victimizations were equally likely to be reported to the police. Approximately one in four stalking victims reported some form of cyberstalking, such as e-mail (83 percent) or instant messaging (35 percent). Many (46 percent) stalking victims felt the fear of not knowing what would happen next. Nearly three in four stalking victims knew their offender in some capacity. More than half of stalking victims lost five or more days from work (Baum et al., 2009, p. 1).

Thanks to the efforts of victims' rights groups, stalking laws were enacted, stalking awareness and assistance programs are common, and statistics about stalking are readily available. As with all crimes, there is still much work to be done, but the progress in dealing with a crime that was previously ignored is phenomenal.

What do you think still needs to be done to prevent or reduce stalking incidents in the United States? What other crimes do you think should receive similar efforts by victim awareness and victims' rights groups?

Offender Restitution

Resulting from enhanced awareness and/or legal mandate, many judges are requiring offenders to make restitution for the harm they have caused victims. Monetary offender restitution requires offenders to make financial reparations to their victim. These payments may be made directly to the victim or may be paid to the court or community correctional officials for transfer to the victim. Offender restitution is similar to a fine in that moneys are paid to the community by the offender, but differ from traditional fines in that they are paid into programs specifically designated to aid crime victims. Service-offender restitution requires offenders to perform a specified number of hours of service for the victim to compensate for the harm that they caused. Service-community restitution usually requires a number of hours of community service as payment to the community for the criminal's victimizing behavior (Doerner and Lab, 2012).

Victims' Rights

In the 1980s and 1990s, advocates of **victims' rights** pushed for victims to have more participation in the criminal justice system. They called for victims to be made aware of and have input into plea bargain agreements, sentencing outcomes, and the release of offenders from prison. In response to these demands, the Victims of Crime Act was passed by Congress in 1984. This legislation provided millions of dollars in funding that helped establish many state compensation programs. In 1990, the Crime Control Act contained the Victims' Rights and Restitution Act and the Victims of Child Abuse Act. Among other things, these acts provided for victims of federal offenses to be notified of court proceedings, to be allowed to confer with governmental attorneys, and to receive restitution.

As of 1997, twenty-nine states had enacted victims' rights provisions within their constitutions (Doerner and Lab, 2012). In addition, many states and the federal government now require a **victim impact statement** to be provided to a court prior to sentencing. Actions at the state and federal levels have also made it easier for victims of crimes to hold their victimizers accountable in civil court for the harm done to them. O. J. Simpson was acquitted in the infamous "trial of the century" murder trial, but the families of victims Nicole Brown Simpson and Ronald Goldman were successful in their civil litigation against him. Unfortunately, a federal law allowing rape victims to sue their assailants in federal court instead of state court was struck down as unconstitutional by the US Supreme Court on May 15, 2000 (*US v. Morrison*, 99-5; *Brzonkala v. Morrison*, 99-29).

The victims' rights movement of the 1980s and 1990s helped educate the public about victims' issues, which also helped promote crime-prevention and victim advocacy efforts. In addition to education on how to avoid victimization and counseling on how to cope with victimization, programs in dispute resolution were also initiated. **Dispute resolution** programs enable offenders and victims to meet with arbitrators to resolve issues outside of (and sometimes instead of) criminal prosecution and/or civil litigation. Dispute resolution efforts that seek to help offenders and victims return to their pre-offense status are termed restorative justice (Karmen, 2010).

Summary

The costs of criminal victimizations run into the billions of dollars each year. These costs reflect only the value of property taken and do not reflect the costs of medical treatment. They do not reflect the greater costs of economic hardship, physical pain and suffering, or the emotional trauma experienced by victims and their families. Nor do they indicate the costs to society resulting from the fear of victimization.

In understanding victims' issues, it helps to understand the various types of victimization. Whether victimization is imposed by strangers, occurs in the workplace, or happens within domestic situations influences both the impact and means of dealing with victimization. Special populations of individuals who are particularly vulnerable to victimization require specific attention from criminal justice practitioners and scholars. Hate-crime legislation is one means of trying to deal with offenders who select their victims based on biases against certain groups or communities.

The problem of victimization in US society can be responded to by several means. These include crime prevention, victim assistance programs, victim compensation, offender restitution, and victim empowerment. The development of programs to aid victims is the direct result of the victims' rights movement and subsequent federal and state legal actions. Although there is still a long way to go, we have come far in a short period of time in understanding and coping with the problem of victimization.

Discussion Questions

1. Explain why the costs of victimization are high not only for individual victims but for other members of society.
2. Contrast the various types of victimization that occur within the family with those that occur within the workplace or that are perpetrated by strangers.
3. Debate the pros and cons of enacting hate-crime laws. If hate-crime laws are enacted, should they be the province of the state or federal government? Justify your view.
4. Discuss the various programs available within your state and community to deal with victimization.
5. Discuss the accomplishments of the victims' rights movement. Describe what you think the future accomplishments in this area will be and why they will occur.

14

Dealing with the Law Abiding

Throughout this text we have examined the different approaches to the study of crime and criminality and have presented different perspectives on the nature of crime and criminal behavior. Chapters 12 and 13 revisited those earlier discussions by assessing responses to offenders and victims. This chapter focuses on how these diverse views apply to members of society who do not commit criminal acts.

Justice in the Eyes of the Law Abiding

The purpose of government is to maintain order and promote stability within society. All other governmental activities are derived from this primary function (Magleby and Light, 2009). Criminal justice systems were created as governmental components to facilitate this basic obligation of government. While there are many forms of government (ranging from **democracy** to tyranny), each must have a means of making and enforcing law in order to continue to exist.

According to Frank Schmalleger (2011), social reality is interpreted according to the cultural experiences and personal interests of the observer. How people view the relationships among society, offenders, victims, and the justice system influences their belief in the justice system and ultimately their commitment to society. Just as the influences or lack of social bonds, strains, and social controls may explain criminal behaviors (Hirschi, 1969; Reckless, 1967), so too do they explain law-abiding behaviors.

The Politics of Justice

The United States is a nation bound by political traditions rather than ethnic or cultural traditions such as those found in many nations. This does not mean that issues such as ethnicity and culture are not important. Rather, it means that according to our governmental institutions, issues such as race, creed, color, religion, and national origin are not supposed to factor into public decision-making (Cummings and Wise, 2006).

Whereas a nation such as Sweden is composed of a relatively small homogeneous population, the United States has great **diversity** in ethnicity, cultural traditions, religious perspectives, socioeconomic status, and political ideologies. What this means for the criminal justice system is that not only do we not have the common ethnic or cultural heritage that helps bind other nations, but our common bonds of democracy and personal **freedom** are often disputed as well. The result is that justice in the United States is extremely political in nature.

Pause for a moment and think about the myriad political views held by those with whom you associate. Each of the approximately 307 million people thought to reside in the United States has his or her own individual perspective on how government (local, state, and federal) should operate, what should be lawful, how laws should be enforced, and how lawbreakers should be treated. Those who view the United States from an elitist perspective have very different views from those who view it from the perspective of political pluralism (the reader may wish to refer back to the social conflict discussions in Chapter 7). Partisan politics influences how the different levels of government are perceived and how they function. Sexism, racism, and classism (all of which have differing definitions depending on who is doing the defining) impact the political process (Greenberg and Page, 2009).

Determining what the balance will be between promoting crime control and protecting individual freedoms is difficult. A group who argues for personal liberties may see governmental involvement as abusive while another group may see those same governmental actions as ensuring such liberties (Hunter and Barker, 2011). Throughout this text, we have presented many different theoretical perspectives on why people become criminal. Chapter 12 presented differing means of dealing with criminal offenders. There are just as many disagreements on how government should deal with the law abiding.

The product of diversity is disagreement. No matter how tolerant individuals may claim to be, they tend to think less of those with whom they disagree than they do of those who share their views. Ensuring social stability requires that citizens have confidence in their governments (Greenberg and Page, 2009). Defining acceptable morality is even more complex (Montague, 1995). For these reasons, the administration of justice in the United States will continue to be highly politicized.

The Social Responsibility Perspective

The last quarter of the twentieth century saw an increasing conservatism of the American public and governmental entities in regard to crime control and dealing with offenders. Jerome Skolnick (2000) represents many **liberals**, and perhaps the majority of criminologists, who assert that this "get tough on crime mentality" is creating large prison populations, the policies are both economically and socially costly, and they are ineffectual in preventing crime. John Dillulio (2000) represents **conservatives**, and quite a number of criminologists, in his support for policies that have gotten dangerous criminals off the streets, lowered crime rates, and allowed the public to express their condemnation of criminal acts.

At the heart of this disagreement among respected criminologists, as well as within the US citizenry, is their perception of accountability. These disagreements hark back to the classical school's focus on the law and punishing those who knowingly violate the law (Barlow, 2000). This view is compatible with political conservatism in which a smaller, less intrusive government that holds people individually accountable for their actions is preferred (Cummings and Wise, 2006). Political conservatives tend to promote individual responsibility.

Schmalleger (2011) refers to this emphasis on an individual's accountability for his or her actions as *social responsibility*. This outlook stresses accountability in civil and noncriminal matters. While acknowledging that social forces may impact decisionmaking, social responsibility proponents argue that people still must be held accountable to society. In addition, criminals are punished to enforce system values. While social programs may help remove some factors that might lead to crime, they are seen as having little impact on deterring criminals from committing crimes. Therefore, strict law enforcement and harsher penalties reassure law-abiding citizens who hold to this perspective (Hancock and Sharp, 2004).

The **social responsibility perspective** is popular not only with political conservatives, but also with moderates and some liberals who believe that punishment is the only means of obtaining compliance from certain offenders. Indeed, the view of social responsibility advocates is based on punishment not just as deterrence, but as a means of atonement so that offenders may regain entry into society. At the very least, society is seen as being safe from victimization while the offender is incapacitated and/or incarcerated.

Perhaps the greatest benefit of this perspective to ordinary citizens is that it gives them a "sense of justice," that is, they believe that evildoers will be punished for their crimes. Victims of criminal acts, as well as the whole of society, find comfort in the belief that the governments they pay their taxes to will enact vengeance on their behalf (Montague, 1995). By exacting vengeance, government promotes stability not only by deterring criminals or would-be criminals from future crime, but also by preventing citizens from "taking the law into their own hands" by seeking personal vengeance.

Another major benefit of this perspective is that it reinforces within the citizenry the idea that they as individuals are accountable to society for their actions. This emphasis serves to ensure compliance with governmental edicts and social norms, as well as with criminal codes. In addition, accountability promotes self-reliance and self-worth, which are seen as enabling individuals and groups to achieve success within society.

The Social Problems Perspective

Just as positive criminology challenges classical criminology in regard to individual responsibility and punishment, so the **social problems perspective** challenges the social responsibility perspective (Schmalleger, 2011). Social problems such as poverty, discrimination, poor education, family violence, the breakup of traditional social institutions, and poor socialization are seen as leading to crime. Since these are social problems, society, not the individual, should be held accountable for criminal behavior.

Instead of strict law enforcement and harsh penalties, social programs designed to ease the burdens of the poor and of other groups who have previously experienced social injustice are preferred. Many advocates of the social problems perspective are political liberals who support government intervention because they believe that society as a whole is responsible for the actions of individuals within that society. These advocates prefer promoting social **mores** and norms as well as sharing in the responsibility for society and the community by creating government-sponsored programs to address perceived social ills (Magleby and Light, 2009). Strict law enforcement is seen as being counterproductive to developing a just and equitable society (Skolnick, 2000).

Proponents of the social problems perspective call for more governmental intervention to ease the burdens on the poor and protected classes. Critics of the social problems perspective argue that its supporters are seeking to punish the law abiding by infringing on their individual rights (such as gun ownership) and view these efforts as "coddling criminals" and promoting immorality. Some conservative political activists have gone so far as to accuse advocates of gun control of using crime issues to promote their political agenda. Proponents respond that any inconveniences to the middle class and the affluent are necessary concessions to social well-being and should therefore be tolerated.

The greatest benefit of the social programs perspective is that it seeks to prevent crime before it occurs by addressing societal issues that may promote crime. While the poor and members of disadvantaged social groups are usually targeted by these programs, the advantages are believed to extend to all members of society. Those who support the social responsibility perspective tend to approve of programs such as Head Start, Social Security, Medicare, and Medicaid. Indeed, highly criticized programs such as welfare are usually attacked because of perceptions of mismanagement, abuse, and corruption rather than the premise of whether society should help those in need.

Critics of social programs usually do not object to governmental efforts at addressing social ills; it is the perceived inequities in the methods in which the programs are applied that rankle. Providing help is sanctioned as long as it does not create dependence or reward irresponsibility (Greenberg and Page, 2009). Defenders respond that it is better to have a humane system with some flaws than to neglect those who are needy. They argue that individual account-ability cannot be imposed on all members of society if all of its members are not able to fully participate in society. Therefore, the social ills (poverty, homelessness, hunger, inadequate medical care, racism, sexism, homophobia, religious intolerance, elitism, etc.) must be addressed by governmental pro-grams supported by the tax dollars of those who can afford to pay for them. Critics respond that such interventions are intrusive and place undue burdens on the working class and lower middle class (Cummings and Wise, 2006). They are also seen as creating a "social crutch" that causes the poor as well as others to become reliant upon government programs.

Depending on one's religious, political, and personal ideologies, choosing between the two perspectives may be very easy or quite difficult. Just as it is difficult to decide what correctional technique should be applied to an offender, so it is difficult to decide what obligations members of society should have toward other members. Ultimately, both perspectives promote individual responsibility and accountability to society: The social responsibil-ity perspective does so by calling for good citizens to comply with the law and do their part. The social problems perspective does exactly the same. It is not the intent or the caring that differs; it is the process by which it is applied.

The Social Engineering Perspective

The debate over social responsibility and social problems is further stirred by those who believe that neither perspective adequately addresses the problems of US society. Critics of these perspectives believe that stressing individual accountability only exacerbates the frustration and feelings of injustice expe-rienced by the poor and the oppressed. In like manner, trying to fix social problems by enacting governmental programs such as Equal Employment Opportunity and welfare are but minor efforts that do not address the underly-ing problems inherent in capitalism. Instead, critics believe social engineering is called for to ensure that society is properly structured. The **social engineer-ing perspective** is the view that society is so badly flawed that it must be reworked by those best equipped to do so.

Critical and radical criminologists, as well as adherents of the political far left, argue for stronger measures than those found within welfare capitalism. Some social engineering advocates urge that the United States become more socialistic by using governmental intervention to redistribute wealth and pro-mote international egalitarianism. Others see **communism** as the only fair solution to eliminate the legacy of greed, corruption, and oppression that cap-italism has created (Bohm and Vogel, 2011). Less extreme proponents of social engineering do not call for adopting **socialism** or communism as an economic system but do see the need for increased government intervention and the increased use of social institutions to bring about social changes (see the social control arguments of Chapter 7).

Such ideas of using education and governmental pressures to impose social changes on the law-abiding masses are not new: During the 1800s, Native Americans and immigrants were forced to become "Americanized" or suffer harsh consequences from the government, social institutions, and private citizens. In the late 1800s, **social Darwinism** encouraged poverty and governmental neglect as a means of eliminating the unfit from society. In the 1950s, McCarthyism sought to rid the nation of leftists who were believed to threaten the moral decency and economic stability of US society. Today voices from both the left and the right seek to impose their views on the majority (Hunter and Barker, 2011).

Calls for equitable treatment of women, gays and lesbians, and minorities have received support throughout the nation. Cultural diversity has been recognized as an integral aspect of life in the United States. While there has often been disagreement over the methods to use (such as reliance on Equal Employment Opportunity enforcement versus maintaining affirmative action), the disagreements are mostly over process and anticipated effects rather than fairness and equality. However, despite a "confused consensus" among Americans in general, many on both the left and the right are dissatisfied.

Political correctness, religious conservatism, and civil rights activism are but some of the many issues that are debated across the country. The nature and role of government itself receive endless scrutiny. In election years, Democrats, Republicans, and a multitude of smaller parties cajole voters with promises of what will happen if they are elected and threats of what will not if they are defeated. Regardless of party, politicians and political pundits are increasingly concerned about the indifference and skepticism of the electorate, without realizing that it is they who have created that alienation. As our society continues to develop, many Americans will continue to be unhappy with the directions that are or are not being taken, and this unhappiness will impact the administration of justice.

Administering Justice on Behalf of the Law Abiding

This section describes various activities on the part of government that are designed to influence the opinions and behaviors of the law abiding. While these events are characterized within the US system of justice, they are not unique to the United States but may be found in any nation regardless of political structure.

Condemning and Punishing Crime

When nation-states came into being, the government accepted responsibility for exacting vengeance on behalf of those who had been harmed by criminal actions, which not only enabled government to administer justice uniformly, but also kept citizens from having to achieve their own revenge (Roshier, 1989). As we have discussed, it is a basic human emotion to strike back at those who have done harm to us or our loved ones. If governmental agencies (police, courts, or corrections) are not perceived as exacting justice on behalf of their constituents, there will most assuredly be people who feel a need to impose their own justice on those who have offended against them.

The act of condemning and punishing crime is a fundamental responsibility of government (Packer, 1968). It is through punishment that government demonstrates to the victims, their friends, their families, and the public in general that the government can and will exact vengeance on their behalf (Montague, 1995). This support from government is also displayed in public calls for sympathy for victims, as well as calls for new criminal sanctions. The responses to the Oklahoma City bombing in 1995, the dragging death of James Byrd Jr. by white racists in 1998, the murder of Matthew Shepard in 1998, and the Columbine High School massacre in 1999 are examples of how government can show support for crime victims. Despite criticisms of then-president Bill Clinton on other justice issues, he was always quick to offer his personal support and the more important figurative condolences of the nation to victims of sensational crimes. While some may criticize such actions as political posturing, they also send a message of compassion and sympathy that benefits the victims as well as concerned citizens across the nation.

Wooing Constituents

Seeing lawbreakers punished is also a means of maintaining citizen support for criminal laws and government in general (Packer, 1968). While we have stressed that punishment is a classical approach that is more appropriate to a conservative political **ideology**, that does not mean that moderates and liberals do not sanction its use. Indeed the successful effort on the part of liberal Democrats to enact federal and state hate-crime legislation exemplifies such support. Conservative Republicans also do the same, as evidenced by federal carjacking laws that were enacted despite the fact that every state in the union has laws against auto theft, robbery, kidnapping, and murder that would cover any carjacking incident. In these cases, the goal is not to necessarily correct a void in the law, but to make points with political constituents. Another motive may be to extend governmental influence into areas that were previously considered to be outside government's sphere of influence.

Promoting Social Change

In addition to showing constituents that they are tough on a particular category of crime, politicians use the criminal justice system to maintain control over the population (Packer, 1968). An unspoken message is "do what we feel to be appropriate voluntarily or we will enact a law that makes compliance mandatory." Federal hiring regulations, protection of voting rights, and sexual harassment prohibitions are illustrations of governmental interventions to halt social wrongs that were not being addressed.

Governmental intervention in a behavior that has previously been considered to be lawful may come about because of technological advancements, for instance the development of the Internet, social movements such as civil rights, less dramatic changes in the social mood like increased fear of victimization, or the efforts of "moral entrepreneurs" who successfully lobby for new laws to halt a behavior that they consider to be evil or inappropriate. Regulation of pornography and nude dancing, limitations on the sale of alcoholic beverages, restrictions on tobacco, and regulation of firearms are examples of this strategy (Siegel, 2010).

In short, just as lawbreakers are punished if they do not conform to the legal codes imposed by government, the law abiding are punished with new legal codes if they do not yield to governmental pressures to change. Enacting criminal codes is not the only means by which the law-abiding populace is pressured to change its behavior. Civil procedures and administrative rulings may serve the same purpose. But perhaps the most successful means that political, social, and economic leaders have for imposing their will on the populace is media exposure.

Despite denial by the news and entertainment media, they are instrumental in shaping Americans' outlook on what is and is not socially acceptable behavior. Social change may be more readily accomplished by statements and actions on the political stage and in the media than through the enactment of laws. In fact, the successful application of law often involves a great deal of public debate and media coverage (consider the debates over gun control, school prayer, and abortion) both prior to and after the passage of the law. Politicians may not have to use legal codes; they may be able to use social condemnation of opponents and the support of their allies in the news and entertainment media to accomplish the same purposes.

Rewarding Compliance

The rewards to law-abiding citizens that are provided by the criminal justice system are many: public safety, which enables us to conduct our daily business and to let our children play in our neighborhoods; an orderly society, in which, despite diverse opinions on myriad political, social, and economic issues, we are able to participate in social activities with only limited fear of terroristic

Reality Check: Symbolic Reassurance

For many years, Ronald D. Hunter (1995, 1996) has advocated an alternative explanation of how and why justice is administered. He refers to this perspective as **symbolic reassurance**. The concept of symbolic reassurance builds on the importance of the *idea* of justice. The basic premise of this theory is that the criminal justice system not only provides guidelines for society to follow but also punishes evildoers to affirm the belief of the law abiding in the system. The mass citizenry are law abiding not because they fear the law, but because they believe in it. Therefore, universal conformity is not attained through threats of prosecution but by reassuring the law abiding that the system of justice is working.

This principle may even be taken to the extreme by asserting that to a large degree, it does not matter what is being done as long as the public perceives that *something* is being done. Symbolic reassurance asserts that the criminal justice system exists not to deal with lawbreakers but to reassure the law-abiding public. As long as a few offenders get occasional punishment (the more severe, the better), the public, especially the middle class, will remain compliant, even if they are not totally satisfied.

There are many means of dealing with criminal and deviant behavior. No one theory will emerge as the miracle solution to the problem of crime, which is a normal social phenomenon. What is truly important is that law-abiding citizens believe that they are being served and therefore do not have to take the law into their own hands. Serious social unrest—society-wide distrust that threatens the existence of governmental entities, not the isolated and short-term threats exemplified by urban riots or actions of fringe groups—will occur only if governmental institutions fail to symbolically reassure the general populace.

activities; low crime rates compared to other Western democracies; and, despite minimal amounts of crime, protection of individual freedoms. Indeed it is not the acts of justice (i.e., punishment of offenders) but the *idea* of justice that unites society.

Summary

The United States has great diversity in ethnicity, cultural traditions, religious perspectives, socioeconomic status, and political ideologies. What this means for the criminal justice system is that not only do we lack the common ethnic or cultural heritage that helps bind other nations, but our common bonds of democracy and personal freedom are often disputed as well. The result is that justice in the United States is extremely political in nature.

Political conservatives place emphasis on an individual's accountability for his or her actions. This social responsibility outlook stresses accountability in civil and noncriminal matters. Strict law enforcement and harsh penalties are seen as reassuring by law-abiding citizens who hold to this perspective. The social problems perspective holds that it is society, not the individual, who should be held accountable. Instead of strict law enforcement and harsh penalties, social programs designed to ease the burdens of the poor and other groups who have previously experienced social injustice are preferred. The debate over social responsibility and social problems is further stirred by those who believe that neither perspective adequately addresses the problems of US society. Social engineering is the view that society is so badly flawed that it needs reworking.

The act of condemning and punishing crime is a fundamental responsibility of government. While there is considerable disagreement among politicians, criminal justice practitioners, and citizens as to how the criminal justice system operates, government must demonstrate to the public that it will exact vengeance on behalf of victims and society as a whole. Government also uses legal sanctions (or the threat of new legal codes) to encourage citizens to comply with changes that those in power wish to create within society. The greatest reward for compliance on the part of law-abiding citizens is social stability. Therefore, it is not specific actions of the justice system but the idea of justice that unites society.

The concept of symbolic reassurance asserts that in addition to providing legal guidelines for citizens to follow, lawbreakers are punished to affirm the belief of the law abiding in the system. Rather than obtaining compliance through general deterrence, compliance is gained by reassurance that the system is working for them.

Discussion Questions

1. Describe how political disagreements have an impact on the administration of justice in the United States.
2. Compare and contrast the three perspectives on criminal justice.
3. Describe how law-abiding citizens are influenced by governmental and social institutions to conform to social policies and norms.
4. Describe the premise of symbolic reassurance, and explain how it may be applied within US society.

15

Theory in Practice

We are now in the fifteenth and final chapter of this theory text. Some of you have gained insights that will benefit you as a researcher, practitioner, policymaker, or taxpayer. Others are perhaps just happy to be almost done. Either way, you will find that this course has been a beneficial experience.

However, the more important question at this time is, how do we apply all these theories? Which are useful and which are useless? How you answer those questions is based upon your self and world views. Those views determine your philosophies in regard to social responsibilities, governmental controls, and how to properly address crime and criminality.

Controlling and Preventing Crime

Individual and Social Accountability

The social responsibility outlook is most compatible with classical criminology. Deterrence theorists emphasize individual accountability and focus on making crime less pleasurable through the use of punishment. Opportunity theories focus on environmental and situational factors that bring criminals and victims together.

The social problems perspective is compatible with positive criminology. Biological and psychological theories seek to understand why individuals act as they do in order to explain the human behaviors that produce criminality. Social structure theories focus on the problems within society and seek to address them in order to reduce or eliminate the inequities that are felt to produce criminal behaviors. Social process theories attempt to explain the different ways in which people are pushed or pulled into committing crimes based

237

upon their social attachments and their perceptions of how they are viewed within society.

The social engineering perspective is compatible with the social conflict theories. Non-Marxist theories view the conflicts between competing interest groups as normal social behaviors. However, the actions taken by those holding power may result in social engineering efforts designed to impose their views upon society as well as maintaining or increasing their group's power. Marxist theorists see capitalism as the base cause for all crimes. Their efforts are geared toward increased governmental controls of the private sector, redistributing wealth through progressive taxation, and greater governmental intervention to protect those in need.

The Different Levels of Crime Prevention

In 2010 Ronald D. Hunter presented different levels of crime prevention and victimization avoidance strategies. He divided potential crime locales into three levels: *micro*—specific individuals, groups, businesses, and similar neighborhood sites; *meso*—individuals, groups, and sites in larger communities, small cities, rural counties, and remote areas; and *macro*—collectives of individuals, groups, and sites within large cities, populous counties, states, nations, and international settings. The level at which an individual or site is located directly impacts the crime-prevention techniques utilized, as well as their success (Hunter, 2010, p. 211).

The micro-level of crime prevention. Hunter used the categories of primary, secondary, and tertiary prevention to describe prevention strategies appropriate at the micro-level. *Primary prevention* involves reducing a site's, or individual's, or small group's vulnerability or a motivated offender's perceptions of opportunity in order to keep crimes from occurring. *Secondary prevention* entails reducing an obvious vulnerability on the part of potential victims or crime sites, or addressing community or area issues that might encourage at-risk individuals or groups to engage in criminal activities. *Tertiary prevention* includes dealing with individuals or sites that have been victimized, or apprehending and dealing with those individuals or groups who have committed crimes within a community or local area (Hunter, 2010, p. 212).

Victim-based prevention techniques at the micro-level seek to prevent crimes from occurring by reducing vulnerability or target attractiveness. Victim-based secondary prevention strategies seek to address identified or obvious vulnerabilities by promoting awareness among potential victims (individuals, groups, neighborhoods, etc.). Victim-based tertiary prevention techniques at the micro-level seek to reduce the trauma of victimization for individuals and to reduce the potential for further victimization of individuals, specific groups, or crime sites.

Offender-based primary prevention techniques at the micro-level emphasize reducing potential offenders' perceptions of success. Potential offender–based secondary prevention techniques at the micro-level are geared to reducing the likelihood of individuals or groups within an area or community to be drawn into criminal behaviors. Actual offender–based tertiary prevention techniques at the micro-level include the myriad correctional methodologies that attempt to keep individual offenders from reoffending.

As can be seen, these techniques are compatible with the deterrence and opportunity theories discussed in Chapter 4, the social disorganization theories explained in Chapter 7, as well as the victimization theories discussed in Chapter 11.

The meso-level of crime prevention. Meso-level crime prevention focuses on potential crime targets and victims within larger communities, small cities, suburbs, rural counties, and remote areas such as parks and tourist attractions that draw large numbers of visitors. The differences in prevention methodologies at the meso-level are based not on a particular individual, group, or crime site, but on categories of individuals, groups, or crime sites in larger and more diverse domains.

The micro-level prevention techniques described above are also applicable at the meso-level. Programs such as neighborhood watch, community development, civic awareness, and police-community initiatives are especially relevant and should be expanded to address the challenges presented by larger cultural, geographical, and political areas. The primary differences would be in the use of business regulations, zoning requirements, city and county ordinances, as well as special districts and intergovernmental task forces to apply primary prevention strategies to different groups at dissimilar locations.

Meso-level strategies are compatible with deterrence, opportunity, social disorganization, and victimization theories used within micro-level prevention strategies. In addition, several of the other social structure theories are useful as the scale and complexity of preventing and controlling crime increase.

The macro-level of crime prevention. The macro-level of crime prevention addresses individuals, groups, and sites within large cities, populous counties, states, nations, and international settings. Crime prevention is addressed by community and local entities. Densely populated metropolises, global business interests, transnational travel, and international relations require greater resources and coordination of crime-prevention efforts.

Due to the impacts of global communications and travel within modern societies as well as the increased potential for organized crime and international terrorism, the coordination of crime-prevention efforts requires increasing involvement on the part of states, nations, and international organizations. It is at the state and national levels that more serious crimes are defined and

Reality Check: The Need for a Holistic Approach to the Prevention of Drug-Related Crimes

Efforts to deal with the impacts of illegal drugs may be broken down into five categories: education, interdiction, strict enforcement, treatment, and legalization.

Education. These efforts focus primarily upon promoting awareness of the negative impacts of illegal drug use on individuals and their families. These may be through television campaigns or the ubiquitous DARE (Drug Abuse Resistance Education) programs found in most communities. While these programs may be classified as a macro-level approach that is primary in nature, their effectiveness as a drug-prevention strategy is questionable.

Interdiction. As with education, this is a combined approach that may be seen as macro and primary in nature by those seeking to keep illegal drugs from being shipped to their country, and micro and tertiary by those seeking to halt drug traffickers who are operating within their communities.

Strict enforcement. This approach may also be seen as primary and macro in regard to the concept of general deterrence. However, the effects are more realistically viewed as tertiary and micro-level in nature.

Treatment. Dealing with individuals who are addicted to illegal drugs is an important and obligatory response. While policies and funding for treatment programs may be of a broad scope, these programs are by necessity micro and tertiary in their application.

Legalization. The concept of legalization is controversial in that it is felt to send a message that drug use is acceptable and that the harm from such use is to be ignored. However, arguments of equal merit contend that drug abuse should be dealt with as a medical problem. They also point out that legalization would eliminate criminal organizations that develop in response to legal prohibitions. Compromise strategies that stress partial legalization and refocusing of efforts on the more dangerous drugs are more realistic.

The mixture of diverse prevention strategies at different levels in the "war on drugs" is an example of how local though global practices should be utilized. Unfortunately, they suffer from a lack of coordination of efforts and from competition for limited resources.

laws are enacted to prevent or reduce their occurrence (and to reassure the law-abiding populace that order is being maintained). In addition to crime legislation to provide for general deterrence, states and nations develop policies and programs designed to eliminate social ills that serve as catalysts for crime. Tertiary prevention at the macro-level has been the predominant, and arguably the least effective, strategy utilized in US crime prevention. While progress has been made in the areas of treatment, restorative justice, and victim-offender mediation, the focus of tertiary prevention at all levels has been specific deterrence through the punishment of offenders.

Recommendations for the Future

In order to advance crime-prevention efforts, we as members of a global society that emphasizes local responses to crime and criminality must understand that just as there is limited agreement in regard to what constitutes crime, there is less agreement in how to respond to crime. No one solution or emphasis of specific levels of response will succeed.

Future crime-prevention efforts must be international in scope but must also provide for individual responses at the local level. More important, they must be comprehensive rather than competitive in their application. Our theoretical orientations, practices, and evaluation efforts must be integrated into a holistic crime-prevention model in order to advance crime prevention in the future.

Discussion Questions

1. Explain how human nature may relate to the social accountability/ responsibility perspectives regarding crime control.
2. Explain how different levels of crime prevention complement one another.
3. Discuss whether the actions of the criminal justice system are really theory driven.

Glossary

Active precipitation   When individuals or groups engage in behaviors that are provocative or instrumental in causing their victimization.

Adjudication   The legal process by which an individual is found guilty and a punishment is determined.

Age-graded theory   A theory based upon the premise that a deviant personality was not necessarily developed at an early age.

Aggravating circumstances   Relevant issues about the commission of a crime that may result in a more severe punishment for the offender of a specified crime.

Alibi   Verification from others that the accused could not have committed the crime because he or she was either elsewhere or physically incapable of committing the crime.

Anomie   Normlessness and apathy experienced by those unable to cope with the rapid social changes that occur around them.

Assault   Unwanted and intentional physical contact made by one person against another.

Atavism   Asserts that criminals are throwbacks to an earlier era in human development and their criminal behavior is the result of primitive urges.

Atheism   A belief system that denies that God exists. It may be practiced to the point of "religious fervor."

Atonement   The idea that an offender must "pay his or her debt to society" so that, having atoned for the crime, he or she can then reenter society with a clean slate.

Behavioral theories   Psychological theories that examine learning experiences. In criminology, they focus on processes that lead to criminal behavior.

Bioconditioning theory   Merges biology, behavioral psychology, and classical criminology into a holistic explanation of criminality. Individuals' personalities are influenced by these physical features that shape how they see themselves as well as how others see them.

Biocriminology   The study of biological influences, such as physiological disorders, genetics, and environmental factors, that influence criminality.

Bioenvironmental theory   Argument that human behavior is the product of complex and constantly changing interactions between the physical environment and the social environment.

Biosocial theories   The scientific study of relations of social species and their relationships with the environment, and the study of the relations between biological and social factors.

Burglary   The unlawful entry into a building, vehicle, or machine with the intent to commit some type of criminal action.

Caring   The act of showing compassion and empathy for others. It is often the basis of a person's belief system.

Capital punishment   The use of the death penalty as punishment for having committed serious crimes. Usually reserved for those having committed heinous murders.

Certainty   The likelihood of being caught, adjudicated, and punished is perceived as high enough to discourage both the offender and similar-minded individuals.

Child abuse   Mistreatment or neglect of a child by a parent or legal guardian.

Class conflict   Competition among the various socioeconomic classes. Conflict theorists, especially Marxists, see this as a power struggle between the "haves" and the "have-nots" that leads to hostility and resentment on the part of the lower classes that will eventually lead to revolution.

Classical conditioning   The behavioral process by which a learned reaction becomes automatic and internalized.

Classical school   Promotes punishment of individuals for their criminal behaviors based upon the crimes they committed. Punishment is seen as serving as a means of deterrence from future crime for the specific offender and others.

Codes of criminal procedure   Delineate how government officials will enforce the substantive laws. Ensure that due process of law is followed.

Coercion   Threats or force applied by another person capable of causing the accused or the accuser's loved ones harm in order to force them to comply.

Cognition   The mental process involved in acquiring knowledge.

Cognitive scripts model   Individuals recall past experiences from memory to deal with new situations.

Cognitive theories   Focus on how the mental processes, such as thinking and moral development, affect one's behavior.

Commitment to conformity theory   Short-term stimuli that influence behavior are controlled by the individual's commitment to a normal society.

Communism   A sociopolitical movement based upon the principles that social class and capitalism harm the poor and the working class. It aims to replace private property with public ownership of the modes of production.

Community corrections   Alternative sanctions that allow offenders to remain within the community under correctional supervision.

Community service   A common sentence for lesser offenders. This compulsory service in public projects may involve menial tasks (e.g., picking up trash, washing police cars) or actually using job skills (carpentry, mechanical abilities) to benefit the community.

Compatible victimology theory   Theoretical application that uses a multidisciplinary approach to victimology. Provides for divergent perspectives in the study of victimization.

Concentric zone theory   Uses the tendencies of large cities to expand radically from their central business districts as a means of describing how social disorganization occurs.

Conceptual absorption theory   Argues that we already have integration within criminological theories. The concepts used to explain the behaviors of criminal offenders are compatible and, in some cases, the same as those used by other theories.

Conceptual integration theory   Argues that criminological theories are already integrated and provides a framework to show how other theories complement one another .

Concordance   A key concept in twin studies research. It is the term used in genetics for the degree to which related pairs of subjects show a particular behavior or condition.

Conflict perspective   Society is a collection of diverse groups that are in constant conflict. Criminal law is a means of protecting the power of the upper class at the expense of the poor.

Conflict theory   An attempt to identify society's power relations and draw attention to their roles in promoting criminal behavior.

Conscience   The moral values one has that guide an individual's thoughts and actions. It can lead to feelings of pride when integrity has been maintained and remorse when it has not.

Conscious   Pertaining to Freud's theory, one of three levels of the mind. The conscious mind is the aspect of the mind of which people are most aware.

Consensus perspective   Crimes are behaviors that are essentially harmful to the majority of citizens and there is agreement that these crimes should be controlled or prohibited by criminal laws.

Conservatives   Those who support individual actions or systemic efforts that try to preserve existing norms and traditions. In law, they seek to follow the framers' original intent.

Containment theory   Explores how the strengths of inner and outer controls push individuals toward conformity or criminality.

Control balance theory   Merges concepts from social control, social learning, rational choice, and anomie to explain how predisposition, provocation, opportunity, and constraint determine behavior.

Corporate crimes   Criminal activities conducted during the course of doing business or that result from inappropriate business practices.

Crime event theory   Focuses on the situational factors that triggered a criminal event rather than the relationship between the victims and offenders.

Crime prevention   Programs designed to reduce the vulnerability of citizens to victimization or prevent crimes from occurring.

Crime statistics   Data collected by surveys or reports such as the National Crime Victimization Survey or the Uniform Crime Reports that enable crime trends to be measured and evaluated.

Crime typologies   Frameworks and theoretical constructs used to describe and compare different forms of criminal behavior.

Criminalization theory   Examines the conditions under which cultural and social differences between authorities and subjects will probably result in conflict.

Criminal law   Legal code that attempts to control public behavior by defining what constitutes a crime.

Criminal personality theory   The belief that social environment has little impact on the development of criminal behavior. Instead the criminal is accountable for his or her actions.

Criminological theory   Any theory of human behavior that seeks to explain the causes and consequences of crime and criminal behavior.

Criminologist   An individual who studies criminology and criminal justice from a scientific perspective in order to understand and explain crime, its causes, and its impacts.

Criminology   The scientific approach to the study of crime as a social phenomenon, that is, the theoretical application involving the study of the nature and extent of criminal behavior.

Critical theory   Perspective based on structural Marxism that emphasizes that the social order is dominated by class interests and that crime is the product of social inequality.

Critical victimology theory   Focuses on inequitable social and economic conditions that are thought to influence the incidence of crime and victimization.

Culture   A system of norms and beliefs that are followed by a racial, ethnic, religious, or social group. These may become the standards for an entire nation or society.

Culture conflict theory   The perspective in social science that emphasizes social, political, or material inequality of the lower class as a means of explaining why members may act differently from middle-class norms.

Cultural deviance theory   Identifies the aspects of lower-class life that produce street crimes by adding the concept of culture to Shaw and McKay's (1942) social disorganization theory.

Darwin's theory of evolution   A theory of evolutionary development that claims that all species, including humans, developed from lower life-forms. It is the basis for scientific explanations of the existence of life on earth.

Decriminalization   Refers to redefining certain criminal behaviors and making them either lesser offenses or lawful.

Defiance theory   Explains how lower-class delinquency may be perpetuated due to sanctions that are deemed to be unfair or too harsh.

Deindividuation   A situational instigator in which the loss of self-awareness and of personal accountability by members within a group can lead to behaviors that would not normally be carried out by individuals.

Delinquency development theory   Asserts that there is continuity in criminal behavior that reaches from early childhood into the adult years depending upon family and social influences.

Delinquent subcultures   Group norms counter to unattainable middle-class culture arise and persist in the lower-class areas of large urban cities due to poverty and social inequality.

Democracy   A government based upon the consent of the people. Citizens have input through the elective process. Due to size constraints, most democracies are representative democracies rather than pure democracies.

Determinate sentencing   The assessment of a specific number of years in prison. This may be by designated term or by a calculated formula based upon the sentence.

Determinism   The theory that all events, including human choices and decisions, have sufficient causes. The idea that factors beyond a person's control determine behavior.

Deterrence   The application of punishment to an offender in order to alter behavior or prevent misconduct. It can be either general or specific in nature.

Deviant places hypothesis   Focuses on those areas in which social disorganization and crime tend to flourish thus causing a deviant place.

Differential anticipation   People commit crimes whenever and wherever expectations of gain from the criminal act exceed expected losses.

Differential association theory   People learn to commit crime through their association with others. The nature and extent of these associations, in comparison to contrary exposures to others, determine behaviors.

Differential opportunity   Theory based on the premise that the opportunities for lower-class youth to reach the American dream are blocked, causing them to resort to illegitimate means.

Differential reinforcement   Criminal behavior and attitudes are more likely to be learned when they are rewarded by friends and family. When anticipated rewards exceed potential punishment, crime occurs.

Differential social control   Explains how a person who is "different" can come to accept the label he or she takes on prior to the actual involvement in a criminal act.

Dispute resolution   Programs that enable offenders and victims to meet with arbitrators to resolve issues outside of criminal prosecution and/or civil litigation.

Distributive justice The concept that justice seeks to distribute rewards and punishment in an equitable manner in which merit is considered as well as need.

Diversion programs In order to avoid criminal prosecution, the offender receives counseling, attends school, obtains job training, acquires employment, or performs other mandatory actions.

Diversity A combination or variety, mostly to do with culture or people.

Domestic violence Acts of violence or abuse against a person living in one's household.

Due process Each individual who is charged with violating a criminal law must be accorded the full protection of the law during the investigation, prosecution, and adjudication of his or her case.

Duress Factors out of their control caused the accused to violate the law to avoid a greater harm (such as breaking into a remote mountain cabin to escape a blizzard).

Economic philosophies Class division in a capitalist society is based on economic standing. The elite, who are seen to have the power and prestige, are dominant in society and control all aspects of life.

Egalitarianism A belief system that emphasizes human equality in how people are treated and how basic necessities are distributed.

Ego The conscious state of the personality that operates on the "reality" principle, which orients the person toward the real world in which he or she lives.

Egoism The view that morality ultimately rests on one's self-interest. If it is seen as beneficial to the individual, it is deemed to be appropriate.

Elder abuse Mistreatment or neglect of the elderly, generally by a caregiver. It may include psychological, physical, material, active, or passive abuse.

Electra complex The unconscious sexual feelings that female children are said to naturally have toward their fathers.

Elite Members of the upper class who are viewed as having control over society.

Elitist theory Sees society's elite as forcing concessions from the middle class to placate the lower class.

Empiricism The method and practice of seeking knowledge based upon the application of scientific observations.

Entrapment Occurs when the police or their agents actually entice someone into committing a criminal act that he or she would not have contemplated doing on his or her own.

Environmental factors Biological and social influences on human behavior. They explain the relationship between nature and nurture in determining one's actions.

Equity All similar crimes must be punished in a similar manner (allowing for legal considerations such as mitigating and aggravating circumstances).

Equivalent group hypothesis Victims of crime often exhibit the same behaviors and lifestyle characteristics as their offenders.

Ethical system An individual or group philosophy that guides one in addressing questions about concepts such as good and bad, right and wrong.

Ethics The discipline that defines moral principles and how they should be properly applied.

Ethnicity A specific identity, background, trait, or association usually based upon race, religion, or national origin.

Expectancy theory Expectations about consequences and reinforcement of behaviors play major roles in decisionmaking.

Felony Any offense punishable by more than one year of incarceration in a state or federal prison.

Feminist theory Relates to the effect of gender and the inequitable treatment of women within society. Provides insight from the female perspective on social inequality and crime.

Fines Monetary value set by the judge that offenders must pay to the court.

Focal concerns theory Asserts that the lower class has a separate identifiable culture distinct from middle-class values that focuses on survival within its social environment.

Freedom Being at liberty to do as you want within limitations imposed by society to protect others.

Free will The concept that individuals are free to make their own choices and to act on those choices.

Freudian psychology Freud adopted the idea of the unconscious and argued that some behaviors could be explained by traumatic experiences in early childhood.

Frustration-induced criminality Individuals become accustomed to rewards for certain behaviors. When those rewards are not provided, individuals become frustrated and act out. The greater the expectations are, the greater the frustration at being denied.

Functional responsibility theory The perspective that everyone within society has a responsibility to conduct him- or herself appropriately. Crime usually occurs when both victim and offender engage in inappropriate behaviors.

General deterrence Punishment is administered to an offender to make others, who may be contemplating similar acts, aware that they risk suffering the same punishment.

General paradigm theory According to Vila, a theory must include biological, sociocultural, and developmental factors in the explanation for all types of crimes.

General strain theory Explains how inner stresses and strains can cause criminal behavior in all classes of people, not just the lower class.

General victimology theory Utilizes a multidisciplinary approach to investigate the causes of victimization and the search for effective remedies.

Genetics The branch of biology that deals with heredity, especially the mechanisms of hereditary transmission and the variation of inherited characteristics among similar or related organisms.

Grim determinism The belief that God has ordained certain behaviors and nothing can prevent them from occurring.

Group conflict theory Postulates that conflict between groups should be viewed as one of the principal and essential social processes upon which the continuance of society depends.

Hard determinism Strongest version of determinism. Hard determinists reject free will. Human behavior is the product of influences of which the individual has no control.

Hate crimes Acts based not on situational factors but on animosity toward individuals who are deemed to be "different."

Have-nots Those who do not have power and control due to their low standing in society.

Haves Those who have power and control because of their high social standing in society.

Hedonistic calculus The weighing of pain, imposed by society for a criminal act, against the pleasure received from committing the crime.

Holistic incorporation Attempt to adapt multifactor perspectives in order to more readily explain criminal behaviors.

Hostile attribution model Previous influences on mental development can cause some people to interpret actions as hostile and threatening. Because of their flawed perceptions of hostility, they respond aggressively to situations that do not warrant aggression.

Human nature Characteristics shared by all human beings, usually innate behaviors, but often influenced by social development.

Human nature theory Genetic makeup, intelligence, and body type have considerable impact on human behavior.

Human rights The idea that there are universal rights for all humankind, principally the rights to food, shelter, and freedom from persecution.

Id The innate urges and impulses thought to underlie all behavior. It is a permanent unconscious state and responds to the "pleasure principle," which causes one to seek and maintain his/her own pleasure regardless of the expense to others.

Identity Distinct moral and emotional characteristics of an individual. Worldview and self-image are major influences.

Identity theory Can also be called enviro-classical conflict theory. It draws from a variety of approaches that might ordinarily be seen as incompatible to explain how nature and nurture influence how individuals perceive themselves.

Ideology An internal belief system or set of guiding principles for an individual or group.

Imitation Modeling behavior that is learned through observation of others, including criminal behavior.

Incapacitation Preventing offenders from further criminal behavior by removing their ability to commit a specific crime. Incarceration is the more commonly used means of incapacitation.

Incarceration Imprisoning criminal offenders for a period of time based on the seriousness of the crime committed.

Indeterminate sentencing Sentencing process in which an offender is given a range of years to serve in a correctional facility. The amount of time actually served is determined by the inmate's response to correctional efforts. A positive response results in a shorter period of incarceration.

Index crimes Data collected by Uniform Crime Reports. These include murder and non-negligent manslaughter, forcible rape, robbery, aggravated assault, burglary, larceny/theft, arson, and motor-vehicle theft.

Individual difference theories The emphasis of these theories is the use of individual-level data to research crime and criminality.

Insanity The inability to make appropriate decisions due to a mental defect or condition. Criminal justice is concerned with whether the accused was insane at the time of the crime and/or incapable of assisting in preparation of his or her own legal defense.

Instrumental Marxism Views capitalism as the root of social conflict and crime. Proponents argue that capitalist elites are the real criminals within society.

Integrated biological theories Stress the importance of physiological factors' interrelationships with other factors in determining an individual's behaviors.

Integrated conflict theories Criminological explanations premised on the conflictive nature of society.

Integrated control theories Use the social control perspective as the foundation of their integrated approaches.

Integrated learning theories Emphasize social learning theory as the foundation for multifactor explanations of criminal behavior.

Integrated psychological theories Explain how social factors can influence individuals' self-perceptions.

Integrated sociological theories Include a combination of integrated learning theories, integrated control theories, integrated strain theories, and integrated conflict theories to explain criminal behaviors.

Integrative delinquency theory Shoemaker's (2009) view that social controls affect self-image. Low self-control can influence susceptibility to criminality.

Interactionist perspective Accepts that criminal law defines the actions constituting a crime, but views criminal law as being influenced by those who hold social power to reflect their interests.

Interdisciplinary model A multifactor approach whereby more than one possible area of inquiry is considered. It emphasizes the interaction of various individual and environmental influences on crime and criminality.

Interest group competition Political pluralism. Relating to group conflict, it serves to hold all groups in check and to keep any one from becoming too powerful.

Just deserts The idea that society needs to see that criminals receive the punishment they deserve based upon the harm that they caused.

Justice The quality of being fair or just to all people regardless of their place within society.

Justicology Myron's (1970) terminology for the study of the criminal justice system, its components, and processes.

Labeling theory Individuals will often accept the labels assigned to them by those in authority, especially when the labeling is done by loved ones.

Larceny/theft Unlawful taking of another's property in order to deprive that individual of ownership or use.

Law A system of codified rules and guidelines enacted by an empowered legislative body that is enforced by different institutions and agents of social control.

Law abiding Those citizens who conduct themselves by keeping within the confines of the law.

Left realism Pragmatic critical approach that acknowledges that criminals may be found at all levels of society. This research seeks to scientifically demonstrate how social inequities produce criminal activities at all levels. It advocates providing solutions within the existing quasi-capitalistic social order.

Legal model One of the five models of criminology. Uses a legal orientation based upon free will and rational thinking to determine punishment. This is the basis for the US system of justice.

Liberals Those who hold to a political and/or social philosophy that the increased use of government is necessary and appropriate to regulate economic, social, and political conditions within a democratic society. Focus is on addressing social inequities that are seen to cause crime rather than punishing offenders.

Lifestyle theory Holds that people may increase or decrease their potential to become victims of crime based upon their lifestyles.

Lower-class culture The view that certain groups and individuals tend to persist in a state of poverty because they have distinct beliefs, values, and ways of behaving that are incompatible with economic success.

***Mala in se* crimes** There is a consensus among the population that these are evil actions in and of themselves and should be prohibited.

***Mala prohibita* crimes** Behaviors or actions that are illegal solely because of bans imposed by legislative bodies (usually influenced by moral entrepreneurs) that found such activities were hazardous to society.

Mandatory sentencing Refers to the automatic imprisonment for a specific period of time of an offender convicted of a designated crime (such as use of a firearm in a felony). Exists in several states.

Marxist theory Political, social, and economic philosophy articulated by Karl Marx that biases resulting from class divisions in capitalist societies will inevitably lead to conflict between the working class and the elite. The view is advanced that the dominant class influences all aspects of life and that a classless society should be created.

Medical model   Attributes criminal behavior to internal and external influences that limit or prohibit rational thinking and/or freedom of choice. Focus is on biological and psychological reasons for criminal behavior.

Mental disorders   Physiological and/or psychological impediments that impair one's ability to cope with life events in an appropriate manner.

Mental illness   Condition of the mind that may cause a person to think or act irrationally or without comprehension. This condition can range from mild emotional distress to outright insanity.

Middle-class measuring rod   Theoretical view that delinquency is due to status frustration and an inability to achieve success in a legitimate manner. Delinquency is seen as a function of the social and economic limitations suffered by less fortunate youth.

Misdemeanors   Offenses punishable by a fine or incarceration of one year or less in a city or county jail.

Mitigating circumstances   Relevant issues that may have played a role in the commission of a crime and might result in a more lenient sentence than would be imposed for a similar crime.

Moral development theory   A cognitive theory that explains how offenders may have failed to grow morally. Kohlberg (1969) offers six stages of moral development.

Morality   Ethical standards of conduct that are generally accepted as right or proper within a culture or society.

Mores   Established customs, traditions, and practices that a social group of people accept as proper and follow.

Multifactor approaches   Combining two or more theories in an attempt to apply a particular theoretical framework to other explanations for criminal behavior.

National Crime Victimization Survey   A survey of randomly selected participants designed to learn about crimes not reported to the police. It is believed by advocates to provide a more credible set of data on the type and frequency of criminal victimization than the Uniform Crime Reports.

National Incident-Based Reporting System (NIBRS)   This program, which began in 2004, is an expansion of the Uniform Crime Reports program coordinated by the Federal Bureau of Investigation. It is more detailed in its analysis and gathers information on more crimes than the UCR system. By 2011, approximately 20 percent of US law enforcement agencies were participating.

Neoclassical school   A revision of classical criminology. The new concepts made allowances for issues that might impact the rationality and/or the free will of offenders. Issues include aggravating and mitigating circumstances, immaturity, insanity, duress, ignorance, and chemical impairment.

Neo-Marxist theories   Are more pragmatic than Marxist theories and tend to provide empirical rather than subjective support for their arguments. Proponents are seen as left realists.

Neutralization theory   Also known as drift theory. Youths learn ways to rationalize their delinquent actions. It is seen as an explanation of why youths drift in and out of criminal behavior as well as why they usually do not become adult offenders.

Non-Marxist conflict theories   Theories that see competition and conflict among interest groups, rather than consensus and stability, as governing the social order.

Norm   A standard, model, or pattern regarded as typical.

Occupational crimes   Crimes committed in the course of one's employment. They may be on behalf of or against the offender's employer.

Oedipus complex   The unconscious sexual feelings that male children are said to naturally have toward their mothers.

Operant conditioning   Uses rewards and punishment to reinforce certain behaviors, and is the dominant learning theory in behavioral psychology.

Organized crimes   Criminal activity that is committed in an orderly and continuous fashion by a group or organization created to accomplish that purpose.

Overcriminalization   When there are so many laws in place that law enforcement is impaired and respect for the law is diminished, crime is said to go up. In part this is due to new laws that lead formerly law-abiding people to become offenders.

Parole   Early release from prison of an inmate who is then subject to continued monitoring as well as compliance with certain terms and conditions for a specified period.

Passive precipitation   Victims unwittingly contribute to their victimization through action (or inaction) that makes them more vulnerable.

Peacemaking theory   Offers the precepts of nonviolence, social justice, inclusion, correct means, ascertainable criteria, and categorical imperative to try to create a more fair and equitable justice system.

Penology   The study of punishment, treatment, and correctional techniques.

Personal factors theory   Social, physical, and psychological factors of individuals help to provide an understanding of their susceptibility to criminal victimization.

Personality studies   The study of emotions, attitudes, and behavioral responses of individuals in order to predict future behaviors.

Physiological disorders   Any of a number of genetic, neurological, or other biological influences that may seriously impact human behavior.

Political model   Views crime as the product of conflicts among competing interests, groups, and political organizations within society.

Political/state crimes   Criminal activities committed by government officials for economic profit, to gain or maintain political power, or to harass or suppress political opposition.

Politics   Who gets what, when, where, and how. The art of trying to influence others to support an individual's, a group's, or a political party's perceptions of what is best.

Positive school   Calls for scientific analysis rather than legal actions. Rather than punishment based upon the severity of the crime, the positive school called for treatment based upon the needs of the offender.

Postmodernism   Argues that the modern emphasis on scientific rationality has reduced the importance of humanistic thinking, causing a multitude of social ills.

Preconscious   Pertaining to Freud's theory, one of three levels of the mind. The preconscious mind is said to contain elements of experiences that are outside our awareness but can be brought back to consciousness at any time.

Prevention   Actions designed to keep potential offenders from committing a crime (primary), to deter individuals exhibiting propensities toward criminal activities from doing so (secondary), or responding to offenders who actually committed crimes (tertiary).

Primary victimization   Refers to personalized or individualized victimization in which the victims were selected for victimization based on personal attributes.

Probation   A means of keeping a person under community supervision without incarceration.

Procedural laws   Regulate how to uphold and/or enforce substantive laws.

Projection   Freudian concept in which individuals with repressed desires deny their desires and behaviors. Instead, they attribute those desires or behaviors to others.

Property crimes Crimes in which a person or group intentionally deprives another person of his or her right to that property by either destroying or taking the property.

Proximity hypothesis Similar to equivalent group hypothesis in that it considers the influence of the victim's lifestyle on his or her vulnerability to crime.

Psychoanalysis Developed by Sigmund Freud, who was concerned with the medical treatment of functional disorders that seemed to be unrelated to any organic cause. In psychoanalysis a patient is encouraged to talk freely about whatever comes to mind. The therapist then explores the associations among the issues raised to help the patient deal with them.

Psychodynamic theories Examine unconscious behaviors that are believed to cause criminal behavior.

Psychometry Examines personality and how one adapts to life's demands and problems.

Psychopathology The study of individuals who exhibit psychopathic, sociopathic, or antisocial behaviors.

Public order crimes Activities that are illegal because they are deemed to be disruptive or to interfere with socially accepted behavior.

Punishment The act or process of punishing, imposing, and/or applying a sanction as retribution for a crime.

Radical Islam A fundamentalist form of Islam that promotes a devotion to the sacred law, a rejection of Western influences, and the transformation of faith into political ideology.

Radical theory Believes that capitalist society should be replaced by communism. Only through the creation of the "new society" can the evils of poverty and crime be eliminated.

Reaction formation A person acts out in extreme ways regarding certain issues. These behaviors are often a result of repression.

Reasonable doubt Beyond a reasonable doubt is the standard of proof required in most criminal cases within an adversarial legal system. To meet this standard, proof must be so convincing that a reasonable person having heard all the facts in a case would believe the defendant to be guilty of the crime.

Recidivism A measure of the effectiveness of rehabilitation programs or the deterrent effect of punishment by observing how many former offenders return to criminality after their release from correctional supervision.

Rehabilitation The main concept of the positive approach to criminal behavior. The underlying basis of rehabilitation is that criminal behavior results from sociological, psychological, or physical imperfection.

Reintegration A newer strategy advocated by positivists that allows offenders to either remain within the community or be placed within the community prior to their release from correctional custody.

Reintegrative shaming theory Braithwaite's theory that compassionate shaming is a means of enforcing moral standards as well as encouraging offenders to rejoin the law-abiding community.

Relative deprivation The idea that individuals assess their situation based on those around them. If they determine that others are better off than they are, they may become frustrated and anomic.

Religion The beliefs and practices concerning the existence, nature, and worship of a deity or deities and divine involvement in the universe and human life.

Repression The ability to keep feelings below the surface of consciousness. These repressed feelings, which may include hostility and sexual feelings, may unconsciously cause an individual to act out in an unexpected manner.

Restitution Compensation for the harm incurred by the victim due to his or her loss. This is seen as a means of lessoning the impact on the victim and as a means of atonement on the behalf of the offender.

Restorative justice Another strategy that is being used for lesser offenses, this is a peacemaking approach that uses meditation in lieu of judicial sanctions to seek to restore both the victim and the offender to their precrime status.

Retribution The act of punishing or taking vengeance against an offender for his or her wrongdoing.

Rewards Favorable outcomes used to reinforce certain behaviors.

Robbery The felonious taking of property from a person in his or her presence, against his or her will, by violence or intimidation.

Routine activities theory The daily and/or normal activities of offenders and victims may bring them into contact with one another. Focuses on reducing opportunity rather than motivation to commit crimes.

Science The study of the physical and natural world and phenomena, especially by using systematic observation and experimentation.

Secondary victimization Occurs when the societal response to victimization is callous, negative, or stigmatizing. Such behaviors can actually have a more devastating impact on crime victims than the primary victimization.

Secular humanism A philosophy or worldview that stresses ethics and human values without reference to religion or spirituality. It is argued that secular humanism is actually a religion without a deity.

Self-concept How an individual perceives herself/himself. Individuals' worldviews and the perceived views of others (particularly family members) influence how they see themselves.

Self-control theory Merges control theory with rational choice, routine activities, and biological and psychological explanations. The theory states that people with low self-control are predisposed to committing crimes if opportunity arises.

Self-defense The action by which a person justifiably protects himself/herself and/or others from injury arising out of assault or attack by a person perceived to be capable of rendering harm.

Self-derogation theory An integrated theory that combines sociological and psychological theories to explain how the need for self-esteem may cause a person to engage in criminal behavior if legitimate opportunities are blocked.

Self-esteem Confidence and satisfaction that a person feels with him- or herself.

Self-report surveys Supplement to the two primary sources of crime data. Provide an alternative to obtaining data that cannot be derived from official statistics. However, the validity is questionable due to the dependence on individuals and/or groups acknowledging their unlawful activities.

Self-view A view of one's self; specifically, regard for one's own interests.

Severity Harm or injury that is deemed to be of a more serious nature is viewed as having a higher severity than less harmful occurrences.

Sex Designation of gender within society, which determines how individuals sees themselves and how they are treated. Formerly, designations were male and female based upon reproductive organs. However, these boundaries have been expanded by modern definitions such as transgender designations.

Sexual assault The uninvited touching of the genitals, the unwilling touching of the genitals of another, or the penetration of another in a sexual manner.

Situational factors theory Belief that certain situational factors may lead to specific criminal events. Environmental influences, geographic location, and prevention strategies are assessed to determine vulnerability. These are integral to rational choice theory.

Situational instigators   Provides support for the view that behaviors may be situational and that circumstances of the situation may override previously developed prohibitions. Obedience to orders from an authority figure exemplifies these effects.

Skepticism   A questioning attitude toward knowledge, facts, or opinions/beliefs stated as facts. While skepticism can be dogmatic rejection of factual proofs, in scientific inquiry it is the practice of confirming causal relationships rather than jumping to conclusions.

Social bonds   Elements that include attachment to families, institutions, and social norms and activities and the belief that they are important in resisting crime.

Social bond theory   The belief that the self-control of an individual can be built by manipulating the processes of socialization and social learning. The stronger social bonds are, the greater the resistance to criminal influences.

Social conflict theory   Non-Marxists view crime as the natural product of societal power struggles. Marxists and critical theorists call for the restructuring of society in order to achieve a just and equitable social order.

Social contract   A commitment between an individual and society. The individual has an obligation to abide by laws enacted by society's legislative bodies, and the state has the responsibility to provide fair and equitable treatment of that person in exchange for compliance.

Social control theories   Propose that people's relationships, commitments, values, norms, and beliefs encourage them not to break the law. If people are tied to their community and have moral codes, they are less likely to commit deviant acts.

Social Darwinism   A nineteenth-century theory that the social order is the product of natural selection. Therefore, helping the poor was a violation of survival of the fittest.

Social development theory   Integrated control theory that incorporates social learning and structural modeling to explain how children are socialized through family interactions.

Social disorganization   Shaw and McKay's attempt to explain crime and delinquency as a product of transition or change in the urban environment. Certain communities remained "disorganized" regardless of who migrated into or out of them.

Social ecology theory   The successor to Shaw and McKay's (1942) social disorganization model. It abandoned the idea of concentric zones and focused on the social ills, particularly social inequality, that plagued certain areas of large cities.

Social engineering perspective   The view that society is so badly flawed that it must be reworked by those (who think that they are) best equipped to do so.

Socialism   Political theory or system in which the means of production and distribution are controlled by the people and operated according to equity and fairness rather than market principles.

Social justice   The promotion of principles of equity and fairness in the distribution of society's resources. This is seen as necessary in order to have a just society that recognizes the dignity of every human being.

Social learning   The concept that humans learn through associations with others. As learning takes place, both good and bad behaviors may be reinforced. This is the basis of all the social learning theories of criminality.

Social norms Specifications of proper and appropriate behavior generally supported and shared by members of a social group.

Social problems perspective   Poverty, discrimination, poor education, family violence, breakup of traditional social institutions, and poor socialization are seen as leading to crime.

Social process theories   Criminal behavior is a function of a socialization process. Offenders turn to crime as a result of peer group pressure, family problems, poor school performance, legal entanglements, and other situations that gradually steer them to criminal behaviors.

Social reaction theories   Focus upon reactions of individuals, groups, and society as a whole to people who are different from the norm. Reactions to those who are different can lead to criminal responses that may then be reinforced due to labeling and stigmatization.

Social reality theory   Argues that conflict is intertwined with power and that differential distribution of power produces conflict, which is rooted in the competition for power.

Social reinforcement   A component of social reaction theories that explains how socialization is reinforced by the frequency and duration of contacts with significant influences within society.

Social responsibility perspective   The conservative view that an individual is accountable for his or her actions in society.

Social structure theories   The premise that the lower classes engage in criminal and deviant behavior to a higher degree than the middle class does because of inequitable social conditions.

Sociological model   Focuses on criminal behavior as resulting from social conditions that restrict legitimate opportunities for the poor to achieve success.

Sociology of law   The sociological understanding of how laws are created, enacted, modified, and applied.

Soft determinism   Views behavior as having biological (nature) or sociological (nurture) characteristics. In this perspective, an individual's freedom of choice may be limited by either nature or nurture.

Special populations   Groups of people who deserve special attention in order to overcome bias, blocked opportunities, and other social challenges. These might be women, young people, gays and lesbians, elderly, and the disabled.

Specific deterrence   The offender who has committed the criminal behavior is punished in order to teach her/him that the benefits received from the act were not worth the costs of the punishment for the crime.

Spouse abuse   Traditionally an intentional assault resulting in injury to a married female by her spouse. In modern US society, it may refer to assault or abusive behavior against a domestic partner regardless of gender or marital status.

Status theory   Power and prestige are seen to be key issues within the conflict that exists in society.

Strain theory   Focuses on the problems of the lower classes within society. Emphasizes an individual's inability to reach higher goals or values because of his or her economic standing in society.

Structural functionalism   Holds that society as a whole is sound but that there are anomalies that impact upon individuals and groups, leading to criminality. The emphasis is to identify conditions that may cause criminal behavior and seek to eliminate them.

Structural Marxism   View that capitalist society produces social inequities that lead to crime, but considers other social influences.

Structure/process theories   Emphasize the use of aggregate-level data to research crime and criminality.

Sublimation   Negative drives are diverted to activities that are approved by the super-ego.

Substantive law   Codified law that defines what is criminal and what the sanctions for violations will be.

Superego   The force of self-criticism and conscience. The moral aspect of a person's personality, used to judge his or her behavior.

Swiftness   In criminal justice, swiftness focuses on the speed in which a criminal is arrested, convicted, and punished for his/her behavior. Swiftness, along with severity and certainty, is a basic tenet of deterrence theory.

Symbolic interactionist theory   Theory that explains how individuals and groups interact, focusing on the creation of personal identity through interaction with others. Of particular interest is the relationship between individual action and group pressures.

Symbolic reassurance   Theory that the criminal justice system provides guidelines for society to follow, then punishes evildoers to affirm the belief in the system by those who are law abiding.

Tertiary victimization   Occurs when the public or society as a whole is considered to be the victim of criminal activity.

Typologies   Frameworks and theoretical constructs used to describe and compare different forms of criminal behaviors.

Unconscious   Pertaining to Freud's theory, one of three levels of the mind. The unconscious mind contains biological desires and urges that cannot readily be experienced as thoughts.

Uniform Crime Reports (UCR)   The most frequently cited source of crime statistics based upon crimes reported to the police, compiled and published annually by the Federal Bureau of Investigation.

Utilitarianism   A social ideology that, in their laws and actions, governing bodies should seek to achieve the most utility or good for the greatest number of people.

Vengeance   The act of or desire for taking revenge; retributive punishment by a government or family on behalf of the victim.

Victim assistance   Programs that provide services for victims of crime to cope with the effects of criminal acts against them.

Victim awareness   Programs developed to help educate the public about victims' issues, crime prevention, and victim advocacy efforts.

Victim compensation   Programs in which victims of crimes are eligible for financial support from governmental agencies.

Victim impact statement   Information given to the judge before sentencing by the victim or a member of the victim's family regarding the harm that was done to him or her.

Victimization   The subsequent effects of crimes on their victims.

Victimless crimes   Behaviors that do not have any direct victims but are criminalized because they are deemed to be socially unacceptable.

Victimology   The study of crime victims and issues related to victimization.

Victim precipitation   Concept that a victim could be a contributing factor to his or her successive victimization.

Victim precipitation theory   The idea that the victim's actions could possibly influence or actually cause his or her victimization.

Victims' rights   Legal protections and political advocacy that supports awareness of rights for crime victims and their input in plea bargain agreements, sentencing outcomes, and the release of offenders from prison.

Victim typology   Characteristics based on physical, social, and psychological disadvantages that could result in potential victimization.

Violent crimes   Intentional actions that cause some form of bodily injury or death to another.

Worldview   One's perspective on life; a comprehensive and personal conception of humanity and the world.

Xenophile   Someone who is drawn to those who are unlike him or her and who is antagonistic toward those who are similar.

Xenophobe   Someone who fears and dislikes people who are different from him or her.

Youth   The period between childhood and adulthood, described as the period of physical and psychological development from the onset of puberty to maturity and early adulthood.

References

Adherents.com. (2011). Religions_By_Adherents. http://www.adherents.com/Religions _By_Adherents.html. Retrieved March 15, 2011.

Adler, E. S. and Clark, R. (2007). *How It's Done: An Invitation to Social Research*, 3rd ed. Belmont, CA: Wadsworth Publishing.

Adler, F., Mueller, G. O. W., and Laufer, W. S. (1998). *Criminology,* 3rd ed. Boston: McGraw-Hill.

Agnew, R. (1985). A revised strain theory of delinquency. *Social Forces* 30:47–87.

Akers, R. L., and Sellers, C. S. (2009). *Criminological Theories: Introduction, Evaluation, and Application,* 5th ed. New York: Oxford University Press.

Albanese, J. (2004). *Criminal Justice,* 3rd ed. Needham, MA: Allyn and Bacon.

American Psychiatric Association. (1994). *Diagnostic and Statistical Manual of Mental Disorders,* 4th ed. *(DSM-IV).* Washington, DC: American Psychiatric Association.

Amir, M. (1971). *Patterns in Forcible Rape.* Chicago: University of Chicago Press.

Anderson, E. (1999). *Code of the Street: Decency, Violence, and the Moral Life of the Inner City.* New York: W. W. Norton.

Anderson, J. R., and Bower, G. H. (1973). *Human Associative Memory.* Washington, DC: Winston and Sons.

Arrigo, B. A. (1999). *Social Justice/Criminal Justice: The Maturation of Critical Theory in Law, Crime and Deviance.* Belmont, CA: West/Wadsworth.

Bandura, A. (1977). *Social Learning Theory.* Englewood Cliffs, NJ: Prentice Hall.

Bandura, A., and Walters, R. (1959). *Adolescent Aggression.* New York: Ronald.

Barkan, S. E. (2012). *Criminology: A Sociological Understanding,* 5th ed. Boston: Prentice Hall.

Barlow, H. D. (2000). *Criminal Justice in America.* Upper Saddle River, NJ: Prentice Hall.

Bartol, C. R., and Bartol, A. M. (2011). *Criminal Behavior: A Psychosocial Approach,* 5th ed. Upper Saddle River, NJ: Prentice Hall.

Bartollas, C. F., and Schmalleger, F. J. (2010). *Juvenile Delinquency,* 7th ed. Boston: Prentice Hall.

Baum, M., Catalano, S., Rand, M., and Rose, K. (2009). *Stalking Victimization in the United States.* Washington, DC: Bureau of Justice Statistics.

Beccaria, C. (1963). *Essay on Crimes and Punishments.* Translated with an introduction by H. Paolucci. New York: Macmillan.

Bell, R. (2011). George Stephanopoulos interviews "Love Wins" pastor Rob Bell. ABC's *Good Morning America*. Aired March 15, 2011.

Bentham, J. (1948). *An Introduction to the Principles of Morals and Legislation*. Edited by L. I. Lafleur. New York: Hafner.

Berkowitz, L. (1962). *Aggression: A Social-Psychological Analysis*. New York: McGraw-Hill.

Bernard, T. J., Snipes, J. B., and Gerould, A. L. (2009). *Vold's Theoretical Criminology*, 6th ed. New York: Oxford University Press.

Black, R. W. (1999). Girlfriend: McKinney told of killing. *The Daily Camera*, October 29. http://homes.thedailycamera.com/extra/shepard/29bshep.html. Retrieved May 7, 2011.

Blau, J., and Blau, P. (1982). The cost of inequality: Metropolitan structure and violent crime. *American Sociological Review* 147:114–129.

Bohm, R. M. (1982). Radical criminology: An explication. *Criminology* 19:565–589.

Bohm, R. M., and Vogel, B. L. (2011). *A Primer on Crime and Delinquency Theory*, 3rd ed. Belmont, CA: Wadsworth/Cengage.

Bonger, W. (1969). *Criminality and Economic Conditions*. Introduction by A. T. Turk. Bloomington: Indiana University Press.

Booth, A., and Osgood, D. W. (1993). The influence of testosterone on deviance in adulthood: Assessing and explaining the relationship. *Criminology* 31(1):93–117.

Bordua, D. J. (1958). Juvenile delinquency and "anomie": An attempt at replication. *Social Problems* 6:230–238.

Braithwaite, J. (1989). *Crime, Shame and Reintegration*. Cambridge: Cambridge University Press.

Brantingham, P. J., and Brantingham, P. L. (2008). Crime Pattern Theory. In R. Wortley and L. Mazerolle, eds., *Environmental Criminology and Crime Analysis*, pp. 78–93. Cullompton, UK: Willan.

Brantingham, P. L., and Brantingham, P. J. (1991). Introduction to the 1991 Reissue: Notes on Environmental Criminology. In P. L. Brantingham and P. J. Brantingham, eds., *Environmental Criminology*, pp. 1–26. Prospect Heights, IL: Waveland Press.

Briar, S., and Piliavin, I. (1965). Delinquency, situational inducements, and commitment to conformity. *Social Problems* 13:35–45.

Brooks, D. (2001). *Bobos in Paradise: The New Upper Class and How They Got There*. Upper Saddle River, NJ: Prentice Hall.

Bryman, A. (2008). *Social Research Methods*. New York: Oxford.

Bureau of Justice Statistics. (2000). *National Crime Victimization Survey, 1999*. Washington, DC: US Government Printing Office.

Bureau of Justice Statistics. (2010). Alcohol and crime: Data from 2002 to 2008. http://bjs.ojp.usdoj.gov/content/acf/29_prisoners_and_alcoholuse.cfm. Retrieved May 5, 2011.

Bureau of Justice Statistics. (2011). Criminal victimization in the United States, 2008 statistical tables. Washington, DC: US Government Printing Office.

Burgess, R. L., and Akers, R. L. (1966). A differential association-reinforcement theory of criminal behavior. *Social Problems* 14:128–147.

Cart, J. (1999). Killer of gay student is spared death penalty; Courts: Matthew Shepard's father says life in prison shows "mercy to someone who refused to show any mercy." *Los Angeles Times*, November 5, p. A1.

Caspi, A., McClay, J., Moffitt, T. E., Mill, J., Martin, J., Craig, I. W., Taylor, A., and Poulton, R. (2002). Role of genotype in the cycle of violence in maltreated children. *Science* 297:851–854.

Chesney-Lind, M., and Sheldon, R. G. (2004). *Girls, Delinquency, and Juvenile Justice*, 3rd ed. Belmont, CA: Wadsworth.

Chilton, R. (1964). Continuity in delinquency area research: A comparison of studies for Baltimore, Detroit and Indianapolis. *American Sociological Review* 29:71–83.

Christiansen, K. O. (1974). Seriousness of Criminality and Concordance Among Danish Twins. In R. Hood, ed., *Crime, Criminology, and Public Policy*. New York: Free Press.

Clarke, R. V. (ed.). (1997). *Situational Crime Prevention: Successful Case Studies*, 2nd ed. Albany, NY: Harrow and Heston.

Cleckley, H. (1976). *The Mask of Sanity*, 5th ed. St. Louis: Mosby.

Clinard, M. B., and Quinney, R. (1986). *Criminal Behavior Systems: A Typology*, 2nd ed. Cincinnati, OH: Anderson.

Cloward, R. A., and Ohlin, L. E. (1960). *Delinquency and Opportunity*. New York: Free Press.

Cohen, A. K. (1955). *Delinquent Boys: The Culture of the Gang*. New York: Free Press.

Cohen, L., and Felson, M. (1979). Social change and crime rate trends: A routine activities approach. *American Sociological Review* 44:588–608.

Colvin, M., and Pauly, J. (1983). A critique of criminology: Toward an integrated structural-Marxist theory of gender and delinquency. *American Journal of Sociology*. 89:513–551.

Conklin, J. E. (2003). *Why Crime Rates Fell*. Sudbury, MA: Allyn and Bacon.

Cornish, D. B., and Clarke, R. V. (1986). *The Reasoning Criminal: Rational Choice Perspectives on Offending*. New York: Springer.

Creswell, J. W. (2008). *Research Design: Qualitative, Quantitative, and Mixed Methods Approaches*, 3rd ed. Thousand Oaks, CA: Sage Publications.

Cummings, M. C., and Wise, D. (2006). *Democracy Under Pressure: An Introduction to the American Political System*, 10th ed. Fort Worth, TX: Harcourt Brace College.

Currie, E. (2000). The Myth of Leniency. In J. H. Skolnick and E. Currie, eds., *Crisis in American Institutions*, 11th ed. Needham Heights, MA: Allyn and Bacon.

Dabbs, J., and Morris, R. (1990). Testosterone and antisocial behavior in a sample of 4,462 men. *Psychological Science* 1:209–211.

Dahrendorf, R. (1959). *Class and Class Conflict in Industrial Society*. Palo Alto, CA: Stanford University Press.

Dalgaard, O. S., and Kringlen, E. (1976). A Norwegian twin study of criminality. *British Journal of Criminology* 16:213–332.

Dalton, K. (1961). Menstruation and crime. *British Medical Journal* 2:1752–1753.

Daly, K., and Chesney-Lind, M. (1988). Feminism and criminology. *Justice Quarterly* 5:497–538.

Dantzker, M. L. (1998). *Criminology and Criminal Justice: Comparing, Contrasting, and Intertwining Disciplines*. Woburn, MA: Butterworth-Heinemann.

Dantzker, M. L., and Hunter, R. D. (2012). *Research Methods for Criminology and Criminal Justice: A Primer*, 3rd ed. Sudbury, MA: Jones and Bartlett.

Darwin, C. (1871). *Descent of Man*. London: John Murray.

Davenport, G. M. (1999). *Working with Toxic Older Adults: A Guide to Coping with Difficult Elders*. New York: Springer Press.

David, O., Hoffman, S., Sverd, S., Clark, J., and Voeller, K. (1976). Lead and hyperactivity, behavior response to chelation: A pilot study. *American Journal of Psychiatry* 133:1155–1158.

Denno, D. (1993). Considering lead poisoning as a criminal defense. *Fordham Urban Law Journal* 20:377–400.

Dillulio, J. J., Jr. (2000). Instant Replay: Three Strikes Was the Right Call. In J. H. Skolnick and E. Currie, eds., *Crisis in American Institutions*, 11th ed. Needham Heights, MA: Allyn and Bacon.

Dodge, K. A. (1993). Social-cognitive mechanisms in the development of conduct disorder and depression. *Annual Review of Psychology* 44:559–584.

Doerner, W. G., and Lab, S. P. (2012). *Victimology*, 6th ed. Burlington, MA: Elsevier/Anderson.

Domhoff, G. W. (1998). *Who Rules America? Power and Politics in the Year 2000*, 3rd ed. Mountain View, CA: Mayfield.

Driver, E. D. (1972). Introductory Essay. In Charles Goring, *The English Convict: A Statistical Study*, 1913 ed. reprint. Montclair, NJ: Patterson-Smith.

Dugdale, R. (1877). *The Jukes: A Study in Crime, Pauperism, Disease, and Heredity*. New York: Putnam.

Durkheim, E. (1933). *The Division of Labor in Society*. London: Free Press of Glencoe.

Durkheim, E. (1984). *The Division of Labor in Society*, 2nd ed. New York: Free Press.

Dye, T. R., and Zeigler, H. (1999). *The Irony of Democracy*, 11th ed. Fort Worth, TX: HAJ College and School Division.

Economist, The. (2010). Rough justice in America: Too many laws, too many prisoners. July 24, pp. 26–29.

Elliott, D. S., Huizinga, D., and Agerton, S. S. (1985). *Explaining Delinquency and Drug Use*. Beverly Hills: Sage.

Eysenck, H. J. (1977). *Personality and Crime*. London: Routledge and Kegan Paul.

Eysenck, H. J., and Eysenck, M. W. (1985). *Personality and Individual Differences*. New York: Plenum.

Eysenck, H. J., and Eysenck, M. W. (1996). Personality and crime: Where do we stand? *Psychology, Crime and Law* 2:143–152.

Eysenck, H. J., and Gudjonsson, G. H. (1989). *The Causes and Cures of Criminality. New York: Plenum.*

Farrington, D. (1988). Psychobiological factors in the explanation and reduction of delinquency. *Today's Delinquent*, 37–51.

Fayetteville (North Carolina) *Observer-Times*. (1991). Drunk driving charge dismissed: PMS cited. June 7, p. 3A.

Federal Bureau of Investigation. (1999). *Crime in the United States, 1998*. Washington, DC: US Government Printing Office.

Federal Bureau of Investigation. (2010a). *Crime in the United States, 2009*. Washington, DC: US Government Printing Office.

Federal Bureau of Investigation. (2010b). *Hate Crime Statistics, 2009*. Washington, DC: US Government Printing Office.

Felson, M. (2002). *Crime in Everyday Life*, 3rd ed. Thousand Oaks, CA: Sage Publications.

Fink, A. E. (1938). *The Causes of Crime: Biological Theories in the United States, 1800–1915*. Philadelphia: University of Pennsylvania Press.

Fishbein, D. H. (1990). Biological perspectives in criminology. *Criminology* 28:27–72.

Fishbein, D. H. (1992). The psychobiology of female aggression. *Criminal Justice and Behavior* 19:99–126.

Fogel, D. (1975). *We Are the Living Proof: The Justice Model for Corrections*. Cincinnati, OH: Anderson.

Freud, S. (1948). The Ego and the Id. In *Complete Psychological Works of Sigmund Freud*, Vol. 19. London: Hogarth.

Frost, L., Moffitt, T., and McGee, R. (1989). Neuropsychological correlates of psychopathology in an unselected cohort of young adolescents. *Journal of Abnormal Psychology* 98:307–313.

Fuller, J. R. (1998). *Criminal Justice: A Peacemaking Perspective*. Boston: Allyn and Bacon.

Gaines, L. K., and Miller, R. L. (2009). *Criminal Justice in Action*, 5th ed. Belmont, CA: Wadsworth.

Gallup Organization Website. (2000). Crime tops list of Americans' local concerns. June 21. http://www.gallup.com/poll/2800/Crime-Tops-List-Americans-Local-Concerns.aspx. Retrieved December 15, 2010.

Gallup Organization Website. (2010). Americans still perceive crime as on the rise. http://www.gallup.com/poll/144827/Americans-Perceive-Crime-Rise.aspx. Retrieved May 7, 2011.

Gavin, H. (2008). *Understanding Research Methods and Statistics in Psychology*. Thousand Oaks, CA: Sage Publications.

Glaser, D. (1956). Criminality theories and behavioral images. *American Journal of Sociology* 61:433–444.

Glueck, S., and Glueck, E. (1950). *Unraveling Juvenile Delinquency*. New York: Commonwealth Fund.

Glueck, S., and Glueck, E. (1956). *Physique and Delinquency*. Cambridge: Harvard University Press.

Goddard, H. (1912). *The Kallikak Family: A Study in the Heredity of Feeblemindedness*. New York: Macmillan.

Goddard, H. (1914). *Feeblemindedness: Its Causes and Consequences*. New York: Macmillan. Reprint. New York: Arno Press, 1972.

Goldstein, P. J. (1995). The Drugs/Violence Nexus: A Tripartite Conceptual Framework. In J. A. Inciardi and K. McElrath, eds., *The American Drug Scene*. Los Angeles: Roxbury.

Goring, C. (1913). *The English Convict: A Statistical Study*. London: His Majesty's Stationery Office. Reprint. Montclair, NJ: Patterson Smith, 1972.

Gottfredson, M., and Hirschi, T. (1990). *A General Theory of Crime*. Palo Alto, CA: Stanford University Press.

Gould, S. (1981). *The Mismeasure of Man*. New York: W. W. Norton.

Greenberg, E. S., and Page, B. I. (2009). *The Struggle for Democracy*, 9th ed. New York: Pearson/Longman.

Greenleaf, J. W. (2010). Sexual abuse and the rotten apple theory. *Another Voice: Reflections About Contemporary Catholic Belief and Practice*, September 27. http://anothervoice-greenleaf.org. Retrieved April 15, 2011.

Hagan, F. E. (2006). *Essentials of Research Methods in Criminal Justice and Criminology*, 2nd ed. Columbus, OH: Allyn and Bacon.

Hagan, F. E. (2011). *Introduction to Criminology: Theories, Methods and Criminal Behavior*, 7th ed. Thousand Oaks, CA: Sage Publications.

Hagan, J. (2003). A power control theory of gender and delinquency. In F. T. Cullen and R. Agnew, eds. *Criminological Theory: Past to Present (Essential Readings)*, 2nd ed. Los Angeles: Roxbury Publishing.

Hancock, B. W., and Sharp, P. M. (2004). *Criminal Justice in America: Theory, Practice, and Policy*, 3rd ed. Upper Saddle River, NJ: Prentice Hall.

Hare, R. D. (1970). *Psychopathy: Theory and Research*. New York: Wiley.

Hare, R. D. (1991). *The Hare Psychopathy Checklist—Revised*. Toronto: Multi-Health Systems.

Hare, R. D. (1996). Psychopathy: A clinical construct whose time has come. *Criminal Justice and Behavior* 23:25–54.

Hare, R. D., Hart, S. D., and Harpur, T. J. (1991). Psychopathy and the DSM-IV criteria for antisocial personality disorder. *Journal of Abnormal Psychology* 100:391–398.

Hart, S. D., and Dempster, R. J. (1997). Impulsivity and Psychopathy. In C. D. Webster and M. A. Jackson, eds., *Impulsivity: Theory, Assessment and Treatment*. New York: Guilford.

Haviland, W. A. (2002). *Cultural Anthropology*, 10th ed. Belmont, CA: Wadsworth.

Heimer, K., and Matsueda, R. L. (1994). Role-taking, role-commitment and delinquency: A theory of differential social control. *American Sociological Review* 59:400–437.

Henggeler, S. (1989). *Delinquency in Adolescence*. Newbury Park, CA: Sage Publications.

Herrnstein, R. (1973). *I.Q. in the Meritocracy*. Boston: Little, Brown.

Herrnstein, R., and Murray, C. (1994). *The Bell Curve: Intelligence and Class Structure in American Life*. New York: Free Press.

Hill, D., and Sargent, W. W. (1943). A case of matricide. *Lancet* 244:526–527.

Hippchen, L. (1978). *Ecologic-Biochemical Approaches to Treatment of Delinquents and Criminals*. New York: Von Nostrand Reinhold.

Hirschi, T. (1969). *Causes of Delinquency*. Berkeley: University of California Press.

Hirschi, T., and Hindelang, M. S. (1977). Intelligence and delinquency: A revisionist review. *American Sociological Review* 42:57–87.

Hooten, E. A. (1939). *Crime and the Man*. Cambridge: Harvard University Press.

Hornsey, M. J. (2008). Social identity theory and self-categorization theory: A historical review. *Social and Personality Psychology Compass* 2:204–222.

Huesmann, L. R. (1997). Observational learning of violent behavior: Social and biosocial processes. In A. Raine, P. A. Breunan, D. P. Farrington, and S. A Mednick, eds., *Biosocial Bases of Violence*. New York: Plenum.

Hunter, R. D. (1995). Symbolic reassurance: Why we punish. Paper presented at the Academy of Criminal Justice Sciences Annual Meeting, Boston, March.

Hunter, R. D. (1996). Symbolic reassurance: How and why the system really works. Paper presented at the Southern Criminal Justice Association Annual Meeting, Richmond, VA, October.

Hunter, R. D. (2010). Crime prevention: Micro, meso and macro levels. In B. S. Fisher and S. P. Lab, eds., *Encyclopedia of Victimology and Crime Prevention*. Thousand Oaks, CA: Sage Publications.

Hunter, R. D. (2011). Presidential address: The future of justice studies. *Justice Quarterly* 28:1–14.

Hunter, R. D., and Barker, T. (2011). *Police-Community Relations and the Administration of Justice*, 8th ed. Boston: Prentice Hall.

Hutchings, B., and Mednick, S. A. (1977). Criminality in adoptees and their adoptive and biological parents: A pilot study. In S. A. Mednick and K. O. Christiansen, eds., *Biological Bases in Criminal Behavior*. New York: Gardner Press.

Jacobs, P. A., Brunton, M., and Melville, M. (1965). Aggressive behavior, mental subnormality, and the XYY male. *Nature* 208:1351–1352.

Jayson, S. (2010). Tired of the baby boomers: Other generations are weary of their place in culture. *USA Today*, November 18, pp. 1D–2D.

Jeffery, C. R. (1956). The structure of American criminological thinking. *Journal of Criminal Law, Criminology, and Police Science* 45:658–672.

Jeffrey, C. R. (1971). *Crime Prevention Through Environmental Design*. Beverly Hills, CA: Sage Publications.

Jeffery, C. R. (1977a). *Crime Prevention Through Environmental Design*, 2nd ed. Beverly Hills: Sage Publications.

Jeffery, C. R. (1977b). Criminology as an interdisciplinary behavioral science. *Criminology* 16:153–156.

Jeffery, C. R. (1990). *Criminology: An Interdisciplinary Approach.* Englewood Cliffs, NJ: Prentice Hall.

Jensen, A. R. (1969). How much can we boost IQ and scholastic achievement? *Harvard Educational Review* 39:1–123.

Johnson, H. A., and Wolfe, N. T. (1996). *History of Criminal Justice,* 2nd ed. Cincinnati, OH: Anderson Publishing Co.

Johnson, R. (1972). *Aggression in Man and Animals.* Philadelphia: Saunders.

Jones, D. A. (1986). *History of Criminology: A Philosophical Perspective.* Westport, CT: Greenwood.

Kaplan, H. B. (1975). *Self Attitudes and Deviant Behavior.* Pacific Palisades, CA: Goodyear.

Kaplan, H. B., and Fukurai, H. (1992). Negative social sanctions, self-rejection and drug use. *Youth and Society* 23:275–298.

Kaplan, H. B., and Johnson, R. J. (1991). Negative social sanctions and juvenile delinquency: Effects of labeling in a model of deviant behavior. *Social Science Quarterly* 72:98–122.

Karmen, A. (2010). *Crime Victims,* 7th ed. Belmont, CA: Wadsworth/Cengage Learning.

Katz, J. (1988). *Seductions of Crime: Moral and Sensual Attractions in Doing Evil.* New York: Basic Books.

Katz, J., and Chambliss, W. J. (1995). Biology amid crime. In J. F. Sheley, ed., *Criminology: A Contemporary Handbook,* pp. 275–303. Belmont, CA: Wadsworth.

Kershner, J., and Hawke, W. (1979). Megavitamins and learning disorders: A controlled double-blind experiment. *Journal of Nutrition* 109:819–826.

Klockars, C. (1980). The contemporary crisis of Marxist criminology. In J. Inciardi, ed., *Radical Criminology: The Coming Crisis,* pp. 92–123. Beverly Hills, CA: Sage Publications.

Kohlberg, L. (1969). *Stages in the Development of Moral Thought and Action.* New York: Holt, Rinehart, and Winston.

Kohlberg, L., Kauffman, K., Scharf, P., and Hickey, J. (1973). *The Just Community Approach in Corrections: A Manual.* Niantic, CT: Connecticut Department of Corrections.

Kornhauser, R. (1978). *Social Sources of Delinquency.* Chicago: University of Chicago Press.

Krassner, M. (1986). Diet and brain functions. *Nutrition Reviews* 44:12–15.

Krohn, M. D. (1986). The web of conformity: A network approach to the explanation of delinquent behavior. *Social Problems* 33:581–593.

Lander, B. (1954). *Towards an Understanding of Juvenile Delinquency.* New York: Columbia.

Lavergne, G. M. (1997). *A Sniper in the Tower: The True Story of the Texas Tower Massacre.* New York: Bantam.

Lemert, E. (1951). *Social Pathology.* New York: McGraw-Hill.

Lilly, J. R., Cullen, F. T., and Ball, R. A. (2007). *Criminological Theory: Context and Consequences,* 4th ed. Thousand Oaks, CA: Sage Publications.

Liska, A. F., and Messner, S. F. (1999). *Perspectives on Crime and Deviance,* 3rd ed. Upper Saddle River, NJ: Prentice Hall.

Lombroso, C. (1920). *The Female Offender.* New York: Appleton.

Lombroso-Ferrero, G. (1972). *Criminal Man According to the Classification of Cesare Lombroso.* Montclair, NJ: Patterson-Smith.

Lovan, D. (2011). God, science are not exclusive, astronomer says. *Tallahassee Democrat,* February 12, p. 6.

Lykken, D. (1996). Psychopathy, sociopathy, and crime. *Society* 34:30–38.

Lynam, D., Moffitt, T., and Stouthamer-Loeber, M. (1993). Explaining the relation between IQ and delinquency: Class, race, test motivation, school failure, or self-control? *Journal of Abnormal Psychology* 102:187–196.

Magelby, D. B., and Light, P. C. (2009). *Government by the People*, 23rd ed. New York: Pearson Longman.

Martin, R., Mutchnick, R. J., and Austin, W. T. (1990). *Criminological Thought: Pioneers Past and Present*. New York: Macmillan.

Martinson, R. (1974). What works: Questions and answers about prison reform. *Public Interest*, 35:22–54.

Marx, K., Engels, F., and Malia, E. (1998). *The Communist Manifesto*. New York: Signet Classic.

Matsueda, R. L. (1992). Reflected appraisals, parental labeling, and delinquency: Specifying a symbolic interactionist theory. *American Journal of Sociology* 97:1577–1611.

Matza, D. (1964). *Delinquency and Drift*. New York: Wiley.

Matza, D., and Sykes, G. M. (1961). Juvenile delinquency and subterranean values. *American Sociological Review* 26:712–719.

Mawby R. I., and Walklate, S. (1994). *Critical Victimology*. Thousand Oaks, CA: Sage Publications.

Maxfield, M. G., and Babbie, E. R. (2009). *Basics of Research Methods for Criminal Justice and Criminology*, 2nd ed. Belmont, CA: Wadsworth Publishing.

McBurney, D. H., and White, T. L. (2007). *Research Methods*, 7th ed. Belmont, CA: Wadsworth Publishing.

McCandless, N. J., and Conner, F. P. (1999). Working with terminally ill older women: Can a feminist perspective add new insight and direction? *Journal of Women and Aging* 11:101–114.

Mead, G. H. (1934). *Mind, Self and Society*. Chicago: University of Chicago Press.

Meadows, R. J. (2010). *Understanding Violence and Victimization*, 5th ed. Upper Saddle River, NJ: Pearson Prentice Hall.

Mednick, S. A., and Christiansen, K. O. (1971). *Biosocial Bases in Criminal Behavior*. New York: Gardner.

Mendelsohn, B. (1976). Victimology and contemporary society's trends. *Victimology* 1:8–28.

Merali, Z. (2011). Physics of the divine. *Discover*, March, pp. 49–53.

Merton, R. K. (1968). *Social Theory and Social Structure*, revised and enlarged ed. New York: Free Press.

Messerschmidt, J. W. (1986). *Capitalism, Patriarchy and Crime: Toward a Socialist Feminist Criminology*. Totowa, NJ: Rowman and Littlefield.

Messner, S., and Rosenfield, R. (1994). *Crime and the American Dream*. Belmont, CA: Wadsworth.

Milgram, S. (1963). Behavioral study of obedience. *Journal of Abnormal and Social Psychology* 67:371–378.

Miller, W. B. (1958). Lower-class culture as a generating milieu of gang delinquency. *Journal of Social Issues* 14:5–19.

Mills, C. W. (2000). *The Power Elite*, 2nd ed. Los Angeles: Getty Trust.

Mischel, W. (1986). *Introduction to Personality*, 4th ed. New York: Holt, Rinehart and Winston.

Moffitt, T. E. (1993). Adolescence-limited and life-course-persistent antisocial behavior: A developmental taxonomy. *Psychological Review* 100:674–701.

Monohan, J. (1996). Mental illness and violent crime. *NIJ Research Preview*. Washington, DC: National Institute of Justice.

Montague, P. (1995). *Punishment as Societal Defense*. London: Rowman and Littlefield.

Moore, R. (2011). *Cybercrime: Investigating High-Technology Computer Crime,* 2nd ed. Burlington, MA: Elsevier/Anderson.

Morrison, B. (2005). Special report: Eric Rudolph writes home. *USA Today,* July 5. http://www.usatoday.com/news/nation/2005-07-05-rudolph-cover-partone _x.htm?POE=NEWISVA. Retrieved May 7, 2011.

Muscular Dystrophy Association. (2011). Neuromuscular diseases in the MDA program. http://www.mda.org/disease/. Retrieved May 5, 2011.

Myren, R. A. 1970. Education in criminal justice: A report prepared for the Coordinating Council for Higher Education. State University of New York at Albany: Unpublished manuscript.

National Crime Prevention Council. National Crime Prevention Council home page. http://www.ncpc.org. Retrieved May 7, 2011.

National Institute on Drug Abuse. (2010). Drug abuse at highest level in nearly a decade. *NIDA Notes* 23 (3). http://www.nida.nih.gov/NIDA_notes/NNvol23N3 /tearoff.html. Retrieved May 5, 2011.

Needleman, H., Reiss, J., Tobin, M., Biesecker, G., and Greenhouse, J. (1996). Bone lead levels and delinquent behavior. *Journal of the American Medical Association* 275:363–369.

Neisser, U., et al. (1996). Intelligence: Knowns and unknowns. *American Psychologist* 51:77–101.

Newman, O. (1972). *Defensible Space: Crime Prevention Through Urban Design.* New York: Macmillan.

New York Times. (1999). Third defendant is convicted in dragging death in Texas. November 19. http://www.nytimes.com/1999/11/19/us/third-defendant-is-convicted -in-dragging-death-in-texas.html?ref=jamesjrbyrd. Retrieved May 5, 2011.

Office of the Undersecretary for Democracy and Global Affairs. (2007). Trafficking in persons report. Washington, DC: US Department of State.

Olweus Bullying Prevention Program. (2011). What is bullying? http://www.olweus .org/public/bullying.page. Retrieved May 5, 2011.

Olweus, D. (1993). *Bullying at School: What We Know and What We Can Do.* Oxford, UK: Blackwell Publishers.

Olweus, D. (2009). Testosterone and Adrenaline: Aggressive Antisocial Behavior in Normal Adolescent Males. In S. A. Mednick, T. E. Moffitt, and S. A. Stack, eds., *The Causes of Crime: New Biological Approaches.* Cambridge, UK: Cambridge University Press.

Packer, H. L. (1968). *The Limits of the Criminal Sanction.* Palo Alto, CA: Stanford University Press.

Pearson, F. S., and Weiner, N. A. (1985). Toward an integration of criminological theories. *Journal of Criminal Law and Criminology* 76:116–150.

Pelfrey, W. V. (1980). *The Evolution of Criminology.* Cincinnati, OH: Anderson.

Piaget, J. (1932). *The Moral Judgment of the Child.* New York: Harcourt, Brace.

Polk, K. (1957). Urban social areas and delinquency. *Social Problems* 14:320–325.

Pollack, J. M. (2012). *Ethical Dilemmas and Decisions in Criminal Justice,* 7th ed. Belmont, CA: Wadsworth/Cengage Learning.

Quinney, E. R. (1964). Crime, delinquency, and social areas. *Journal of Research in Crime and Delinquency* 1:149–154.

Quinney, R. (1970). *The Social Reality of Crime.* Boston: Little, Brown.

Quinney, R. (1974). *Criminal Justice in America: A Critical Understanding.* Boston: Little, Brown.

Quinney, R. (1980). *Class, State and Crime,* 2nd ed. New York: Longman.

Quinney, R. (1991). The Way of Peace: On Crime, Suffering, and Service. In H. E. Pepinsky, ed., *Criminology as Peacemaking.* Bloomington: Indiana University Press.

Reaves, B. A. (1993). Using NIBRS data to analyze violent crime. *Bureau of Justice Statistics Technical Report.* Washington, DC: US Department of Justice.

Reckless, W. (1967). *The Crime Problem.* New York: Appleton-Century-Crofts.

Reckless, W., Dinitz, S., and Murray, E. (1957). The "good boy" in a high delinquency area. *Journal of Criminal Law, Criminology and Police Science* 48:18–25.

Reid, S. T. (2011). *Crime and Criminology,* 13th ed. New York: Oxford University Press.

Reiss, A. (1951). Delinquency as the failure of personal and social controls. *American Sociological Review* 16:196–207.

Roberson, C., and Wallace, H. (1998). *Introduction to Criminology.* Incline Village, NV: Copperhouse.

Roizen, J. (1997). Epidemiological issues in alcohol-related violence. In M. Galanter, ed., *Recent Developments in Alcoholism,* Vol. 13. New York: Plenum.

Roshier, B. (1989). *Controlling Crime: The Classical Perspective in Criminology.* Chicago: Lyceum.

Rowe, D., and Osgood, D. W. (1984). Hereditary and sociological theories of delinquency: A reconsideration. *American Sociological Review* 49:526–540.

Ruby, Charles L. (2002). The definition of terrorism. *Analyses of Social Issues and Public Policy* 2002:9–14.

Ryan, J. (1972). IQ—The Illusion of Objectivity. In K. Richardson and D. Spears, eds., *Race and Intelligence.* Baltimore: Penguin.

Sampson, R. J., and Laub, J. H. (1993). *Crime in the Making: Pathways and Turning Points Through Life.* Cambridge: Harvard University Press.

Sampson, R. J., and Wilson, W. J. (2003). A Theory of Race, Crime, and Urban Inequality. In F. T. Cullen and R. Agnew, eds., *Criminological Theory: Past to Present (Essential Readings),* 2nd ed. Los Angeles: Roxbury Publishing.

Schafer, S. (1968). *The Victim and His Criminal.* New York: Random House.

Schauss, A. (1980). *Diet, Crime and Delinquency.* Berkeley: Parker House.

Schmalleger, F. (2011). *Criminal Justice Today,* 11th ed. Upper Saddle River, NJ: Prentice Hall.

Schmalleger, F. (2012). *Criminology Today: An Integrative Introduction,* 6th ed. Boston: Prentice Hall.

Schoenthaler, S., and Doraz, W. (1983). Types of offenses which can be reduced in an institutional setting using nutritional intervention. *International Journal of Biosocial Research* 4:74–84.

Scott, S. L. (2011).What makes serial killers tick? The Crime Library. http://www.crimelibrary.com/serialkillers/notorious/tick/victims_1.html. Retrieved May 7, 2011.

Sellin, T. (1938). *Culture Conflict and Crime.* New York: Social Science Research Council.

Sellin, T., and Wolfgang, M. E. (1964). *The Measurement of Delinquency.* New York: Wiley.

Shaw, C. R., and McKay, H. D. (1942). *Juvenile Delinquency and Urban Areas.* Chicago: University of Chicago Press.

Sheldon, W. (1949). *Varieties of Delinquent Youth.* New York: Harper and Row.

Sherman, L. W. (2003). Defiance Theory. In F. T. Cullen and R. Agnew, eds., *Criminological Theory: Past to Present (Essential Readings),* 2nd ed. Los Angeles: Roxbury Publishing.

Shevky, E., and Bell, W. (1955). *Social Area Analysis: Theory, Illustrative Application and Computational Procedures.* Stanford: Stanford University Press.

Shockley, W. (1967). A "try simplest cases" approach to the heredity-poverty-crime problem. *Proceedings of the National Academy of Sciences* 57:1767–1774.

Shoemaker, D. J. (2009). *Theories of Delinquency,* 6th ed. New York: Oxford University Press.

Siegel, L. J. (2010). *Criminology: Theories, Patterns and Typologies,* 10th ed. Belmont, CA: Wadsworth/Cengage Learning.

Skolnick, J. H. (2000). Wild Pitch: Three Strikes, You're Out and Other Bad Calls on Crime. In J. H. Skolnick and E. Currie, eds., *Crisis in American Institutions,* 11th ed. Needham Heights, MA: Allyn and Bacon.

Sourcebook of Criminal Justice Statistics. (1999). Washington, DC: US Government Printing Office.

Stark, R. (1987). Deviant places: A theory of the ecology of crime. *Criminology* 25:893–911.

Stewart, R. (1999). Murder case forces Jasper to revisit horror of slaying in June. *Houston Chronicle,* January 24. http://www.chron.com/disp/story.mpl/special/jasper /killing/217740.html.

Sutherland, E. H. (1939). *Principles of Criminology.* Philadelphia: Lippincott.

Sutherland, E. H., and Cressey, D. R. (1978). *Criminology,* 10th ed. Philadelphia: Lippincott.

Tarde, G. (1912). *Penal Philosophy.* Boston: Little, Brown.

Taylor, I., Walton, P., and Young, J. (1973). *The New Criminology: For a Social Theory of Deviance.* London: Routledge and Kegan Paul.

Territo, L., Halsted, J. B., and Bromley, M. L. (2004). *Criminal Justice in America: A Human Perspective,* 6th ed. Boston: Prentice Hall.

Thornberry, T. P. (1987). Toward an interactional theory of delinquency. *Criminology* 25:863–891.

Time. (1966). Nation: The madman in the tower. *Time.* August 12. http://www.time .com/time/magazine/article/0,9171,842584,00.html. Retrieved May 7, 2011.

Time. (1979). Law: Getting off? May 28, p. 57. http://www.time.com/time/magazine /article/0,9171,947318,00.html. Retrieved May 7, 2011.

Tittle, C. R. (1995). *Control Balances: Toward a General Theory of Deviance.* Boulder, CO: Westview Press.

Torcaso v. Watkins, 367 U.S. 488 (1961).

Tremoglie, M. P. (2011). How state budget battles could mean more criminals back on the streets. *Accuracy in the Media Special Report.* March 14. http://www.aim.org /aim-column/how-state-budget-battles-could-mean-more-criminals-back-on-the -streets/#_ftn9. Retrieved May 7, 2011.

Truman, J. L., and Rand, M. R. (2010). *Criminal Victimization, 2009.* Washington, DC: Bureau of Justice Statistics. http://bjs.ojp.usdoj.gov/content/pub/pdf/cv09.pdf. Retrieved May 5, 2011.

Trunell, E. P., Turner, C. W., and Keye, W. R. (1988). A comparison of the psychological and hormonal factors in women with and without premenstrual syndrome. *Journal of Abnormal Psychology* 97:429–436.

Turk, A. T. (1966). Conflict and criminality. *American Sociological Review* 31:338–352.

Turk, A. T. (1977). Class, conflict and criminalization. *Sociological Focus* 10:209–220.

Udry, R., Talbert, L., and Morris, N. (1986). Biosocial foundation for adolescent female sexuality. *Demography* 23:217–227.

University College London/Jill Dando Institute of Security and Crime Science. (2011). About us. http://www.ucl.ac.uk/jdi/about-us. Retrieved May 10, 2011.

Veblen, T. B. (1998). *The Theory of the Leisure Class* (Great Minds Series ed.). Amherst, NY: Prometheus.

Vila, B. (1994). A general paradigm for understanding criminal behavior: Extending evolutionary ecological theory. *Criminology* 32:311–360.

Violence Against Women Grants Office. (1998). *Stalking and Domestic Violence: The Third Annual Report to Congress Under the Violence Against Women Act*. Washington, DC: Violence Against Women Grants Office.

Vito, G. F., and Holmes, R. M. (2007). *Criminology: Theory, Research, and Policy*, 2nd ed. Sudbury, MA: Jones and Bartlett.

Vito, G. F., Kunselman, J. C., and Tewksbury, R. (2008). *Introduction to Criminal Justice Research Methods: An Applied Approach*. Springfield, IL: Charles C. Thomas.

Vold, G. (1958). *Theoretical Criminology*. New York: Oxford University Press.

von Drehle, D. (2010). What's behind America's falling crime rate. *Time*, February 22. http://www.time.com/time/magazine/article/0,9171,1963761,00.html#ixzz1GcH ya5vn.

von Hentig, H. (1941). Remarks on the integration of perpetrator and victim. *Journal of Criminal Law, Criminology and Police Science* 31:303–309.

von Hentig, H. (1948). *The Criminal and His Victim: Studies in the Socio-Biology of Crime*. New Haven: Yale University Press.

Wallace, H. (1998). *Victimology: Legal, Psychological and Social Perspectives*. Boston: Allyn and Bacon.

Wallace, H. (2006). *Victimology: Legal, Psychological and Social Perspectives*, 2nd ed. Boston: Allyn and Bacon.

Weber, M. (1953). Class, status, party. In R. Bendix and S. M. Lipset, eds., *Class, Status and Power*. New York: Macmillan.

Weis, J., and Hawkins, J. D. (1981). *Reports of the National Juvenile Justice Assessment Centers: Preventing Delinquency*. Washington, DC: US Department of Justice.

Weis, J., and Sederstrom, J. (1981). *Reports of the National Juvenile Justice Assessment Centers: The Prevention of Serious Delinquency*. Washington, DC: US Department of Justice.

Wilson, J. Q. (1975). *Thinking About Crime*. New York: Vintage.

Wilson, J. Q., and Herrnstein, R. (1985). *Crime and Human Nature*. New York: Simon and Schuster.

Wilson, J. Q., and Kelling, G. L. (1982). Broken windows: The police and neighborhood safety. *Atlantic Monthly*, March, pp. 29–38.

Witkin, G. (1998). Why crime is down (special report): The real story. *US News and World Report*, May 25, pp. 28–40.

Wolfgang, M. E. (1958). *Patterns of Criminal Homicide*. Philadelphia: University of Pennsylvania Press.

Wolfgang, M. E., and Ferracuti, F. (1967). *The Subculture of Violence*. London: Social Science Paperbacks.

Wolraich, M., Lindgren, S., Stumbo, P., Stegink, L., Appelbaum, M., and Kiritsy, M. (1994). Effects of diets high in sucrose or aspartame on the behavior and cognitive performance of children. *The New England Journal of Medicine* 330:303–306.

Wray, H. (1997). Born bad? *US News and World Report*, April 21, pp. 72–80.

Wunderlich, H. (1978). Neuroallergy as a Contributing Factor to Social Misfits: Diagnosis and Treatment. In L. Hippchen, ed., *Ecologic-Biochemical Approaches to Treatment of Delinquents and Criminals*, pp. 229–253. New York: Van Nostrand Reinhold.

Yochelson, S., and Samenow, S. E. (1976). *The Criminal Personality*, Vol. 1. New York: Jason Aronson.

Zax, D. (2010). Crime rates fell despite recession—But why? *Fast Company,* September 14. http://www.fastcompany.com/1688851/in-the-midst-of-recession-crime-rates-fell-reports-fbi.

Zeleny, L. D. (1933). Feeblemindedness and criminal conduct. *American Journal of Sociology* 38:564–576.

Zimbardo, P. G. (1970). The Human Choice: Individuation, Reason, and Order Versus Deindividuation, Impulse, and Chaos. In W. J. Arnold and D. Levine, eds., *Nebraska Symposium on Motivation, 1969.* Lincoln: University of Nebraska Press.

Zimbardo, P. G. (1973). The Psychological Power and Pathology of Imprisonment. In E. Aronson and R. Helmereich, eds., *Social Psychology.* New York: Van Nostrand.

Zimmer, C. (2011). The brain. *Discover: Science, Technology and the Future,* March, pp. 28–31.

Index

About the Book

This concise but thorough introductory textbook bridges the gap between theory and the real world of crime and criminal justice. In clear, accessible prose, the authors discuss the full gamut of issues and concepts typically covered on the introductory course syllabus.

Building on the basics of the first edition, this revised and updated edition also:

- Uses real-world examples to illustrate theory
- Discusses cutting-edge crime-prevention strategies
- Highlights the impact of crime on both victims and offenders
- Addresses the challenges of homeland security for local police
- Reflects the impact of changing criminal law on the criminal justice system

Ronald D. Hunter is professor of criminology and criminal justice at Georgia Gwinnett College. He is a past president of the Southern Criminal Justice Association and of the Academy of Criminal Justice Sciences. **Mark L. Dantzker** is professor of criminal justice at the University of Texas, Pan American. He is also a practicing clinical psychologist. Both authors are former police officers.